A Sign and a Witness:
2,000 Years of Hebrew Books and Illuminated Manuscripts

קודם קריאת המגילה
מברך

בָּרוּךְ אַתָּה יְיָ אֱלֹהֵינוּ מֶלֶךְ אֲשֶׁר קִדְּשָׁנוּ
בְּמִצְוֹתָיו וְצִוָּנוּ עַל
מִקְרָא מְגִלָּה ;

בָּרוּךְ אַתָּה יְיָ שֶׁעָשָׂה נִסִּים
לַאֲבוֹתֵינוּ בַּיָּמִים
הָהֵם וּבַזְמַן הַזֶּה ;

בָּרוּךְ אַתָּה יְיָ שֶׁהֶחֱיָנוּ וְקִיְּמָנוּ
וְהִגִּיעָנוּ לַזְּמַן הַזֶּה ;

וְאַחַר קְרִיאָתָהּ מְבָרֵךְ הָרַב
אֶת רִיבֵנוּ

A Sign and a Witness

2,000 Years of Hebrew Books and Illuminated Manuscripts

Edited with an Introduction by
LEONARD SINGER GOLD

The New York Public Library and
Oxford University Press, *New York & Oxford*

The New York Public Library is grateful to Edith and Henry Everett for their commitment to the Library. Without their generosity, the exhibition "A Sign and a Witness" and this publication would not have been possible.

On the front cover: "Gates of Mercy" from the liturgy for the Day of Atonement (Yom Kippur), in a fourteenth-century Maḥzor from Germany. NYPL, Jewish Division, **P, fol. 353v (Ex. no. 59)

On the back cover: Part of the Haggadah with the end of Psalm 116 and the first word of Psalm 117, in a Spanish festival prayerbook of the thirteenth or early fourteenth century. Staatsbibliothek Preussischer Kulturbesitz, Orientabteilung, Berlin (West), Ms. Hamilton 288, fol. 30v (Ex. no. 55)

Frontispiece: Blessings recited before reading the Scroll of Esther at Purim, in an Esther Scroll copied and illustrated by Raphael Montalto, Netherlands, 1685/86. NYPL, Spencer Collection, Heb. Ms. 2 (Ex. no. 16)

Copyright © 1988 by The New York Public Library, Astor, Lenox and Tilden Foundations

Exhibition dates:
October 15, 1988 – January 14, 1989

An indemnity for this exhibition has been provided by The Federal Council on the Arts and the Humanities.

Co-published by
The New York Public Library,
Astor, Lenox and Tilden Foundations
and
Oxford University Press
Oxford New York Toronto
Delhi Bombay Calcutta Madras Karachi
Petaling Jaya Singapore Hong Kong Tokyo
Nairobi Dar es Salaam Cape Town
Melbourne Auckland
and associated companies in
Berlin Ibadan

Distributed by
Oxford University Press, Inc.,
200 Madison Avenue, New York, N.Y. 10016.
Oxford is a registered trademark of Oxford University Press.
All rights reserved. No part of this publication may be reproduced, stored in a retrieval system, or transmitted, in any form or by any means, electronic, mechanical, photocopying, recording, or otherwise, without the prior permission of Oxford University Press, Inc.
Printed in the United States of America

A Sign and a Witness is a publication in the Oxford University Press series Studies in Jewish History (see series listing on p. 223).

Library of Congress Cataloging-in-Publication Data:

A Sign and a witness.
   (Studies in Jewish history)
   Published in conjunction with an international exhibition, held at the New York Public Library, Oct. 15, 1988 – Jan. 14, 1989.
   Bibliography: p.
   Includes index.
   1. Manuscripts, Hebrew – History.
2. Printing – History – Hebrew.   3. Hebrew literature, Modern – Publishing.   4. Hebrew imprints – Exhibitions.   5. Illumination of books and manuscripts, Jewish – Exhibitions.
I. Gold, Leonard Singer, 1934–
II. New York Public Library.   III. Series.
Z115.4.S54   1988   090'.74'01471   88-22358
ISBN 0-87104-409-9 (pbk.)
ISBN 0-19-505619-1 (Oxford University Press: pbk.)

Contents

Acknowledgments

MANY PEOPLE have had a part in making this exhibition and book a reality. I thank them all heartily and beg forgiveness of any whose names I have inadvertently failed to mention. Edith and Henry Everett have made a major gift to the Library for this book, the exhibition, and the accompanying public programs. On behalf of all my colleagues, I want to express my deepest appreciation to them. Joy Ungerleider-Mayerson participated at many levels. She helped to conceive the very idea of the exhibition, used her good offices with foreign institutions on our behalf, and visited libraries abroad, examining individual manuscripts and sending back her notes. Hers has truly been a guiding spirit. Dr. Vartan Gregorian, President of The New York Public Library, is largely responsible for creating the climate at the Library in which such a major project could be undertaken. Very early on he expressed his belief that the exhibition should be carried out in a manner befitting the grandeur of the subject, and he has supported our collective effort consistently. I am especially grateful to him for naming me the Library's third Astor Fellow, for 1986–87. The Astor Fellowship enabled me to travel extensively in order to examine Hebrew manuscripts in this country, in Europe, and in the Middle East. To Professor Joseph Gutmann of Wayne State University, Detroit, and Mrs. Gutmann go a large measure of thanks. They offered me the hospitality of their home, and Professor Gutmann undertook to give me what amounted to a seminar tailored to my needs on Hebrew illuminated manuscripts. Professor Bezalel Narkiss of the Hebrew University offered his advice near the inception of planning. I am grateful to him for having counseled me to seek out the very best examples of manuscript illumination available.

Diantha D. Schull, Manager of the Library's Exhibitions Program, has been a wonderful partner, planning work, keeping the project on schedule, thinking of things that would never have occurred to me. Jeanne Bornstein, Research Coordinator, has been with me every step of the way. She is the person of whom I can truly say, "Without her help it would not have happened." Others of the Exhibitions staff whom I thank are Susan F. Saidenberg, Assistant Manager; Jean Mihich, Registrar, and the staff of the Registrar's Office: Caryn Reid, Melitte Buchman, and Sandra Spurgeon; Lou Storey, designer of the exhibition, and Tracy Fell; Myriam de Arteni, Exhibitions Conservation Specialist; and Edward Rime and Suzanne Stallings, Exhibitions

Assistants. I also thank Richard De Gennaro, Director; Gregory Long, Vice President, Public Affairs and Development; Harold Snedcof, Susan Rautenberg, and Carolyn Cohen of the Development Office; Betsy Pinover, Manager of Communications, and Daniela Weiss, Esther Harriott, and Shellie Goldberg of the Public Relations Office; and Myrna Martin, Coordinator of Volunteer Activities. They have been unstinting of time and effort.

Richard Newman, Manager of Publications, was always available for consultation. He has given invaluable assistance in preparing this volume. Barbara Bergeron has edited the manuscript, and Marilan Lund, Coordinator, Graphics Office, has designed the book and graphic materials related to the exhibition. Lisa Ratkus, also of the Graphics Office, and Lili Cassel Wronker have contributed to the exhibition graphics. I thank them all.

I am grateful to David H. Stam, University Librarian at Syracuse University, and to Donald F. Jay, Library of Congress Field Director in Cairo, who in their former capacities at The New York Public Library, as Andrew W. Mellon Director of The Research Libraries and as Associate Director for Public Services, respectively, helped me to procure the time and freedom I needed to pursue the project. I warmly thank their successors, Paul J. Fasana, Andrew W. Mellon Director, and G. Rodney Phillips, Associate Director for Public Services, for their continued encouragement and support. I am grateful to Donald Jay also for the warm hospitality he extended to me when my travels on behalf of the exhibition took me to Cairo.

As I began to explain the idea for the exhibition to people outside the Library, I was heartened by the extent of their enthusiasm. Two old friends and colleagues who were particularly generous with their time and cooperation and who, from the outset, helped to allay my fears about my adequacy for the task were Dr. Menaham Schmelzer, until recently Librarian of The Jewish Theological Seminary of America and now Professor of Medieval Hebrew Literature and Jewish Bibliography there, and Dr. Herbert C. Zafren, Director of Libraries at Hebrew Union College–Jewish Institute of Religion. I am also grateful to Dr. Schmelzer's successor as Seminary Librarian, Dr. Mayer Rabinowitz, and to Rabbi Jerry Schwarzbard, Reference Librarian, Special Collections, of the Jewish Theological Seminary of America.

Others whom I thank for their assistance during my Astor Fellowship travels are Dr. Michael W. Grunberger and Doris Hamburg of The Library of Congress; David Gilner and Arnona Rudavsky of Hebrew Union College–Jewish Institute of Religion; Evelyn M. Cohen of The Jewish Theological Seminary of America; Richard and Beatrice Levy, Boca Raton, Florida; the owners of the Frankfurt Mishneh Torah, who wish to remain anonymous; Dr. Diana Rowland-Smith, Manny Silver, and Yasin Safadi of The British Library; A. D. S. Roberts and R. C. Judd of the Bodleian Library, Oxford; Dr. Stefan C. Reif of Cambridge University Library; Jack V. Lunzer of the Valmadonna Trust, London, and his assistant, George Wright; Glenise A. Matheson and Peter McNiven of the John Rylands University Library of Manchester; Colin MacLaren and A. T. Hall of the Aberdeen University Library; Drs. Jespër Düring-Jørgensen and Ulf Haxen of The Royal Library, Copenhagen; Dr. Kurt Hans Staub of the Hessische Landes- und Hochschulbibliothek, Darmstadt; Dr. Wolfgang Irtenkauf of the Württembergische Landesbibliothek, Stuttgart; Father Leonard E. Boyle, O.P., of the Biblioteca Apostolica Vaticana; Professor Malachi Beit-Arié and Rafael Weiser of the Jewish National and University Library, Dr. Leila Avrin of the Hebrew University, Dr. Martin Weyl, Iris Fishof, and Michael Magen of the Israel Museum, Magen Broshi of the Shrine of the Book, Dr. H. J. Katzenstein and Avraham Rosenthal of the Schocken Institute, and Dr. Nehemia Levtzion of the Ben Zvi Institute, all in Jerusalem; Michel Garel, Monique Cohen, and Andrée Pouderoux of the Bibliothèque Nationale, Paris; Dr. Hartmut-Ortwin Feistel of the Staatsbibliothek Preussischer Kulturbesitz, Berlin; Eva Apor and Dr. István Ormos of the Library of the Hungarian Academy of Sciences, Budapest; and Maria Luisa Cabral, João Gonçalves, and Maria Teresa Duarte Ferreira of the Biblioteca Nacional de Lisboa. Malachi Beit-Arié served in some sense as roving ambassador for the exhibition and also made valuable suggestions. I thank, too, those lenders to the exhibition whose names have not been mentioned above.

I spoke about the exhibition over the telephone with the late Dr. David Goldstein of the British Library when I was in London in January 1987. Although illness prevented him from meeting me, he offered kind words of interest and expressed his hope of writing for this volume. He was never able to do so, for he died later in the year. He is remembered with affection by those who knew him.

Others who assisted me with their generous hospitality during my travels are my cousins Irene and Henry Zucker of Glasgow and Ruth Abrahamson of Tel Aviv and my dear friends Lea and Uri Russak of Zurich. Joan Siegel, now of Travel 57, Ltd., was indefatigable in making my travel arrangements.

I thank all who kindly consented to serve on the International Committee of Advisors. I thank, too, the learned essayists who have contributed to this book, and give special recognition to Sharon Liberman Mintz who volunteered to compile the bibliography. Marc M. Epstein of Sotheby's was of great help in determining valuations. At The New York Public Library, Robert Rainwater, Curator of the Spencer Collection, Susan E. Davis, Curator of Manuscripts and Archives, and Francis O. Mattson, Curator of Rare Books, also cooperated graciously with the loan of items in the collections for which they are responsible. David Cronin, Manager of the Library's Public Education Program, has my gratitude for his work in planning public programs. I owe a special debt to Robert D. Rubic for his fine photography of items from the Library's collections and for his sensitivity to the needs of the project.

I heartily thank my colleagues of nearly twenty-five years, Norman Gechlik, First Assistant in the Jewish Division, and Claire L. Dienstag, Principal Cataloger, and all the staff of the division. Together they made sure that I would not have to worry about the Jewish Division while working on the exhibition. Roberta Saltzman of the division made a special contribution as bibliographic detective and speedy, accurate typist. I wish to acknowledge here my incalculable debt to my predecessors as Chief of the Jewish Division, Abraham Berger and Dora Steinglass. They were my mentors and teachers and helped me to set out on the path which led to the present book and exhibition.

My wife, Stella, has given me her unwavering support. I thank her for it in all the forms it has taken and most particularly for helping me to see what a wonderful opportunity for growth this exhibition would be.

LEONARD SINGER GOLD

Foreword

IN 1897 the newly established Jewish Division of The New York Public Library contained two thousand books in Hebrew and other languages on Jewish subjects. Brought together from the Astor and Lenox Libraries and augmented by rare and classic works purchased with funds provided by Jacob H. Schiff and, later, other donors, that nucleus has steadily grown over the twentieth century, presenting a comprehensive record of the Jewish people in many languages and books in Hebrew and Yiddish on a variety of subjects. Included are rare books and manuscripts, as well as basic resources, periodicals, and newspapers. Today, with over a quarter of a million items, the division is one of the world's most important scholarly resources on Jewish life and history as well as one of the nation's broadest collections of historical, literary, and classic Hebrew texts. A special characteristic of the division is the context in which it exists, as a part of the great research collection of The New York Public Library. Many thousands of works throughout the Library complement the divisional resources.

In 1984 the Library was able to reactivate a long-interrupted tradition of major exhibitions through the restoration of the central exhibition space, the D. Samuel and Jeane H. Gottesman Exhibition Hall. In consideration of the importance of the Jewish Division, an exhibition focused on the heritage of the Jewish people was established as one of the priorities for display in the restored hall. In consideration of the Library's strong connections with sister institutions throughout the world, the project was envisioned as international in scope, placing the Library's collections within the context of worldwide collections of Hebrew manuscripts and books. We owe a great debt of gratitude to Dr. Leonard Gold for taking on the challenging task of turning this idea into a reality.

For nearly four years Dr. Gold has worked to develop the exhibition upon which this publication is based. "A Sign and a Witness: 2,000 Years of Hebrew Books and Illuminated Manuscripts" draws heavily from the Library's significant holdings of Hebraica and augments these with loans of important manuscripts and printed books from other collections in the United States, Europe, and Israel. Visitors to the exhibition will have an unparalleled opportunity not only to view rare treasures, many not shown before in America, but also to see a range of related materials brought together under one roof for the very first time.

It is also due to Leonard Gold that this publication was conceived as a companion volume, one which would reinforce the exhibition and augment its themes. The careful choice of contributors, the editing, and the selection of illustrations were all the result of Leonard's efforts, carried on for four years over and above his regular duties as Dorot Chief Librarian of the Jewish Division and Assistant Director for Jewish, Oriental, and Slavonic Studies.

Many individuals and many institutions have made possible this exhibition and this publication. First and foremost, Edith and Henry Everett, two of the Library's most cherished friends, have made possible the entire project through a generous contribution which underwrites the exhibition, the public programs, and the publication. Their participation with us in a venture of such importance for public education and for scholarship exemplifies the highest qualities of enlightened philanthropy, for which I salute them on behalf of the Library's Board of Trustees and my colleagues within The Research Libraries. Additional grants have come from Mr. and Mrs. Alan Greenberg and from other donors, for which we thank them. The exhibition is also supported by an indemnity from The Federal Council on the Arts and the Humanities.

Special guidance and encouragement on the project have been provided from the outset by Joy Ungerleider-Mayerson, another friend of the Library and of the Jewish Division. Her insights and her energetic assistance have been of inestimable help not only to Dr. Gold but also to my colleagues in the Exhibitions Program and Development Offices. We thank her for her intelligent involvement.

It has been a fortuitous circumstance that "A Sign and a Witness" has coincided with New York's celebration of the fortieth anniversary of Israel. I want to express my admiration of Consul General Moshe Yegar's efforts on behalf of American-Israeli friendship and understanding, and my thanks for his interest in the Library and this project.

Encouragement and cooperation have also been forthcoming from numerous local and foreign officials. These include Mayor Teddy Kollek of Jerusalem, Ennio Troili of the Italian Cultural Institute, Alice M. Whelihan of the Federal Arts and Indemnity Program, R. Wallace Stuart of the United States Information Agency, Ely Maurer of the Department of State, and New York City Mayor Edward I. Koch and his Chief of Staff, Diane Coffey. We also give special thanks to

Dr. Martin Weyl, Director of the Israel Museum, for his early support and his involvement in the evolution of the project.

At an early stage of exhibition planning, an international committee of advisors was organized. I thank them all for their gracious participation: Professor Malachi Beit-Arié, Father Leonard E. Boyle, O.P., Magen Broshi, Michel Garel, the late Dr. David Goldstein, Professor Joseph Gutmann, Dr. Ulf Haxen, Professor Bezalel Narkiss, Dr. Stefan C. Reif, Dr. Menahem Schmelzer, Dr. Gabrielle Sed-Rajna, Professor Colette Sirat, Joy Ungerleider-Mayerson, and Dr. Herbert C. Zafren.

The extent of international cooperation involved in the exhibition and the publication is reflected also in the list of lenders to the exhibition, which includes over twenty-five institutions and private collections. We are grateful to all of the individuals and administrators who have generously lent to this show and assisted with arrangements. In many cases these loans represent the first time that the objects have been allowed to travel, and we are humbly grateful for the opportunity to bring them to New York for public viewing.

Leonard Gold has also been supported in his work on this book and exhibition by many members of the Library staff, including members of the General Research Division, the Special Collections, the Conservation Division, the Exhibitions Program Office, the Publications Office, the Graphics Office, the Public Education Program Office, the Public Relations Office, and the Office of Public Affairs and Development.

The Library is truly a House of the Book. Its main business is to acquire books, to make them available for use, and to conserve them for posterity. It is also a museum of the book, interpreting collections and putting treasures on view. It is sometimes a "workshop of the scholar," the setting in which discoveries are made, new knowledge created, new books born. And, on very special occasions, the Library itself brings a book into being. That is the present case. The House of the Book has drawn upon the riches it has acquired, organized, conserved, and borrowed to present an exhibition, "A Sign and a Witness: 2,000 Years of Hebrew Books and Illuminated Manuscripts." To complete the undertaking it has initiated the publication of this volume, which we hope will serve as a record of an international cultural event of lasting significance.

VARTAN GREGORIAN
President and Chief Executive Officer
The New York Public Library

A Sign and a Witness:
2,000 Years of Hebrew Books and Illuminated Manuscripts

In the illustration captions, "NYPL" refers to The New York Public Library. "Ex. no. —" refers to the number in the Checklist of the Exhibition, which begins on p. 198.

Introduction

THE CENTRALITY of the book in Jewish life was secured by the Pharisaic-Rabbinic revolution some two thousand years ago, which transformed Judaism from a Temple-bound system to a religious culture that could survive and flourish in the most diverse environments. The Mishnah, a collection of early rabbinic opinions put into its final form in about the year 220 of the Common Era, states: "These are the things the fruits of which a man enjoys in this world, and the stock of which remains for him in the world to come, honoring one's father and mother, and charity, and making peace between man and his fellow; but the study of the Torah is equal to them all" (Peah 1:1).

One way in which the transformation was accomplished was by identifying Scripture with the Sanctuary, a tradition begun in antiquity and continued through the Middle Ages. Thus, the Sephardic Bible manuscript is sometimes called *Mikdashyah,* or "Sanctuary of God." The identification is made complete by decorating the Bible manuscript with pictures of the sanctuary implements, which hark back to the time when the Temple stood and embody the promise of a future Messianic Age.

This volume appears on the occasion of The New York Public Library's exhibition "A Sign and a Witness: 2,000 Years of Hebrew Books and Illuminated Manuscripts." (The title is taken from Isaiah 19:20.) It is meant both as a preparation for seeing the exhibition and as a guide to further inquiry. In it experts in various fields share their knowledge in such a way as to orient the novice as well as provide something new for the specialist. Although it contains a checklist of the items exhibited, the book is not a catalog as the term is usually understood. The organizers of the exhibition see the book, instead, as a record of the event and as a resource that will stand on its own merit in the future.

The concept of the exhibition is very ambitious indeed: to display Hebrew books produced in a very broad range of locations over the past two millennia. Never before has such a gathering been brought to public view. It has been made possible only through the generous cooperation of libraries, private collectors, philanthropic foundations, and government agencies in America, Europe, and Israel. Enthusiasm for the project has been infectious. This venture has been the work of many hands, and all deserve credit for the outcome.

Any exhibition requires selection. Selection is determined in part by what is available and in part by deliberate decision. In making choices for the present exhibition, the organizers considered both the corpus of existing material and the interests of the viewing public. On the one hand, the great majority of extant Hebrew manuscripts are undecorated, and most Hebrew printed books must look very dull to the uncomprehending eye. On the other hand, while New York is blessed with more Hebrew readers than many other great cities, most visitors to the exhibition will not know Hebrew, and this is meant to be an exhibition for all. Visual appeal has therefore been an important consideration in making choices, so that what has been brought together is not entirely "representative" of the body of Hebrew literature.

A word about the subject itself is in order. Why the Hebrew book and not the literature of the Jews? That would have had to include expressions in Yiddish, Ladino, Judeo-Arabic, and other Jewish languages, as well as Aramaic, Greek, and the entire gamut of modern European languages. The answer comes down, again, to the need for selectivity. By limiting the subject we hoped to keep the project manageable. Admittedly, selectivity can be frustrating.

The assumptions underlying the exhibition are simple, even though they seem to pull in opposite directions. The first is that the Hebrew book is fundamentally important and merits attention in its own right. The second is that the Jews, the primary exponents of the Hebrew book, always participated in some form of exchange with the cultures surrounding them. The resulting traffic in ideas, which involved both giving and receiving, made the Jews important transmitters of culture, and this was accomplished in large part through the medium of the Hebrew book.

The principle for organizing the material in the exhibition is literary. Within literary categories technical aspects of book production receive consideration. The first category, *In the Beginning* (Gen. 1:1), consists of the Hebrew Bible: the Torah or Five Books of Moses, the Prophets, and the Writings, which are the source of all Jewish teaching. The *Naḥum Commentary,* the Dead Sea Scroll which is the most ancient item exhibited, belongs to this group. The second section, *A Fence around the Law* (Avot 1:1), contains works belonging to the Oral Tradition: the Mishnah, the Babylonian Talmud and the Talmud of the Land of Israel, legal codes, rabbinic responsa and other works of Jewish law. The third group, *Remember This Day* (Ex. 13:3), includes books dealing with prayer and celebration. The fourth, *Tongue of the Wise* (Prov. 15:2), contains works of language and literature, and the last, *The World and the Fulness Thereof* (based on Ps. 24:1), embraces writings which endeavor to understand the world and include philosophy, science, and mysticism.

The volume at hand approaches the Hebrew book differently. A group of experts has been invited to write, each on a topic related to her or his field of specialization which contributes to the general theme. Authors were asked to keep in mind the educated lay person who may not be familiar with the Hebrew language or the Hebrew book. Some writers have provided notes and some have not. Bibliographies for the essays have been incorporated into the single bibliography near the end of the volume. Some of the contributions contain information not published before. Others approach their subject in a novel way, and still others make available for the first time in English material which had previously to be read in other languages.

Professor Cross, who opens the collection with his paper on the Dead Sea Scrolls and their significance for study of the text and canon of the Hebrew Bible, establishes the context for the cornerstone of the exhibition, its oldest manuscript, the *Naḥum Commentary*. Professor Beit-Arié discusses the way Hebrew manuscripts are made, while Professor Schmelzer deals with them as a resource for scholarship. Ms. Cohen treats the decoration of Hebrew manuscripts, and Professor Gutmann traces the way in which today's great collections came into being. Dr. Glatzer writes of Hebrew printing in its infancy. Dr. Rosenfeld concentrates on the sixteenth and seventeenth centuries, the period in which Hebrew printing gained acceptance and spread beyond Italy and the Iberian peninsula. Dr. Grunberger discusses the role that publishers played in nurturing the renascent Hebrew literature of the late nineteenth and early twentieth centuries and, conversely, the influence of certain writers on Hebrew publishing. Dr. Avrin recounts the twentieth-century movement for higher standards of Hebrew book production.

There are three contributions which consider overall aspects of the Hebrew book and therefore go beyond the distinction between manuscript and printed book. It is no accident that two of these are also the essays that deal most directly with the complex cultural relations between Jews and their neighbors. Professor Ruderman describes the changing nature of Christian involvement with the Hebrew book. Mr. Singerman shows through the history of translation into and out of Hebrew the role played by the Hebrew book in the transmission of culture. Chaim Potok, the well-known American Jewish novelist, writes about Hebrew books that have been important in his life.

These essays are by scholars who deal with the book as form and as content. And the Hebrew book is both. The Torah, the first five books of the Hebrew Bible, which contains the basic teaching of Judaism, is read and studied in the synagogue. As a book in scroll form it is also venerated: it is richly clothed, it is held aloft for all to see, it is carried in procession through the congregation so that worshippers may touch it with prayerbooks or prayer shawls. Holiness stems from the teaching, yet the physical book is itself revered.

LEONARD SINGER GOLD
Dorot Chief Librarian of the Jewish Division
The New York Public Library
November 1987

I   FRANK MOORE CROSS

The Dead Sea Scrolls: Light on the Text and Canon of the Bible

In 1947 two young shepherds of the Taʿâmireh tribe discovered ancient manuscripts in a cave in the towering cliffs that line the Dead Sea in the vicinity of the ancient ruin of Qumrân. The seven major documents that belonged to this first find, announced to the world in the spring of 1948, came to be known as the "Dead Sea Scrolls." Another year was to pass before Western scholars were able to explore and excavate the cave—owing to conditions created by the Israeli-Arab war following the establishment of the State of Israel in May 1948. When the cave was finally cleared, it had yielded, including the well-preserved seven scrolls, some seventy documents, most of them highly fragmentary.[1]

The discovery of these ancient manuscripts created a sensation in the scholarly community, and led to heated controversy concerning their date and the identity of the sectarian community which produced them. Soon the story was taken up by the press and popularized, intriguing such distinguished writers as Edmund Wilson, and puzzling such characters as Charlie Brown in *Peanuts*.[2]

The great Isaiah Scroll (1QIsaᵃ), which was dated to the second century B.C.E. by leading palaeogra-phers, presented a form of the text of Isaiah one thousand years older than the medieval manuscripts upon which the received (traditional) text of Isaiah is based. While the date of the Isaiah scroll was sharply disputed initially—for the most part by scholars without epigraphic or palaeographic training—now, forty years later, thanks to a large corpus of documents of the period, we can date the great scroll confidently to 150–125 B.C.E. Another scroll from the cave, a commentary (*péšer*) on Habakkuk, was inscribed, and probably composed, in the early Herodian era (ca. 25 B.C.E.). The commentator perceived in the text of Habakkuk allusions to his own time and, concretely, prophecies of events in the history of his sect, now identified by a consensus of scholars with the Essenes. This document too produced a storm of controversy. The archenemy of the sect, called the "Wicked Priest" in the commentary, who is described as persecuting the sect and its leader, the "Righteous Teacher," was identified by various scholars with various historical figures, priests who flourished in Hellenistic and Roman antiquity in Judaea. Alas, there was (as always) an ample supply of wicked priests, and the veiled language of the commentary furnished insufficiently precise details to identify the villain. In addition to biblical manuscripts and commentaries on biblical works, Cave I, Qumrân, produced apocryphal, juridical, liturgical, and hymnic works, some known (e.g., the Book of Jubilees), but mostly unknown. Among the most important manuscripts is one containing *The Order of the Community*. It reviews the history of the sect (the Essenes, "pious ones"), utilizing the technique of apocalyptic interpretation of Scripture following the same principles used in the commentaries, instructs in doctrine, lays down the laws and halakic lore by which the community lived, and gives the protocols of its "messianic banquet." In short, the scrolls tell us much about the apocalyptic *Weltbild* of the separatist Jewish community and its refraction in their daily life.

In 1952 tribesmen found fragmentary remains of manuscripts in a new cave, hard by Cave I. Archaeologists realized that the first cave was not an isolated, unique cache, and it began to dawn upon them that the manuscripts actually derived from a community with its center at the ruin of Qumrân (Khirbet Qumrân). An expedition of various archaeological schools in Jerusalem was galvanized to explore the caves of the rocky cliffs north and south of Khirbet Qumrân. Of two hundred caves explored, one, Cave III, Qumrân, produced a few fragmentary manuscripts and the famous "Copper Scroll," a list of fabulous treasures, presumably of the Temple of Solomon, and their hiding places. Although some gullible scholars have taken the scroll seriously, no treasures have been located. The document belongs to the genre of fantasy, not to accountancy. The scholars retired from the desert, the bedouin remained. Bedouin discovered Cave IV, Qumrân, located in the marl terrace on which the community center of Qumrân stands. Clandestine digging by the Ta'âmireh was halted before the cave was exhausted, and Cave IV, containing the main remains of the ancient library of the community, was excavated by scientists in September 1952. Caves V and VI were found in conjunction with the discovery of Cave IV, Cave V by scientists, Cave VI by tribesmen. In 1955, during excavations at Khirbet Qumrân, four additional caves in the marl terrace were located and exploited: Caves VII–X. Caves II, III, and V–X have been published as the minor caves of Qumrân.[3]

In 1956 a cave, collapsed in antiquity, was divined by Ta'âmireh shepherds from observation of the flight of bats from crevices. Cave XI, Qumrân, proved to be, along with Caves I and IV, a major cave. The most remarkable of its contents are a Psalms Scroll, which mixes together hymns of the canonical Psalter with apocryphal hymns and unknown compositions, and the great Temple Scroll, published by the late Yigael Yadin.[4] The latter is an astonishing work, composed in the form of instructions directly from God himself, through Moses, designed as an additional book of the Torah. Yadin viewed it as an Essene work; others have argued with some merit that it is "proto-Essene," that is, a work of relatively early date that later influenced the calendar and law of the Qumrân sect. The rigor of the legal interpretations of the Temple Scroll is extraordinary. For example, the priestly and military laws of uncleanness were to be applied not merely to the Temple proper but *mirabile dictu* to the holy city as a whole. Effectively this meant that women could not live in Jerusalem. Men living in Jerusalem, led by priests, could not desecrate the city, so acts which render one unclean had to be performed outside the holy city. In such circumstances, priestly continence was imposed or recommended. Latrines were to be 3,000 cubits (nearly a mile) outside the city, and not to be used on the Sabbath. The lame, blind, or diseased with unclean ailments were excluded not only from the temple but also from the city.[5]

Cave IV, as we have noted above, was the main cache of the ancient library of Qumrân. It contained about 580 manuscripts at latest count; of these about 120 were biblical manuscripts. Every biblical book of the later Hebrew canon is represented with the exception of the Book of Esther, and commentaries are found on the books of Isaiah, Hosea, Nahum, Zephaniah, and Psalms. None of the manuscripts of Cave IV is as well preserved as the best of the Cave I and Cave XI manuscripts, but the riches of this cave are overwhelming, and provide vast source materials for studying the history of the biblical text and the history of Judaism in the Hellenistic and Early Roman era in Palestine. It will be another decade or more before all these manuscripts are published.[6]

Concurrent with the discoveries at Qumrân, and continuing into recent years, were manuscript and papyrus discoveries in other precincts of the Jordan rift. Caves well to the south of Qumrân in the Wadi Murabba'ât were explored by Ta'âmireh in 1951, and produced documents mostly from the era of the Second Jewish Revolt against Rome (132–135 C.E.). In addition to nonliterary documents left behind by slaughtered rebels under the pseudo-Messiah Bar Kokheba, there were some biblical scrolls, including a very important copy of the Minor Prophets.[7] A cave in the Nahal Hever was explored by tribesmen in 1952, and by Israeli archaeologists in 1960 and 1961, along with other caves in the great southern wâdis. Prominent among the finds is a manuscript of a Greek recension of the Minor Prophets, a key document for reconstructing the history of the Greek Bible.[8]

In the early spring of 1962, Ta'âmireh shepherds found a new cave in the Jordan rift north of Jericho, which yielded unique documents, papyri drafted in Samaria in the years immediately before the conquest of Palestine by Alexander the Great (ca. 385–332 B.C.E.). They are the first legal documents of high antiquity found in Palestine, and shed light on a dark century of Persian rule. They also prove important for the reconstruction of the era of the Jewish Restoration.[9]

The most recent discoveries come from the ancient fortress built by Herod the Great at Masada. Major excavations at Masada were carried out under the direction of Yigael Yadin in 1963–64 and 1964–65. The literary finds come from the era of the First Jewish Revolt when the magnificent site was seized and held by Zealots in their last stand against Rome. The fortress fell to the Romans in 73 C.E. when the Jewish contingent committed mass suicide. Sealed in the destruction were fragments of biblical manuscripts, a text of Ben Sira (Ecclesiasticus), and a document known elsewhere only from Qumrân, the "Songs of the Sabbath Sacrifice."[10]

The caves at Qumrân and north and south of Qumrân in the arid wastes of the Jordan rift valley have produced over the years remarkable finds of manuscripts on leather and papyri. There is no reason to believe that these finds are exhausted, and indeed there has been a new, small but important find near Jericho, yet to be announced.

THE QUMRÂN scrolls and the people of the scrolls can be placed within a broad historical framework with relative certitude, thanks to external controls furnished by the archaeologist and the palaeographer. The historian must begin here, for the internal controls pose special problems for the historian, as we have seen, owing to the esoteric language of the sectarian scrolls.

The archaeological context of the community of the Dead Sea, its caves, community center, and agricultural adjunct at 'Ên Feshkhah has been established by six major seasons of excavation (1951–58).[11] The ancient center at Khirbet Qumrân has yielded a clear stratification, and in turn the strata are closely dated by their yield of artifacts, including large quantities of coins. In the era of our interest, the site exhibits three phases. The first of these, so-called Period Ia, consists of the remains of the earliest communal structures. In Period Ib, the settlement was almost completely rebuilt and enlarged. The coin series suggests that the buildings of the second phase were constructed in the time of Alexander Jannaeus, the Hasmonaean who ruled from 103 to 76 B.C.E. The foundation of the community, owing to the extensive rebuilding, is more difficult to date precisely. Obviously it is earlier than Period Ib, and must be placed within the extreme limits of 150–100 B.C.E. and probable limits of 140–120 B.C.E. Period Ib came to an end because of a great earthquake, almost certainly the great earthquake of 31 B.C.E. reported by the historian Flavius Josephus. After a short period of abandonment, the site was reoccupied, rebuilt, and repaired precisely on the plan of the older communal complex; Period II flourished until 68 C.E. when it was stormed by the forces of Vespasian, Roman general and later emperor, in the course of his raid on Jericho.

The center was composed of communal facilities for study, writing, eating, domestic industries, and common stores. The members of the community lived, for the most part, not in the buildings, but in caves and shelters radiating out from the central buildings. The architectural functions of the rooms and structures require a special mode of religious and communistic life which correlates nicely with the institutions and orders laid down in the sectarian writings.

Corroboration of this reading of the archaeological evidence is immediately furnished by palaeographical analysis of the library of Qumrân. The scripts of Qumrân belong to three periods of palaeographical development. A very small group of biblical manuscripts belong to an archaic style whose limits are circa 250–150 B.C.E. A large group of manuscripts are in hands of the Hasmonaean period, between 150–30 B.C.E. Manuscripts *composed* as well as *copied* by the sectarian community begin, most significantly, about the middle of this period, toward 100 B.C.E. Finally, there is a large corpus of Herodian manuscripts dating between 30 B.C.E. and 70 C.E.[12]

The relatively identical conclusions derived from the independent disciplines of the archaeologist and the palaeographer establish the framework within which we must reconstruct the history of the sectarian community. We must look for its origins in the interval between 150 and 100 B.C.E. and its effective demise in the Jewish Revolt against Rome.

Extant classical texts which treat the history of the second century B.C.E. mention four Jewish movements in Judaea, the Hasidim, a pious "congregation" which disappeared in the Maccabaean era, and three orders which emerged no later than the early Hasmonaean era, and presumably have their roots in the Maccabaean period. These are the Essenes, the Pharisees, and the Sadducees. Of these three, only the Essenes can be described as separatist in the radical sense that they separated themselves fully from close contact with fellow Jews. Josephus informs us that the Essenes rejected as unclean even the sacrificial service of the Temple. Pliny (or rather his sources) tells us of the Essene "city" in the wilderness between Jericho and 'Ên Gedi near the shore of the Dead Sea. In the absence of strong counterarguments, this datum is decisive in identifying the sectarians of Qumrân with the Essenes. We know of no other sect arising in the second century B.C.E. which can be associated with the wilderness community. Further, the community of Qumrân, as we know from their writings, was organized precisely as a new Israel, a true sect which repudiated the priesthood and cultus of Jerusalem, and indeed dreamed apocalyptic dreams of establishing a cleansed Jerusalem, a refurbished temple, with a legitimate (i.e., sectarian) cultus, calendar, and priesthood. Neither the Pharisees nor the Sadducees can qualify. The Essenes qualify perfectly.

IN THE BRIEF compass allotted to us in this essay, we can comment on only one or two of the many areas in which the library of Qumrân has enriched our knowledge of early Judaism and its literature. I have chosen to discuss the contribution of the Dead Sea Scrolls to our understanding of the history of the biblical text, and to examine the biblical commentaries, notably the *Pēšer Naḥum,* with a view to discovering the mode of interpretation or exegesis practiced by the community.

The technique of exposition of Scripture in the commentaries and related works grows out of the presuppositions of apocalypticism, and can be understood only within the categories of this special type of eschatological thought. Two major assumptions characterize apocalyptic exegesis. First, all biblical prophecy is normally taken to have eschatological meaning. Moreover, most of Scripture is taken to be prophecy. The "prophets," Moses as well as Amos, the Psalmist as well as Jeremiah, are believed to speak regularly in open or in hidden language of the "last days." Their predictions are not to be understood in simple historical terms of the near future or even the remote future, but apply to "final times," the crisis of the ages in which the historical epoch, "this age," turns into the transhistorical epoch, the new age to come. Second, it must be understood that the apocalyptist commenting on Scripture understood himself to be living in these days of final crisis at the end of days and the dawning of the New Age, so the events of his own time were identified as precisely those events foretold by the prophets of old as coming to pass in the last days.

By assiduously searching the Scriptures the Essenes were able to find allusions to events of current history: the central figures of their

Fragment of the Naḥum Commentary
(Péšer Naḥum). *This Commentary is
unique among published scrolls of the Dead
Sea Scrolls in its naming of historical figures
and its reference to an identifiable event in
history.*
The Shrine of the Book, D. Samuel and Jeane H.
Gottesman Center for Biblical Manuscripts, Israel
Museum, Jerusalem [Ex. no. 28]

own sect and of their own times
were to be found hidden in prophetic
discourse. The life of their sect, its
origin, vicissitudes, and glorious des-
tiny, all had been laid out in the predictions of the ancients. To be sure,
these allusions could be read only by
"those who had eyes to see." Essene
exegesis was necessarily pneumatic,
based on the gift of special eschatological "knowledge." The secrets of
the prophets had to be discovered by
inspired interpreters.

In the Qumrân commentaries certain set forms of exposition and a
traditional body of biblical exposition grew up, stemming no doubt
from a pattern laid down by the
sect's founder, the Righteous Teacher,
but transmitted and supplemented in

the regular study of scholars of the
community, and particularly in the
regular sessions of the sect mentioned
in our sources, where Scripture was
read and systematically expounded.
In a later era (all the commentaries
are of late date) the body of accumu-
lated traditional exegesis was put
into writing in the documents which
have come into our hands.

Essene exegesis describes the
events of its time from within the
myopic outlook of the elect community. The important events of history are those which involve or affect
the sect. This means that major political events (from our point of

view)—Pompey's conquest of Jerusalem, the death of a high priest—are judged significant according to their direct bearing on the life of the sect, while insignificant events (from the historian's perspective)—the rebuke of an Essene leader, the disturbance of a festival—become turning points in world history. In the commentaries the inner history of the sect is bewilderingly mixed with external political events.

Apocalyptic exegesis also makes use of a mythic typology of eras. There is to be a new desert sojourn (life at Qumrân), a new Exodus, a new covenant, a new gift of "the height of Israel," a new Holy War. Parallels with New Testament typological exegesis will be discerned here. A prophet like Moses, a messiah like David, a priest like Aaron or Zadok, are expected. Figures bearing biblical sobriquets, the "Righteous Teacher," the "False Oracle," the "Wrathful Lion," and a dozen others, appear in the "last times," that is to say, in the present days of the sectarian exegete.

One of the most important commentaries found in Cave IV, Qumrân, is the *Nahum Commentary,* in which, along with allusions to persons called by biblical sobriquets, as is usual in the commentaries, we find explicit reference by personal name to two historical figures. In one passage being expounded, Nahum 2:12–14, Nineveh of the Assyrians is described under the figure of a den of lions, lions cut down by the divine sword. The key passages are as follows: (Col. I, l. 2) "[this is

to be interpreted as referring to Deme]trius the Greek king who attempted to enter Jerusalem at the advice of the 'Clever Expositors' . . ."; (l. 3) ". . . the Greek kings from Antiochus until the accession of the rulers of the Kittiyim"; and (ll. 6–7) ". . . this is to be interpreted as referring to the 'Wrathful Lion' . . . [ ] who hangs men alive. . . ."

The exposition deals with a very small unit of Scripture, and in all probability deals with a single series of events, far removed, of course, from the fall of Nineveh of which the prophet Nahum actually sang. We must look for a setting in the framework set by the text itself, in the interval between Antiochus and the establishment of Kittaean rulers in the East. The Antiochus in question is probably Antiochus IV, Epiphanes (175–163 B.C.E.), the Seleucid ruler who desecrated the Temple of Jerusalem, although a later important Seleucid such as Antiochus VII, Sidetes (138–129 B.C.E.), cannot be ruled out. The Kittaean rulers seem clearly enough to be the Roman rulers who arrive on the scene beginning with Pompey, who conquered Jerusalem in 63 B.C.E. In this framework we must look for (1) an attempt by a Greek king named Demetrius to enter Jerusalem, preferably in an attack on a Jewish prince who (2) crucified men alive.

Of the Greek kings named Demetrius, Demetrius III (Eukairos) is the most suitable candidate. His adversary was Alexander Jannaeus, the priest-king of Judaea from 103 to 76 B.C.E. In Jannaeus' reign civil war broke out (93–88 B.C.E.), and in 88 B.C.E. the desperate Jewish rebels against Jannaeus called upon Demetrius Eukairos for succor. Demetrius met Jannaeus at Shechem north of Jerusalem and decisively defeated him. However, Demetrius was not permitted to follow up his victory and take Jerusalem. The Jews who had asked his aid and fought alongside him, in view of the threat to Jerusalem, abruptly went over to the side of their archenemy Jannaeus. When Demetrius was forced to retire in the face of Jannaeus' new strength, Jannaeus turned on the Jewish rebels and, we are told by Josephus, crucified captives in wholesale lots.

This construction, while speculative in part, admirably fits the requirements of the text of the commentary. What does it tell of the history of the Essenes? The "Wrathful Lion" and the events of his time discovered by the sectarians in the prophecy of Nahum certainly belong to "their history," i.e., to the end of days. However, we have no way of knowing whether the terrible events in the reign of Alexander Jannaeus, the illegitimate priest of Jerusalem (to speak from an Essene point of view), belong early or late in the history of the sect. There is no mention of the Righteous Teacher in connection with these events, and no reason to connect the Wrathful Lion with figures of the era of Essene origins such as the wicked priest *par excellence,* whose biblical sobriquet seems to be the "False Oracle."

There is now increasingly agreement among scholars that the archvillain of the sect, the Wicked Priest who persecuted the Righteous Teacher, is to be identified with one of the Maccabaean brothers, Jonathan or Simon. Jonathan usurped the priesthood at the appointment of a Seleucid pretender in 152 B.C.E. After his death at the hands of Tryphon, another Seleucid pretender, his brother Simon, took power and, in the third year of his ascendancy, 140 B.C.E., was proclaimed legitimate high priest, he and his sons after him "until a faithful prophet arise." The proclamation was by the assembly of the Jews, seconded by the Seleucid Demetrius II, and the house of Simon thereby became high priests *de jure* replacing the ancient Zadokite line. Simon and two of his sons came to a violent end in a fortress in Jericho at the hands of his Edomite son-in-law, Ptolemy son of Abubos, military commander of Jericho, in a plot to overthrow the house of Simon. The Commentary on Habakkuk from Cave I describes the end of the Wicked Priest: "God gave into the hand of his enemies to bring him low with a mortal blow. . . ." A commentary on Psalm 37 observes that the Wicked Priest was "given into the hands of 'Violent Foreigners'" (a biblical cliché, *'rysy gwym*). Neither comment fits Alexander Jannaeus. Both appropriately apply to Jonathan *or* Simon. I am inclined to favor Simon. A document called 4Q Testimonia quotes the curse of Joshua on the city of Jericho (Joshua 6:26): "Cursed before the Lord be the man that rises up and rebuilds this city [ ]. At the cost of his firstborn shall he lay its foundation and at the cost of his youngest son shall he set up its gates." The exposition follows: "And behold, cursed is the man of Belial who comes to power to be a trapper's snare to his people. . . ." The next lines are broken but appear to apply to the two sons of the "man of Belial." The best reconstruction, I believe, of several suggested, is to read "and he rose to power and [his sons] . . . [with him], the two of them becoming violent instruments, and they rebuilt again this [city?]." The passage assuredly applies to an archenemy of the sect. The application of the passage to Simon and his sons Judas and Mattathias, and their deaths in Jericho, seems to me almost inevitable. Jonathan was murdered by Tryphon in Transjordan on his way home to Syria; Simon was killed in Jericho while fortifying the city. It is possible, but unlikely I think, that the man of Belial (the "Hellion") is not the Wicked Priest. However, it should be noted that the Testimonia Document lists prophecies of five figures expected by the sect in the last days: a "prophet like Moses," the Star of Jacob and the Scepter of Israel, the priestly and royal Messiahs respectively, the new Levi who "shall teach thy judgments to Jacob, thy torah to Israel," presumably the Righteous Teacher, and the "Man of Belial." In this company the one cursed should be the archvillain of the sect.

THE DISCOVERY of ancient manuscripts in the caves of Qumrân provides the first unambiguous witness to an ancient stage of the Hebrew text of the Bible. The eleven caves

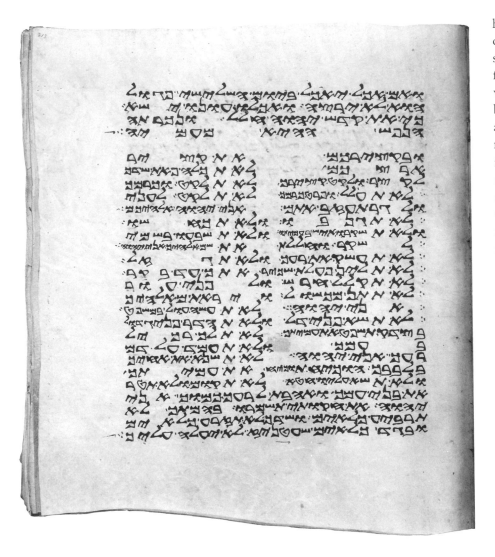

Page of a Samaritan Torah written on parchment in the Land of Israel in the thirteenth century. This page contains the text of Leviticus 19:7–19 in Hebrew in Samaritan script. NYPL, Rare Books and Manuscripts Division [Ex. no. 19]

have yielded some 175 manuscripts of biblical books. The biblical manuscripts of Qumrân differ strikingly from the medieval manuscripts upon which the received or traditional biblical text is based. The number and variety of variant readings are much greater—I am tempted to say incomparably greater—in the case of certain important manuscripts. Further, the textual variation found in these manuscripts is not inchoate, the result of indiscriminate mixing of manuscript readings. There exist at Qumrân discrete and, indeed, recognizable families of textual tradition. Some, despite their many variant readings, clearly belong to the family from which the Rabbinic Recension, which fixed a standard Hebrew text, was derived. This Rabbinic Recension, to which we shall return below, is the immediate ancestor of the masoretic biblical text of the ninth and tenth centuries C.E., the base of the modern Hebrew Bible. Other manuscripts belong to other text types or families with characteristic differences from the Rabbinic Recension. Some manuscripts, for example, the well-preserved scroll of Samuel (4QSam[a]) from Cave IV, Qumrân, contain a text closely allied to the Hebrew manuscript used in Egypt in the third century B.C.E. for translation into Greek, the so-called Septuagint. In the case of the Book of Jeremiah, we possess from Cave IV text types which develop from two different editions of Jeremiah, a short, older edition (4QJer[b]) known hitherto only in Old Greek translation, and a longer edition (by one-seventh) ancestral to the text chosen by the Rabbis for their recension

(4QJer^a). These Hebrew texts, related to the Hebrew text which underlies the Greek translation, settle an old argument among scholars. Many textual critics of the Hebrew and Greek texts of the Bible have argued in the past that the Old Greek or Septuagint basically was translated from a text quite like the traditional text fixed by the Rabbis. The differences in the Old Greek translation were attributable to the errors, biases, omissions, and additions of the translators, not to an underlying Hebrew text which differed from the traditional text. In Jeremiah, for example, the short text was considered an abbreviation and reshuffling of the standard Hebrew text. The new evidence proves the Greek translation to be a faithful witness to its *Vorlage,* not an erratic creation distorted by the vagaries of a willful translator. Such information about the character of the Old Greek translation is of enormous value to the textual critic, who can in effect treat the Old Greek translation as a witness to the Hebrew text in Egypt in the third century B.C.E. It is as if we had discovered another corpus of manuscripts from Egypt, for the new finds teach us how to utilize the surviving Old Greek text. Other Qumrân manuscripts, for example, manuscripts of Exodus and Numbers, reflect a late Palestinian text similar to that preserved in a Samaritan recension of the Pentateuch, and which, thanks to the new evidence, we can trace back to a family branching off from the Palestinian text in the late first century B.C.E. or the first century of the Common Era.

The several variant streams of textual tradition appear to be the product of natural development in isolation in the process of scribal transmission, not of a controlled or systematic *recensio,* revision, or collation at a given time or place. At the same time, in the differing textual families we now know from Qumrân, and from the Rabbinic Recension, the Samaritan Recension, and the *Vorlage* of the Old Greek translation, we can discern traits, some more or less systematic, of each of the textual families. These traits held in common by a given family include especially their "bad genes," an inherited group of scribal mistakes or secondary readings. In addition to these "corrupt readings," as the textual critic terms them, they also include such features as an orthographic style, reworked chronologies, and "modernized" grammar and lexicon. In short, at Qumrân, and in the traditions of the biblical text that broke off from the main Jewish stream before the turn of the Common Era (the Samaritan Recension and the Septuagint), we find several textual families which probably had their origin in local texts, texts transmitted over centuries in separate Jewish communities, in Palestine, Egypt, and Babylonia. None, including the text type ancestral to the Rabbinic Recension, shows evidence of a systematic recension or attempt at stabilization.

The biblical manuscripts from Qumrân differ strikingly from the corpus of biblical manuscripts found in the southern caves, at Murabbaʿât and Ḥever, and in the Zealot bastion at Masada. The latter, "southern group" are of later date, from the late first and early second century of the Common Era. Moreover, in the southern group we find only a single text type, one that shows *every* evidence of the external controls that fixed the text we call the Rabbinic Recension. Indeed, it stands very close to the archetype of this recension. We are led to the conclusion that the Rabbinic Recension of the Hebrew Bible—what we may call the authoritative Pharisaic text—was already fixed by the time of the Roman destruction of Jerusalem in 70 C.E., and that this recension became regnant in the interval between the two Jewish Revolts, when the Pharisaic party came wholly to dominate the surviving Jewish community and rival parties diminished and disappeared. Rabbinic Judaism survived, and with it the Rabbinic Recension.

The Rabbinic Recension was promulgated as a response and solution to a "textual crisis" that developed in Hellenistic and Roman times. The Maccabaean Revolt, initiated in 167 B.C.E., ultimately reestablished an independent Jewish state, which had not existed since the destruction of Jerusalem and the First Temple in 587 B.C.E. In the wake of the Maccabaean victories that led eventually to the full independence of Judaea under the rule of Simon the Maccabee (140–134 B.C.E.), a Zionist revival was fueled, augmented by Parthian expulsions of the Jews. A flood of Jews returned to Jerusalem from Babylon, Syria, and Egypt. By the first century before and the first century of the Common Era, competing local texts and editions of biblical works had found their way to Judaea, causing no little confusion, as reflected in the library at Qumrân. Moreover, the uncontrolled development of the text of individual textual families became intolerable and precipitated a textual crisis when the urgent need for precise doctrinal and legal (halakic) exegesis arose in Hellenistic Judaism. Concurrent with these events was the rise of party strife with the emergence of the Sadducean, Pharisaic, and Essene parties; the subsequent religious disputes between the parties increased the need for a fixed, authoritative text. By the beginning of the first century of the Common Era further sectarian splinters appear, and there is evidence of intense intra-party dispute as well as inter-party and sectarian argument and contention.

These data provide the general time and historical context for the creation of the Rabbinic Recension. Other bits of data, limiting the time frame in which we must place the promulgation of the Rabbinic Recension, are found in the history of the Palestinian recensions of the Greek Bible. In sum, our new evidence points to the first half of the first century of the Common Era as the date of the promulgation of the Rabbinic Recension. In these days the great sage Hillel flourished, and to the school of Hillel we must assign the recensional labors which established the text that would become authoritative in later Judaism.

The new light shed by finds at Qumrân and in the southern caves on the history of the Hebrew Bible and the Greek recensions of the Old Greek Bible enable us to sketch in part the process by which the Rabbinic or "Hillelite" Recension came into existence. The establishment of the text followed a pattern unusual in the textual history of ancient documents. Unlike the recensional activity in Alexandria, which produced a short if artificial and eclectic text of Homer, and quite unlike the recensional activity which gave rise to the conflate *textus receptus* of the New Testament, the activity of the Pharisaic scholars proceeded neither by wholesale revision nor by eclectic or conflating procedures. Instead, the Rabbis selected a single textual tradition, which we term the proto-Rabbinic text, which had been in existence in individual manuscripts for some time. In a given biblical book of the Hebrew Bible, the Rabbis chose exemplars of one textual family or even a single manuscript as a base. They did not collate all the wide variety of textual types available; on the contrary, in some instances they firmly rejected a dominant late Palestinian text. It should be noted, however, that they did not select, in the case of every book, texts having a common origin or local background. In the Pentateuch they chose a short, relatively unconflated text—a superb text from the point of view of the modern critic—quite unlike the late Palestinian text found in many of the Qumrân manuscripts, in the Samaritan Pentateuch, and in such Hellenistic

Jewish works as the Book of Jubilees and the Genesis Apocryphon. On the other hand, they chose relatively late and conflate Palestinian texts of the Major Prophets, Isaiah, Jeremiah, and Ezekiel. In Jeremiah, in fact, they selected the long edition of Jeremiah in preference to the shorter, superior edition.

Thus far, we have discussed the establishment of the text, rather than the stabilization of the canon of the Hebrew Bible. In the remarks that follow we shall comment briefly on the latter. "Canon" will be used here in its strict sense: a fixed list of books of Scripture defined as authoritative for religious doctrine and practice, a list to be neither added to nor subtracted from.

There is no evidence in non-Pharisaic Jewish circles before 70 C.E. of either a fixed canon or text. The Essenes at Qumrân exhibit no knowledge of such, and the same is true of the Hellenistic Jewish community in Alexandria, and of the early Christian communities. The earliest clear definition of a "closed" Hebrew canon is found in Josephus in his apologetic work, *Contra Apionem*, written in Rome in the last decade of the first century of the Common Era. He writes that there was a fixed and immutable number—twenty-two—of "justly accredited" books. Josephus no doubt draws upon his Pharisaic tradition in making his assertion, and presumes in his remarks a well-established doctrine of canon.

I am persuaded by the accumulation of evidence, old and new, that the circumstances that brought on the textual crisis that led to the establishment of the Hebrew text—varied texts and editions, party strife and sectarian division, the systematization of hermeneutic rules and halakic dialectic—were the occasion as well for a canonical crisis, and further that Hillel and his house were central in sharpening the crisis and responding to it. The establishment of the text and the establishment of the canon were thus two aspects of a single if complex endeavor. Both were essential to erect "Hillelite" protection against rival doctrines of cult and calendar, alternate legal dicta and theological doctrines, and indeed against the speculative systems and mythological excesses found in the books of certain apocalyptic schools and proto-Gnostic sects. Such literature abounds in the apocryphal and pseudepigraphic works found at Qumrân. To promulgate a textual recension, moreover, one must set some sort of limit on the books whose text is to be fixed. In choosing one edition of a book over another—in the case of Jeremiah or Chronicles or Daniel—one makes decisions that are at once textual and canonical. Ultimately, the strategies that initiate the establishment of the biblical text lead to the *de facto* if not *de jure* establishment of a canon.

It is not impossible that an old dictum embedded in the Talmud (*Sukkah* 20a) preserves a memory of the role of Hillel and his circle in the events leading up to the establishment of the Hebrew text and canon: "When the Torah was forgotten in Israel, Ezra came up from Babylon and reestablished it; and when it was once again forgotten, Hillel the Babylonian came up and reestablished it. . . ."

If I am correct in perceiving the hand of Hillel in the promulgation of a Pharisaic text and canon, I must nevertheless acknowledge that this canon and text did not immediately supplant other traditions or receive uniform acceptance even in Pharisaic circles. The ascendancy of the "Hillelite" text and canon came with the victory of the Pharisaic party and the Hillelite house in the interval between the Jewish Revolts against Rome. After that the text and canon of the Hebrew Bible—despite rabbinical queries about marginal books from time to time—remained fixed and guarded down to our own day.

Notes

1 These manuscripts now carry the siglum IQ, i.e., Cave I, Qumrân, to distinguish them from later manuscripts found in caves near Qumrân and elsewhere in the Jordan rift. The principal editions of the manuscripts of Cave I are as follows: M. Burrows, J. Trever, and W. Brownlee, *The Dead Sea Scrolls of St. Mark's Monastery*. Vol. I. *The Isaiah Manuscript and the Habakkuk Commentary* (New Haven: American Schools of Oriental Research, 1950); Vol. II, *Plates and Transcription of the Manual of Discipline* (New Haven, 1951); reed. F. M. Cross, D. N. Freedman, and J. A. Sanders from photographs of John C. Trever, *Scrolls from Qumrân Cave I* (Cambridge and Jerusalem: The Albright Institute of Archaeological Research and the Shrine of the Book, 1972); E. L. Sukenik and N. Avigad, *'wṣr hmgylwt hgnwzwt* (Jerusalem: Bialik Foundation and the Hebrew University, 1954), English version, *The Dead Sea Scrolls of the Hebrew University* (Jerusalem: The Hebrew University and the Magnes Press, 1955); N. Avigad and Y. Yadin, *A Genesis Apocryphon* (Jerusalem: Magnes Press and the Shrine of the Book, 1956); and *Qumrân Cave I, Discoveries in the Judaean Desert* I, ed. D. Barthélemy and J. T. Milik (Oxford: Clarendon Press, 1955).

2 See Edmund Wilson, *The Dead Sea Scrolls 1947–1969* (New York: Oxford University Press, 1969), portions of which first appeared in *The New Yorker* magazine.

3 *Les "Petites Grottes" de Qumrân, Discoveries in the Judaean Desert* III, ed. M. Baillet, J. T. Milik, and R. de Vaux (Oxford: Clarendon Press, 1962).

4 *The Psalms Scroll of Qumrân Cave II, Discoveries in the Judaean Desert* IV (Oxford: Clarendon Press, 1965); *The Temple Scroll*, ed. Yigael Yadin, 3 vols. (Jerusalem: The Israel Exploration Society, Institute of Archaeology of the Hebrew University, and the Shrine of the Book, 1983). Two other important manuscripts from Cave XI have been published: *Le Targum de Job de la grotte XI de Qumrân*, ed. J. P. M. Von de Ploeg and A. S. van der Woude (Leiden: Brill, 1971); and *The Paleo-Hebrew Leviticus Scroll (11QPaleoLev)*, ed. D. N. Freedman and K. A. Mathews (Winona Lake, Ind.: American Schools of Oriental Research, 1985).

5 This reading of the Temple Scroll has not gone unchallenged, but I believe with Yadin that it is the plain meaning of the text.

6 Principal editions of texts from Cave IV, Qumrân, are the following: *Qumrân Cave 4: I 4Q158–4Q186, Discoveries in the Judaean Desert* V, ed. John M. Allegro (Oxford: Clarendon Press, 1968); cf. the review (virtually a reedition) of J. Strugnell, "Notes en marge du volume V des 'Discoveries in the Judaean Desert of Jordan,'" *Revue de Qumrân* 26 (1970): 163–276; *Qumrân Grotte 4: II. Discoveries in the Judaean Desert* VI, ed. R. de Vaux and J. T. Milik (Oxford: Clarendon Press, 1977); and *Qumrân Grotte 4: III (4Q482–4Q520), Discoveries in the Judaean Desert* VII, ed. M. Baillet (Oxford: Clarendon Press, 1982). See also J. T. Milik, *The Books of Enoch* (Oxford: Clarendon Press, 1976). Preliminary editions of samples of many Cave IV works have been published. For bibliography see J. A. Fitzmyer, *The Dead Sea Scrolls: Major Publications and Tools for Study.* Sources for Biblical Study 8 (Missoula, Mont.: Scholars Press, 1975). Major preliminary editions include the following: Carol Newson, *Songs of the Sabbath Sacrifice: A Critical Edition.* Harvard Semitic Studies 27 (Atlanta, Ga.: Scholars Press, 1985); and Eileen M. Schuller, *Non-Canonical Psalms from Qumrân: A Pseudepigraphical Collection.* Harvard Semitic Studies 28 (Atlanta, Ga.: Scholars Press, 1986).

7 *Les Grottes de Murabba'ât, Discoveries in the Judaean Desert* II, ed. P. Benoit, J. T. Milik, and R. de Vaux (Oxford: Clarendon Press, 1961). The Minor Prophets scroll was recovered from a cave in the Wâdi Murabba'ât in 1955, after the bedouin finds of 1951 and the excavations of de Vaux in 1952.

8 See D. Barthélemy, *Les Devanciers d'Aquila* (Leiden: Brill, 1965); and B. Lipshitz, "The Greek Documents from the Cave of Horror," *Israel Exploration Journal* 12 (1962): 201–207.

9 See provisionally *Discoveries in the Wâdi ed-Dâliyeh*, ed. P. W. and Nancy L. Lapp. *Annual of the American Schools of Oriental Research* XLI (1974); and F. M. Cross, "Samaria Papyrus 1: An Aramaic Slave Conveyance of 335 B.C.E. Found in the Wâdi ed-Dâliyeh," *Eretz-Israel* 18 (1985): *7–*27 and Pl. II.

10 See Y. Yadin, *The Ben Sira Scroll from Masada* (Jerusalem: Israel Exploration Society, 1965). On the Songs of the Sabbath Sacrifice, see above, n. 7.

11 See the excavator's splendid synthesis of the results of archaeological excavations in R. de Vaux, *Archaeology and the Dead Sea Scrolls.* The Schweich Lecture 1959 (London: Oxford University Press, 1973).

12 On the palaeographical dating of manuscripts from the Qumrân caves, see F. M. Cross, "The Development of the Jewish Scripts," *The Bible and the Ancient Near East: Essays in Honor of W. F. Albright* (Garden City, N.Y.: Doubleday, 1961; Anchor Books, 1965), pp. 133–202 (Anchor, pp. 170–264).

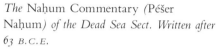

The Naḥum Commentary *(Pešer*
Naḥum*) of the Dead Sea Sect. Written after*
63 B.C.E.
The Shrine of the Book, D. Samuel and Jeane H.
Gottesman Center for Biblical Manuscripts, Israel
Museum, Jerusalem [Ex. no. 28]

Leaf of the Aleppo Codex, *copied in the tenth century, containing the text of 2 Chronicles 35:25 through 36:19. This Bible manuscript was corrected by Aaron ben Moses ben Asher, who lived in Tiberias. He was the last of an important family of masoretes or textual scholars of the Bible. This was the manuscript Maimonides (1135–1204) considered authoritative, and it forms the basis for today's accepted text of the Hebrew Bible. Housed for centuries in the Old Synagogue in Aleppo, the Codex is now in Israel.*

Ben-Zvi Institute for the Study of Jewish Communities in the East, Jerusalem [Ex. no. 2]

Children's primer from the Cairo Geniza,
tenth or eleventh century. Because Hebrew letters were considered sacred, worn books and
documents could not be destroyed. One way of
keeping them was by placing them in a geniza
(literally, "hiding place") or depository adja-
cent to a synagogue. This sheet is one of over
one hundred thousand found in the geniza of
the synagogue at Fostat, Cairo. On the left
the letters alef, bet, and gimel are repeated
in combination with different vowels. The decorations on the right include a seven-branched
candelabrum and eternal light, which had definite Jewish associations, and two six-pointed
stars, which were not specifically Jewish symbols in the Middle Ages. B. Narkiss has written elsewhere that decorative alphabets
sometimes preceded the text of the first portion
of Leviticus, which was traditionally used as a
primer.

*By permission of the Syndics of the Cambridge
University Library, T-S. K5.13 [Ex. no. 29]*

Shelaḥ-Lekha *("Send thou"), weekly Torah reading containing the text of Numbers 13–15 (Egypt, 1106/07). Manuscripts consisting of a single Torah portion are unusual but not unknown.*

The Jewish National and University Library, Jerusalem, Ms. Heb. 8° 2238, fols. 3v–4r [Ex. no. 18]

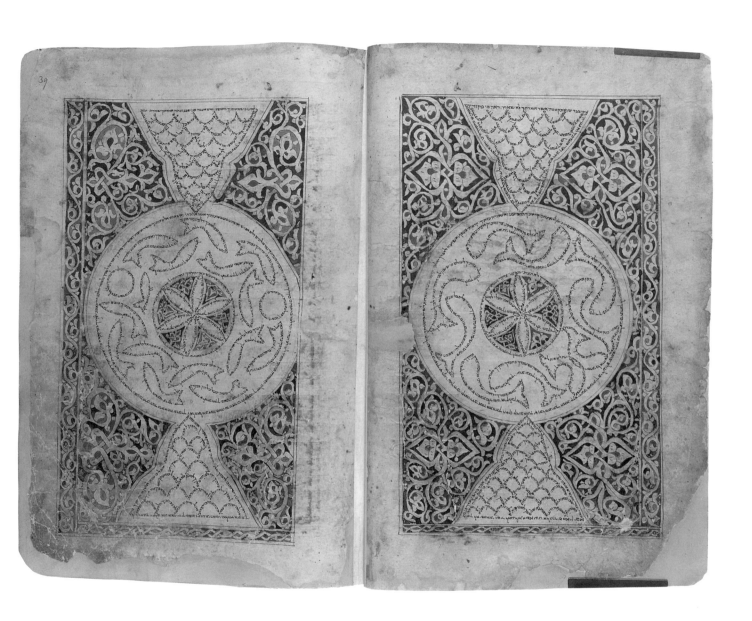

Carpet pages of micrographic writing of verses from Psalms 119 and 121 forming a circular design of fish around a rosette with two mountain-like shapes at top and bottom. From the San'a Pentateuch (Yemen, 1469).
By permission of The British Library, London, Ms. Or. 2348, fols. 38v–39r [Ex. no. 25]

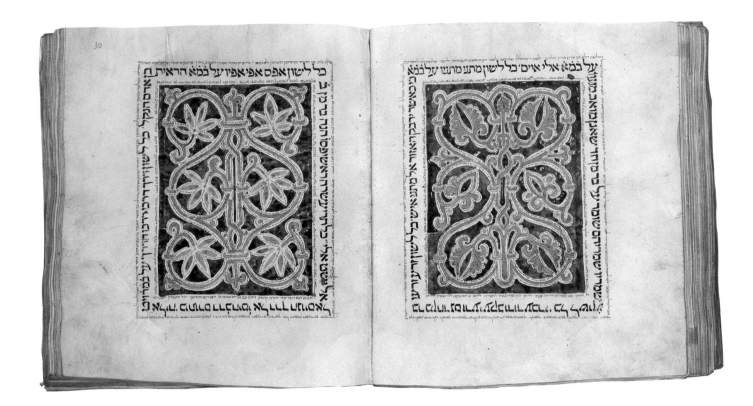

Carpet pages from the Burgos Bible *(Spain, 1260). This is one of the earliest surviving illuminated Hebrew manuscripts from Spain. In it ornate carpet pages are placed before the main sections of the Bible: Pentateuch (*Torah)*, Prophets (*Nevi'im)*, Writings or Hagiographa (*Ketuvim)*. The pages shown here precede the Writings.*
The Jewish National and University Library, Jerusalem, Ms. Hebr. 4° 790, fols. 309v–310r [Ex. no. 4]

Part of the Haggadah with the text of Psalms
116:16–19 and the decorated opening word,
Hallelu ("Praise"), of Psalm 117, in a Spanish festival prayerbook of the thirteenth or early
fourteenth century. Characteristic of the decoration are the use of anthropomorphic and zoomorphic letters and the elongation and
embellishment of ascenders, as in the two
lameds here, and of descenders.
Staatsbibliothek Preussischer Kulturbesitz, Orientabteilung, Berlin (West), Ms. Hamilton 288, fol.
30v [Ex. no. 55]

"*I, Joseph the Frenchman, have illustrated and completed this book.*" Illuminator's colophon in zoomorphic and anthropomorphic letters in the Cervera Bible, *completed in Spain in 1300. The volume also contains a separate scribe's colophon. This manuscript served as the model for the well-known* Kennicott Bible, *produced nearly one hundred and eighty years later.*

Biblioteca Nacional, Lisbon, Ms. 72, fol. 449r [Ex. no. 6]

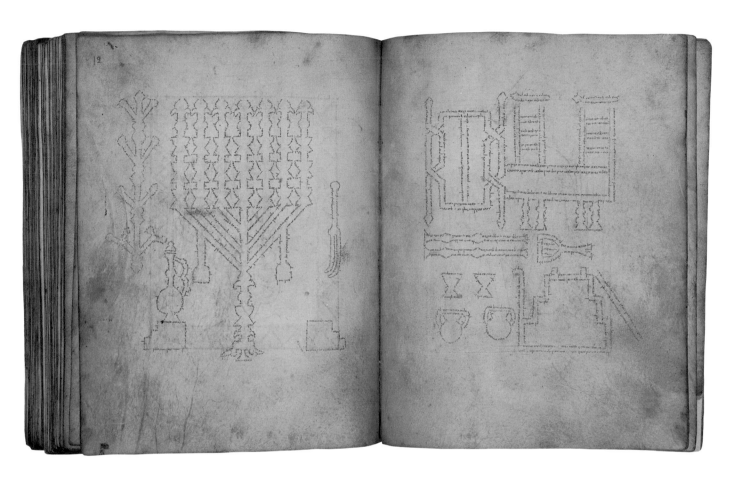

Catalan Maḥzor *of the fourteenth century*
showing sanctuary implements including the
table of showbread, the ark, the altar of burnt
offering, a firepan, pots for ashes, basins for
the blood of sacrifices, two silver trumpets, the
seven-branched lamp or menorah, the jar of
manna, the budding rod of Aaron, etc., all in
micrographic writing.
The Jewish National and University Library, Jeru-
salem, Ms. 8° 6527, fols. 11v–12r [Ex. no. 57]

Scenes from Genesis in the prefatory pages of the Golden Haggadah *including: Lot and his daughters fleeing Sodom, the sacrifice of Isaac, Isaac blessing Jacob, Jacob's dream, Jacob wrestling with an angel, Joseph's dreams, Joseph relating his dreams, and Joseph on the way to his brothers.*
By permission of The British Library, Add. Ms. 27210, fols. 4v–5r [Ex. no. 35]

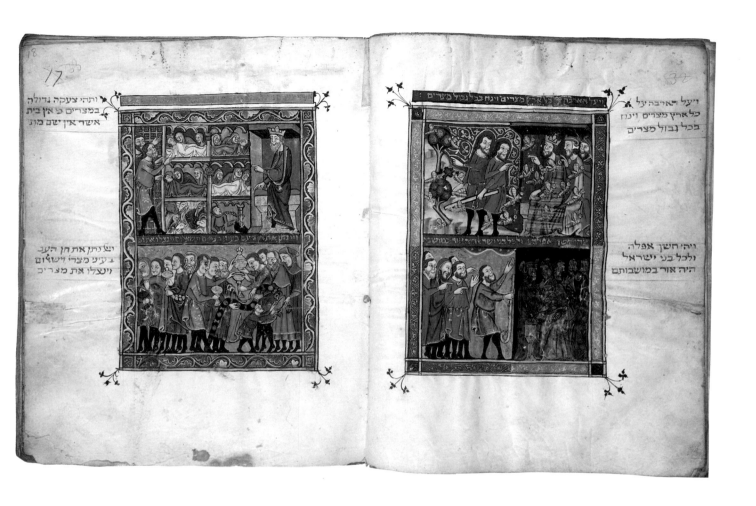

18

17

34

ותהי צעקה גדולה
במצרים כי אין בית
אשר אין שם מת

ויתן את חן העם
בעיני מצרי וישלום
וינצלו את מצרים

ויעל הארבה על
כל ארץ מצרים וינח
בכל גבול מצרים

ויהי חשך אפלה
ולכל בני ישראל
היה אור במושבותם

*Part of a cycle of miniatures of the Passover
story in the* Rylands Spanish Haggadah
*(Spain, mid-fourteenth century). Depicted are
the plagues of locusts, darkness, death of the
firstborn, and the Children of Israel despoiling
the Egyptians (Exodus 12:36).*
The John Rylands University Library of Manchester, Ms. 6, fols. 17v–18r [Ex. no. 34]

Maimonides' great philosophical work Moreh Nevukhim (Guide to the Perplexed) in the Hebrew translation of Samuel ibn Tibbon (1160–ca. 1230), copied and illuminated in Barcelona, 1348. The seated figure in this illustration is holding an astrolabe.
Royal Library, Copenhagen, Cod. Hebr. XXXVII, fol. 114r [Ex. no. 70]

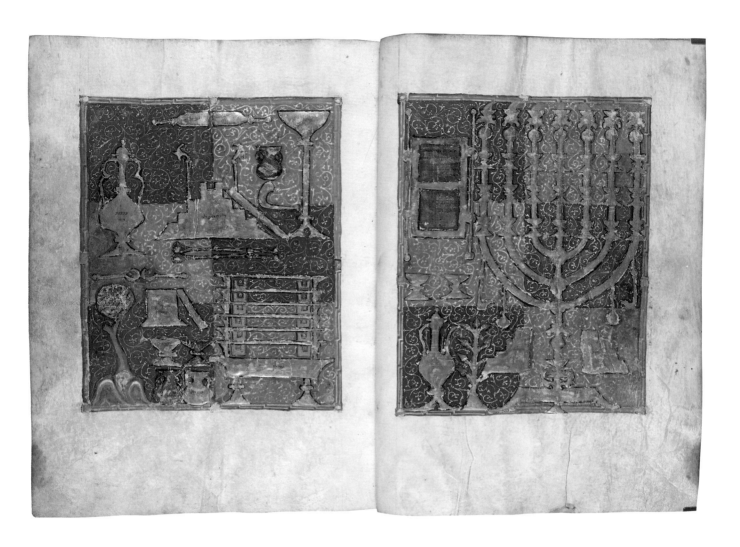

Harley Catalan Bible *showing sanctuary implements. Note in the lower-left corner a tree
atop the cleft Mount of Olives. This is an allusion to the Messianic Age as foreseen in
Zechariah 14:4 and serves to connect the description of the sanctuary as it was with the
belief in a Messianic restoration.*
*By permission of The British Library, London,
Harley Ms. 1528, fols. 7v–8r [Ex. no. 9]*

Colophon of the Lisbon Mishneh Torah,
written by the scribe Solomon Ibn Alzuk for
Joseph ben David ben Solomon ben David ben
Gedaliah the elder 'n Yaḥya, completed in
5232 (1471/72).
By permission of The British Library, London,
Harley Ms. 5699, fol. 434v [Ex. no. 68]

Beginning of the Book of Joshua in the British Library's Lisbon Bible.
By permission of The British Library, London, Ms. Or. 2627, fol. 1v [Ex. no. 12]

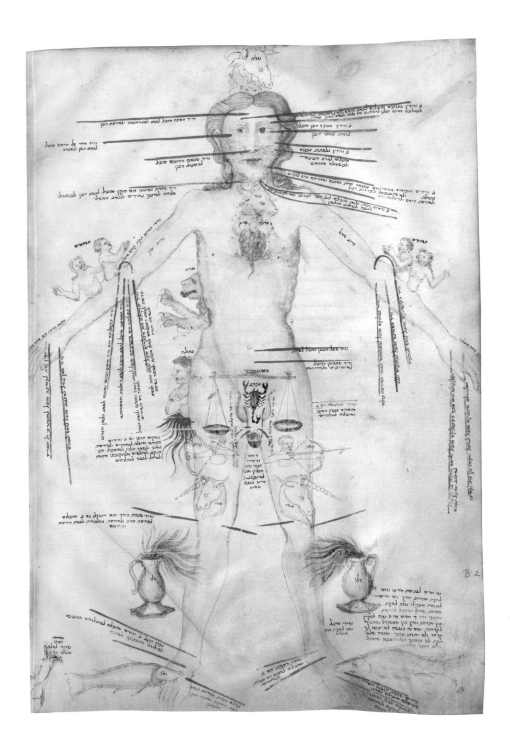

Anatomical diagram showing the relation of the signs of the zodiac to various parts of the body, in a fourteenth-century medical text from Italy.

Bibliothèque Nationale, Paris, Ms. Hebr. 1181, fol. 264v [Ex. no. 71]

2 MALACHI BEIT-ARIÉ

How Hebrew Manuscripts Are Made

AT THE beginning of the Middle Ages, Hebrew books were probably still produced in the form of a roll. This book form of the ancient world was used in biblical times, according to various sources in the Old Testament, where not only the word *Megillah* (scroll, roll) is employed, but also *Sefer* (book). Books were produced in roll form during the Second Temple period in Palestine, as is extensively attested to by the Dead Sea Scrolls, which were usually made of leather.

I. The Early Middle Ages and the Beginning of the Hebrew Codex

According to surviving books and excavated fragments of books in Greek, Latin, and Coptic, preserved and found mainly in Egypt due to her dry climate, a new, more practical book form, the codex, was introduced into Mediterranean civilization during the second century of the Common Era. The revolutionary form, in which a number of papyrus or parchment sheets are folded into quires and stitched together at the center to form a series of opening pages, easily carried, stored, and used, gradually replaced the old form of the roll. By 300 C.E. the codex and the roll were employed equally, according to surviving handwritten books, which also testify that the

new form was first adopted and promoted by the Christians for copying the Bible and Christian literature. By the sixth century the roll was totally rejected for literary texts, and since then has been used only for documentary and liturgical purposes.

Literary evidence, as well as findings, seems to attest that the codex form was adopted by Jews much later, not before the Arabic period and Geonic literary activity, possibly as late as the eighth century. All references to books in post–Second Temple literature, namely the Mishnah and Tosephta, the Palestinian and the Babylonian Talmud, the halakic and Palestinian Midrashim, relate to rolls, as was noted by Rashi in the eleventh century: "All *Sefarim* [books] of the times of the sages were in a roll form, like our Sefer Torah" (his commentary to the Babylonian Talmud, Megillah, 19a).

Indeed, there are several references in this literature, from as early as the second half of the second century, to another form of recording information, called by the Greek term *pinax,* rendered in Hebrew by the word *pinkes,* multileaved wood or waxed wood tablets fastened together to form a sort of notebook. According to literary references, the Romans developed this device by applying

parchment. A passage in the Mishnah, Kelim 24:7, dating from not later than the middle of the second century, refers apparently to a papyrus *pinkes.* Although two later midrashic passages refer to folded notebooks, there is no clear evidence to support the assumption that the codex book was utilized by the Jews during talmudic times, nor are there archaeological findings to suggest it. A long period, from which hardly any Hebrew book has survived, separates the rich and diverse findings of books of the Judaean Desert of the late Second Temple period, and the earliest surviving dated codex manuscripts, from circa 900. Even if one is justified in ascribing to a time earlier than 900 certain undated handwritten, mostly fragmentary, codices—such as Ms Vatican Ebr. 66, *Sifra* with Babylonian vocalization, or the palimpsests found in the Cairo Geniza, in which the upper Hebrew Palestinian texts are written on Christian texts, mainly in Christian Palestinian Aramaic and Greek—the long gap of about eight centuries is reduced by probably no more than a century or two.

From the period of that long gap, only a few dozen papyri and a few leather fragments have survived, most of them excavated in Egypt and dating from the Byzantine period. Of these, not a single fragment derives clearly from a codex, though some of the literary texts probably derive from single leaves. On the other hand, existing fragments attest that apart from the ritual Pentateuch scroll (Sefer Torah), which is used and written to this day, rolls were employed for Hebrew books until approximately the middle of the tenth century. A Latin palimpsest, preserved in Munich, Bayerische Staatsbibliothek Clm 6315 and 29022, was written in Northern Italy in the first half of the eighth century on fragments of a Hebrew roll which contained liturgy for Yom Kippur. Quite a number of fragments of literary rolls were preserved in the Cairo Geniza. However, a major part of them derive not from the regular ancient form of roll—whose sheets are stitched or glued vertically and which is written and read from right to left and rolls from left to right— but from rolls whose sheets are stitched or glued horizontally and which is written and read from top to bottom in one single column and rolls from bottom to top. Such a papyrus roll, which had been used in the ancient world by the Greeks, Romans, and Egyptians for documents only, and was designated by the Latin term *transversa charta,* was indeed known to talmudic sources both for keeping records and for copying liturgy. To designate such a roll, the Tosephta uses the Greek/Latin term *tomos/tomus,* which is replaced by the Hebrew term *takhrikh* in the Mishnah and the Palestinian Talmud. It is interesting to note that the earliest Arabic Korans, as well as other Arabic literary texts, were also written on such rolls, and that the Arabic

A Haggadah from about the year 1000 of the Common Era found in the Cairo Geniza considered the oldest surviving Haggadah. Shown here are the end of Psalm 113 and the beginning of Psalm 114.
Annenberg Research Institute for Judaic and Near Eastern Studies, Merion, Penn., Halper 211 [Ex. no. 32]

term for a codex, *muṣḥaf,* originally designated such a Koran roll.

This Arabic term was borrowed and employed when the codex form was explicitly referred to, apparently for the first time, in Hebrew literature. It appears in the old Hebrew translation (*Hilkhot Re'u*) and in a later version (*Halakhot Gedolot*) of the Babylonian-Aramaic *Halakhot Pesukot* of the late eighth or beginning of the ninth century (the halakah in which the term is employed is missing in the only existing, incomplete codex and Geniza fragments of *Halakhot Pesukot*). The Hebrew terms designating a codex, *miṣḥaf* as well as *diftar,* are found in colophons of the earliest dated Hebrew biblical codices of the tenth century. Like *miṣḥaf,* the term *diftar* too was borrowed from early Islamic Arabic. The additional term derived from the Greek *diftera* (hide), a term used in talmudic literature to designate a certain sort of leather rejected for writing the Torah scroll.

To sum up: existing Hebrew manuscripts in the form of a codex which contain an explicit indication of their time of production date from circa 900 and later. Some codex manuscripts, mostly fragmentary, can be dated up to about a century or, at most, two centuries earlier. Indeed, literary evidence reflects the later adaptation of the codex, which had been introduced as a book form for Greek and Latin texts as early as the second century, and became the usual book form in the fifth century. However, the virtual lack of surviving Hebrew books in any form from late antiquity to the High Middle Ages cannot be attributed only to their destruction by wear and tear or by conquerors and persecutors. One should also consider the possibility that the talmudic and midrashic literature, the so-called Oral Law, was indeed mainly transmitted orally until the Islamic period, as is indicated explicitly in a few talmudic sources, and attested by literary patterns and reciting devices contained in these texts.

II. The Making of Handwritten Books of the High and Late Middle Ages

Hebrew dated (and undated) manuscripts have survived from the tenth century on, and are found in hundreds of collections throughout the world. They represent a rich diversity of technological, scribal, and aesthetic traditions of book production by Jewish scribes and copyists continuing until the invention of printing and the spread of Hebrew printing by the end of the Middle Ages. Hebrew handwritten books were produced in many lands and over vast areas, due to the wide distribution of the Jews in the Orient and the Occident. They were made in Christian Europe; in Moslem Spain, North Africa, the Near and Middle East, and West Central Asia; and in Byzantine Greece and Asia Minor. Our knowledge of the making of Hebrew books and the scripts employed in them derives from the study of the existing dated manuscripts, and is naturally confined to the High and Late Middle Ages: from the tenth century in the Orient;

the late eleventh century in Italy; the late twelfth century in the Iberian peninsula, France, and Germany; and the late thirteenth century in Byzantium and the Maghreb. Therefore, we know the various types of the Hebrew codex and its writings in their established form. Nevertheless, gradual changes in script and some radical shifts in bookmaking techniques can be noticed in most areas.

The variety of scribal practices that medieval Hebrew manuscripts demonstrate can be classified into several geocultural, rather than political, entities, each of which manifests its own combination of techniques and style and shape of script. The following geocultural terms are used to distinguish both specific types of scribal practices and script and the geographical distribution of these practices.

Orient: Egypt, Palestine, Syria, Eastern Asia Minor, Iraq, Iran and its surroundings. At the time of the earliest manuscripts, these territories were incorporated into a single political unit, the Abbasid Caliphate.

Yemen: A subtype within the Orient. Its distinctiveness manifests itself, particularly in the script, as early as the earliest dated documents of the twelfth century.

Persia: A subtype within the Orient which includes Iran and Uzbekistan. Its distinctive characteristics emerged only at the beginning of the fourteenth century.

Sepharad: This entity encompasses vast territories including not only the Iberian peninsula, but also the Maghreb and even regions beyond the Pyrenees, Provence and Languedoc, which share the script and technical practices of Spain and North Africa from at least the beginning of the thirteenth century.

The affinity of these four Islamic territories and types is evident mostly in their scripts, which were influenced by Arabic script and calligraphy.

Ashkenaz: Central and northern France, England, and medieval Germany, and in the Late Middle Ages also Central and Eastern Europe. Some slight differences in script and codicological practices can be discerned between France and Germany.

Italy: Distinctive script and scribal techniques characterized Hebrew manuscripts produced in Italy as early as the time of the earliest dated ones, in the late eleventh century. However, some correlations can be noticed between early Franco-German manuscripts of the late twelfth and early thirteenth century and Italian manuscripts, which hint at the Italian origin of the Ashkenazic type.

Both these types share the background of Western Christian European civilization and are influenced by Latin script.

Byzantium: An independent type, clearly in its script, but also in some scribal practices, shared by manuscripts produced in Western Asia Minor, the Greek islands, Crete, Rhodes, and the Balkans, which constituted the late Byzantine Empire before its decline. This type may have been influenced by Greek script.

A. Writing Material

Medieval Hebrew codices were written on two kinds of material—parchment and paper. Only one large fragment of a papyrus codex was preserved in the Cairo Geniza, which can be dated to the ninth or eighth century. Papyrus was undoubtedly the writing material of biblical times in Palestine, but leather was introduced at the beginning of the post-exilic period at the time of the canonization of the Hebrew Bible. Most of the Dead Sea Scrolls were written on *gevil,* whose hair-side only was treated for writing. Early Hebrew codices in all regions were written on parchment, cattle hides treated so that both the hair-side and the flesh-side were suitable for writing. Rolls were written on only one side, whereas codices were written on both sides of their leaves.

Parchment preceded paper, as papermaking was introduced to the Arabs only at the middle of the eighth century, by Chinese prisoners of war in Samarkand, spread gradually through the Islamic countries, and reached Christian Europe, starting with Italy, only in the last quarter of the thirteenth century. Once introduced and manufactured, paper began to replace the expensive parchment and eventually became the chief writing material in all areas. In the Orient, paper replaced parchment more rapidly, as early as the beginning of the eleventh century. Deluxe copies were produced everywhere on parchment even at the end of the Middle Ages and even thereafter.

Several types of parchment employed in medieval Hebrew manuscripts can be visually distinguished. The differences between them relate mostly to the treatment and the appearance of the hair-side. In Italy the parchment always preserves the natural differences between its two sides: the flesh-side is smooth, glossy, and much brighter, while the rough hair-side, although often scraped, retains its grain. In the Sephardic parchment the rough hair-side is generally not scraped, yet the grain pattern is barely visible. The flesh-side is

bright. In Ashkenaz we see a radical shift in the nature of the parchment. Early manuscripts were written on parchment which, like the Italian, preserved the differences between its sides. By the end of the twelfth century, a new technique was introduced, which minimized the differences between the sides. In Germany, this new technique was adopted gradually and evolved finally into a complete equalization of both sides in the mid-thirteenth century: the hair-side is rubbed and all its hair follicles removed; the flesh-side is also scraped; and both sides are very rough. In France also the minimizing technique was adopted, but there the sides remain distinctive, though sometimes not so clearly. Like the late Ashkenazic parchment, the Oriental shows a resemblance between the hair-side and the flesh-side, but while this effect was achieved in Ashkenaz by scraping both sides, it was accomplished in the Orient by smoothing and glossing. However, although the grain is barely visible in Oriental parchment, its sides differ in color, so it is usually possible to distinguish between them.

While parchment may have been produced by the Jews themselves, as some documents hint, and bears particular characteristics in Hebrew manuscripts, paper was manufactured in gentile papermills and was shared by all scribes. Consequently, Hebrew paper manuscripts do not differ from Arabic, Latin, or Greek paper manuscripts. In the Orient

they were written on Arabic paper and later, in Europe, on Occidental paper. The two kinds of paper, both produced from rags, differ greatly in their morphological patterns. Oriental paper has either no wire-lines at all, or only curly and not easily visible laid-lines; when it has chain-lines, they are grouped in twos, or threes, or twos and threes alternately. Occidental paper has clear and straight laid- and chain-lines, spaced evenly and, from the year 1282 on, watermarks, which were trademarks of the papermills. Just as watermarks in European paper provide a useful tool for dating, some of the patterns in Arabic paper are typical of certain regions and periods, as Oriental Hebrew paper manuscripts demonstrate.

B. *Quiring*

To construct a codex, the scribe or the stationer had to procure a number of sheets of either parchment or paper, of the height but of double the width of the page desired. The sheets were placed on top of each other and then folded down the center. When folded, each sheet would give a sequence of two leaves or four pages. Two sheets laid on top of each other before folding would give four leaves or eight pages, and so on. Later, each set of folded sheets was stitched at the center of its opening, and constituted a quire. A codex was formed by a number of sewn quires. A second set of threads passed horizontally through the first set united the quires. It was taken through them across the spine of the book and secured to the front and back binding covers. The number of sheets folded

Yemenite Pentateuch of 1470 with masoretic notes in decorative micrography. The script is typically Yemenite. Shown is the conclusion of the Torah reading Shemot *(end Exodus 5, beginning 6). Note the instruction for a large winding letter* pe *in the right margin, just below the middle of the page, which is executed in the word* ve-yishpot *in the body of the text on the same line. This is called* pe lefufah, *or "winding pe," and is one of a number of oddly shaped letters prescribed by the Masorah for specific places in the Bible.*

Valmadonna Trust Library, London [Ex. no. 26]

The Moses Book *(Persia, late seventeenth century), a work in Judeo-Persian. The writing is characteristic of Hebrew script from Persia.*
Staatsbibliothek Preussischer Kulturbesitz, Orient-abteilung, Berlin (West), Ms. or. oct. 2885 [Ex. no. 84]

to make a quire in Hebrew manuscripts varies from three to fourteen, but is usually uniform within a manuscript. Naturally, quires at the end of manuscripts, or at the end of parts of them, might be larger or smaller. Manuscripts produced in the same geocultural region share the same composition or compositions of quires, reflecting the degree of conformity and the power of tradition in Hebrew bookmaking. In some regions there was a difference between the composition of parchment quires and that of paper quires, the latter manuscripts showing less regularity and a larger number of sheets.

In the Orient the regular number of sheets in a paper or parchment quire was five (ten leaves, twenty pages), but in Persia and Uzbekistan, at least from the fourteenth century, Hebrew manuscripts were constructed of four-sheet quires (eight leaves). In Ashkenaz, regular quires, made of parchment or paper, were always constructed of four folded sheets (eight leaves). In Italy the regular composition of parchment manuscripts was five sheets (ten leaves). Paper manuscripts had no uniform quiring, and show a variety of compositions, but usually five, six, or eight sheets in a quire. In Sepharad the usual number of folded sheets in parchment codices was four (eight leaves), but around 1275, a secondary, much less common composition of six sheets (twelve leaves) was introduced. Paper manuscripts were frequently constructed of six-sheet quires, and less frequently of eight-sheet quires, but other compositions were also sometimes employed. All parchment codices produced in Byzantium have four-sheet quires, but

paper quires have no uniform composition, though six sheets are most frequent.

The sheets of parchment quires in Hebrew manuscripts are arranged so that hair-side faces hair-side and flesh-side faces flesh-side. Consequently, each opening of a parchment codex has a uniform appearance, hair-side or flesh-side alternately. Quires usually start with the hair-side, but in Italy, and rarely in Sepharad, quires can start with the flesh-side.

In Sepharad, Italy, and Byzantium, quires were sometimes constructed by combining parchment and paper sheets. This practice was introduced after paper had become the cheaper material in these areas, as

Sephardic prayerbook written in Spain in Sephardic square letters in the second half of the fifteenth century.
Bibliothèque Nationale, Paris, Ms. Hebr. 593 [Ex. no. 85]

a compromise between the cheap but less durable paper and the much more expensive but stronger, more durable parchment. Parchment was used for the outer and innermost sheets of quires to protect the sheets of paper placed between the parchment sheets.

C. Ruling

The quires having been prepared, the next step in producing a codex was to rule the pages. The scribe could not start copying texts until horizontal writing and vertical boundary lines were drawn to guide the copying, to ensure the uniformity of the copy, and to help the scribe comply with traditional proportions and layout of the written space. Hebrew manuscripts show a variety of ruling designs and techniques, most of them typical of certain areas and periods. In Ashkenaz and Northern Italy one notices clear shifts of ruling practices in the mid-thirteenth and early fifteenth centuries respectively, while in the Orient and Byzantium a single technique was applied until the end of the Middle Ages.

To guide the drawing of horizontal and vertical lines, and to ensure the uniformity of the ruling pattern within a codex, rows of pricks or small slots were made by knife, compasses, or other metal instruments down the outer margin of the folded quire (in the Orient, Italy, Byzantium, early Ashkenaz, and late Sepharad), or the outer and inner margins of the folded quire (in late Ashkenaz and early Sepharad). Horizontal lines were then drawn across

the width of the unfolded sheet, or the leaf, from prick to prick, as were vertical boundary lines on each side of the written space or column. In paper manuscripts the drawing of the lines was probably guided by ruling-boards.

The lines in Hebrew manuscripts were ruled either by hard point (in all areas, but in Ashkenaz only in early manuscripts, and in the Orient only in parchment manuscripts), or by lead pencil (in late Ashkenaz), by ink (in late Northern Italy), or by ruling-board (in paper manuscripts in the Orient). While lead pencil and ink were applied to each page and ruling-board to each leaf, ruling by hard point was applied in various ways, depending on the ruling unit and the side of the sheet or leaf to be ruled, since hard point can rule successive leaves (or sheets) at one time. Thus, in early Sepharad, pairs of parchment leaves or sheets (sometimes even four) were ruled at one time on the hair-side. In early Ashkenaz, Italy, and Byzantium, each unfolded parchment sheet was ruled individually by hard point on the hair-side, while in the Orient each unfolded parchment sheet was ruled individually on its flesh-side.

D. Copying

Once the ruled parchment or paper quires were prepared, the scribe could start copying the texts requested. For writing he naturally needed a writing instrument and ink. He also employed certain specific techniques to ensure the uniformity of the margins of the copied text, and to indicate the proper order of sheets, leaves, and quires before binding.

1. Writing instruments and inks

Medieval Hebrew scribes employed two kinds of writing implements, the reed pen and the quill pen. The two pens differed in flexibility, which strongly affected the nature of the letter strokes and the style of the script. The reed pen, which was made from reed plants, was more rigid and produced more regular strokes. The quill pen, which was made from birds' feathers, was more flexible and produced varying strokes. The reed pen was used during the High Middle Ages by Hebrew scribes who lived within the Islamic territories, i.e., the Orient, the Maghreb, and the Iberian peninsula. The quill pen was employed by Hebrew scribes living in Christian territories, i.e., France, England, Germany, Italy, and probably Byzantium.

Inks were produced as dry sticks, which were mixed with water before use. In general, the main coloring component in the Orient was lampblack, while in the Occident it was always soluble iron salt. This difference resulted in the different colors of the written texts of Hebrew medieval manuscripts. While the Occidental manuscripts exhibit a variety of shades of brown, from dark to light, and sometimes reddish, yellowish, or even greenish hues, Oriental manuscripts always exhibit dark written text, either black or dark brown.

2. Script

In each of the Jewish cultural areas, scribes employed a characteristic type of script: Ashkenazic, Italian, Sephar-

The Ebermannstadt Pentateuch *(southern Germany, 1290) showing the beginning of Leviticus, with micrographic illumination. Leviticus is written with a verse in Hebrew followed by its Aramaic translation. The upper part of the page contains 1 Kings 8:1–11, which belongs to the* haftarah *or prophetical reading that accompanies the preceding Torah portion. The relation of the architectural design to such south German cathedrals as Regensburg has been pointed out elsewhere by J. Gutmann. The letters are distinctly Ashkenazic. Their shape and the extreme contrast between thick and thin strokes were determined by the use of a quill instead of the reed pen common in Sephardic and Oriental lands. Royal Library, Copenhagen, Cod. Hebr. XI [Ex. no. 20]*

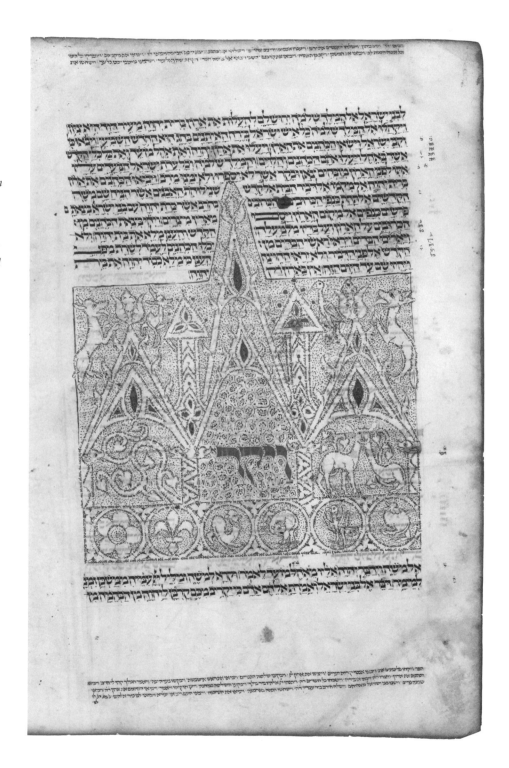

The opening of the Book of Psalms (Italy, fifteenth century) with the commentary of David
Kimḥi (1160–1235) in a fine Italian hand.
The four miniatures showing scenes from the
life of King David suggest, in their anthropomorphic representation of the deity and in the
use of halos, a Christian illuminator.
Staatsbibliothek Preussischer Kulturbesitz, Orientabteilung, Berlin (West), Ms. Hamilton 547 [Ex.
no. 27]

dic, Byzantine, and Oriental (which included two subtypes: Yemenite and, from the fourteenth century on, Persian). These types are known to us in the form established in the High Middle Ages, but the evolution of the Oriental type can be traced in part, due to the survival of papyri and datable epigraphic writings from the beginning of the Middle Ages, and of dated codices and documents from the tenth century. The lack of early dated or datable codices or scripts from the other areas severely hinders our knowledge and understanding of the development of this diversity of types; only from historical information can we infer the factors which contributed to it. Thus, the Ashkenazic script seems to have evolved from the early Italian type, which had probably evolved from the Oriental. The Sephardic script, which was not confined to the Iberian peninsula, but was also employed in the Maghreb, Provence, and Sicily, most probably arose in North Africa.

Within the vast geographical distribution of the Ashkenazic, Sephardic, and Oriental types of script, local variations can be seen, despite the strong tendency toward conformism and conservatism. Some stylistic differences can be observed between the Ashkenazic script employed in France and that in Germany. Local variation can be discerned within the Sephardic type between Iberia (Spain and Portugal), Provence, North Africa, and, to some extent, Sicily and Southern Italy. Within the Orient, apart from the independent Yemenite script and the later Persian subtype, morphological differences exist between northeastern regions and southwestern ones.

These types of medieval Hebrew script should be multiplied by three, as almost each type was employed in three modes of writing: square, semi-cursive, and cursive. Thus, Hebrew medieval manuscripts exhibit a rich and very large variety of handwriting, amounting to some twenty completely different types of script. The difference between the three modes of each type is in the number of strokes needed to produce a letter; more strokes are required to produce square than semi-cursive characters, fewer strokes are needed to write cursive than semi-cursive characters.

The types of Hebrew scripts have not always been confined to their geographical boundaries. The special historical circumstances of medieval Jewry, the expulsion of whole communities by force and the frequent emigrations of individuals by choice, affected the script of many Hebrew manuscripts. These were written, not in the local script of the geocultural area in which they were produced, but in the native script of the immigrant copyists, who usually retained their native scripts for the rest of their productive lives. Thus, we find in Northern Italy, for instance, late medieval Hebrew manuscripts copied in not only the local Italian type, but also in Ashkenazic and Sephardic types or, in Palestine, manuscripts copied in not only the local Oriental type, but also in Sephardic, Ashkenazic, and Byzantine types of Hebrew script. The codicological features, such as writing material, quiring, and ruling techniques, of codices produced by immigrant scribes reflect, however, the local tradition.

3. Scribal devices to maintain the left-hand margin

Although the ruled left-hand margin sets the limit of the lines, it does not guarantee that the lines will in fact end in a straight edge. Unlike Latin scribes, Hebrew copyists attempted to achieve a relatively justified end margin and preserve the uniform page layout of the book. Apart from aesthetic motivation and the influence of Arabic calligraphy, the roots of this marginal neatness are probably found in old halakic rules and practices of writing the ritual Pentateuch scroll. Some devices can be traced back to the scrolls of the Judaean Desert.

To maintain the left-hand margin, Hebrew scribes developed and elaborated a broad range of scribal devices, some common to broad geocultural areas, some unique to one or another region. The Hebrew scribes used three methods: filling out short lines, preventing the margin from being exceeded, and writing protruding words or letters in such a way that the margin boundary was respected.

The scribal devices for filling out short lines included (1) dilating one of the last letters of the last word in the line (the most common device in all areas, most effective with a square script, and particularly used on letters containing a long horizontal upper bar); (2) leaving space before the last word or, particularly in Sepharad, before the last letter of the last word; (3) inserting various graphic signs in the space at the end of the line when that space was too short to accommodate a complete word without protruding considerably into the margin (in the Orient and Sepharad such graphic fillers might consist of certain letters or parts of letters); and (4) filling in the space with as many letters of the next word as could be inserted and then writing the complete word, repeating those letters, at the beginning of the following line (Ashkenazic copyists tend to omit one or more of the strokes of the last letter of the anticipated word).

Devices for preventing the margin from being exceeded included (1) compressing letters of the last word (in the Orient and particularly in Sepharad, scribes might change their semi-cursive script into a cursive one) and (2) dividing final words so that the beginning was written at the end of the line and the rest at the beginning of the following line (this device was practiced only by Yemenite and Italian scribes). Devices for writing exceeding letters or words in such a way that the left margin was retained were (1) writing as much of the last word as possible within the available space, leaving a blank, and then completing the word to the left, in the border of the leaf; (2) writing up to the edge of the text block and then placing the excess letters *above* the word, without

violating the margin; (3) writing words likely to exceed the margin diagonally, usually downward (the favorite practice of Oriental copyists, who made extensive use of it, following Arabic scribes); and (4) writing exceeding letters vertically upward (practiced in Ashkenaz).

4. *Means of ensuring the correct order of the codex*

Since scribes were copying texts on loose folded sheets arranged in quires, and only upon completion of the copy would they give the loose quires to the binder for stitching together, it was necessary to ensure the correct order of the quires at the time of binding. In later times, particularly when writing on paper, which was more vulnerable than parchment, scribes tended to employ additional means to ensure the order of the sheets or leaves within a quire.

These means included numerating the quires by Hebrew letters either at the beginning or at the end of the quire, or at both the beginning and the end. In Oriental manuscripts, additional numerating in Arabic words may occur at the beginning of quires. This numbering of quires ("signatures") was not practiced by Ashkenazic scribes. By the end of the Middle Ages copyists numerated *all* the leaves of the codex.

Another way to ensure the correct order of quires, sheets, or leaves was by the use of catchwords. The most common method was to repeat the first word or words of the quire, or the leaf, at the foot of the preceding page. An alternative method was to repeat the last word of a quire, or a leaf, at the beginning of the follow-

ing page. In the first method, catchwords are placed separately from the copied text (in the Orient they were frequently written diagonally, in Ashkenaz sometimes vertically), are frequently decorated simply, and are sometimes illustrated (in Ashkenaz and Byzantium). Sometimes, particularly in Sepharad, catchwords of both kinds were employed in the first half of a quire and at the end of a quire, as this was sufficient to ensure the order of the sheets within the quire.

AFTER THE TEXT had been copied and the correct order of the loose quires assured, biblical and liturgical manuscripts, and sometimes other texts, had to be vocalized; this was usually done by a professional vocalizer, rather than by the copyist. To biblical texts the Masorah was usually added in the margins, generally by the vocalizer. Deluxe manuscripts were handed over to artists, who added decorations, illuminations, or illustrations. Only after the vocalizers and artists had done their work was the manuscript handed over to the binder, who completed the process of producing a codex.

3 EVELYN M. COHEN

The Decoration of Medieval Hebrew Manuscripts

THE MOST widespread form of painting in the Middle Ages was executed neither on panels nor on walls, but on the pages of manuscripts. Handwritten books, both religious and secular, were decorated throughout this period. Hebrew manuscripts, commissioned by Jews for communal or home use, were often illuminated as well.

Contrary to a widely held misconception, art was permitted among medieval Jewry. The injunction in the second commandment, Exodus 20:4, "Thou shalt not make unto thee a graven image," was generally interpreted in conjunction with the verse that follows it, "Thou shalt not bow down unto them, nor serve them." In fact, Exodus 25 describes the making of the Sanctuary and its ark, which was to be adorned with two cherubim, with wings and human faces, formed from gold. Archaeological evidence has revealed that around the year 250 in Dura Europos, Syria, the walls of a synagogue were covered with biblical scenes and other decorations, while in the Galilean synagogues of the fifth and sixth centuries, mosaic floors were enlivened with representations of ritual objects and even pagan motifs, in addition to stories from the Bible.

In the Christian world, the art of manuscript illumination flourished from late antiquity to the Renais-

sance. Among Jews, however, no examples of decorated manuscripts remain from the early Middle Ages. Although some scholars maintain that works were produced, the earliest extant decorated manuscript bearing a date is a Book of Prophets written in Tiberias in 895 C.E., which is now housed in the Karaite synagogue of Cairo. In Western Europe it was not until the thirteenth century that illuminated Hebrew books seem to have been commonly used. The production of liturgical manuscripts, like Haggadot, for use by individuals parallels a similar development that took place among Christians at that time. In the earlier Middle Ages, books were generally written and illuminated in monastic *scriptoria* or writing shops, for use by either the Church or royalty. In the thirteenth century, with the development of towns, universities, and a middle class, book production shifted to lay workshops, and wealthy individuals commissioned luxurious manuscripts, particularly the Psalter and Book of Hours.

The procedures employed in the illumination of Hebrew manuscripts do not differ from those used in Christian works. Although paper was used in the Islamic East, before the late fifteenth century most manuscripts in the West were written on

animal skins. After the parchment was prepared and cut into sheets, the bifolios were arranged in groupings, known as gatherings or quires, which usually contained four to five sheets. After the leaves were ruled, the scribe, who was responsible for the layout of the page in general, copied the text, leaving blank the areas that were to be painted. The gatherings were then ready to be decorated by the artist, who usually was someone other than the scribe. The drawings were executed first, but before they were painted over, the areas that were to be covered with gold were prepared. Bole, a mixture of gesso and clay, was applied to the folio to form a somewhat raised surface to which the delicate sheets of gold leaf would adhere. The pigments, formed of various minerals and common elements like egg and urine, were then mixed and applied, one color at a time.

Some medieval recipe books still exist which list the ingredients and explain the procedures that were used to create different pigments. One of these was written by Abraham ben Judah ibn Ḥayyim, a Jew. The Portuguese text, written in Hebrew characters, is found in a manuscript in the Biblioteca Palatina in Parma (Ms. De Rossi 945). The colophon states that the treatise was written in 1262, although this copy may have

The Bird's Head Haggadah *(southern Germany, ca. 1300). Note that most, but not all, of the people have bird-like features. The figures on the left are preparing dough for matzah. The males are wearing pointed Jews' hats, which were imposed as a distinguishing mark on Jews in Germany and other lands of the Holy Roman Empire beginning in the thirteenth century.*

Israel Museum, Jerusalem [Ex. no. 33]

been written in the fifteenth century. The document is composed of forty-five parts, with each section describing how to make a specific color. The treatise begins with an account of the production of various types of gold, and continues with the making of blues, reds, greens, yellows, and black. Different recipes and instructions are given for obtaining different shades of color.

Unfinished manuscripts that display the stages of decoration exist in various collections. Perhaps the most revealing example is the *Prato Haggadah* in the Library of the Jewish Theological Seminary of America in New York (Mic. No. 9478). This work, written in Spain around 1300, is an illuminated manuscript in the strictest sense of the word; it is a book that was painted with gold and brilliant colors that reflect light. It is not known why, but the manuscript's illumination was halted abruptly, leaving some folios decorated with only the underdrawings, while others were already fully painted. It is evident that the traditional order was followed of writing the text, executing the drawings, applying the bole, affixing the gold leaf, and finally adding the colors. The leaves were kept in gatherings and the artist worked from the outside in, painting the outer bifolio first and working his way toward the center. The pigments were applied one color at a time, beginning with blue. In one unfinished quire, therefore, the outer side of the bifolio was fully illuminated, while on the inside only blue was applied. Nearer to the center,

the folios have gold and no pigment, then only bole, and finally, in the middle of the gathering, only the drawings have been executed.

Decorations appear to have been commonplace in medieval Hebrew manuscripts, and are discussed in rabbinic literature. Rabbi Meir ben Baruch of Rothenburg (1215?–1293), for example, was asked why he did not protest the widespread inclusion of paintings in prayerbooks. He replied that the drawing of images is not forbidden, although he condemned the presence of illustrations because they distract the worshipper. In fact, few images were strictly prohibited. The Talmud and rabbinic responsa forbid the depiction of the four creatures of the *merkavah* from Ezekiel's vision. These figures, which are frequently represented in Christian works as attributes of the four Evangelists, do however appear in Hebrew manuscripts. A depiction of the Heavenly Chariot is found, for example, in the Ashkenazic *Ambrosian Bible* (Biblioteca Ambrosiana, Milan, Ms. B. 32, Inf.), 1236–38, and in Maimonides' *Moreh Nevukhim* (*Guide to the Perplexed*) from Barcelona, 1348 (The Royal Library, Copenhagen, Cod. Hebr. XXXVII).

In the *Ambrosian Bible* the image of the man from Ezekiel's vision was replaced with that of a bird. In fact, throughout the manuscript an accurate rendering of the human form was avoided. Figures were often portrayed with their heads viewed from behind, or with faces that were left blank, or articulated with the features of animals or birds. This was a specifically Ashkenazic approach

that was prevalent in the thirteenth and fourteenth centuries. The avoidance of realistic human forms was manifested in different ways in the manuscripts from Germany. Not surprisingly, almost all of the people in the *Bird's Head Haggadah* (Israel Museum, Jerusalem, Ms. 180/57) were given bird-like features. In the *Tripartite Mahzor,* which is divided into three volumes housed in Budapest (Library of the Hungarian Academy of Sciences, Ms. Kaufmann A384), London (British Library, Add. Ms. 22413), and Oxford (Bodleian Library, Ms. Michael 619), men were generally represented with human features while women were depicted with animal-like heads. In some manuscripts, however, neither people nor angels were portrayed in a distorted manner, and by the fifteenth century, as is indicated by the *Darmstadt Haggadah* (Hessische Landes- und Hochschulbibliothek, Ms. Or. 8) and the *First Cincinnati Haggadah* (Hebrew Union College, Ms. 444), there was no longer an avoidance of complete representations of humans. In Spain and Italy the accurate depiction of the human form seems never to have been considered problematic.

It is only the personification of God that appears to have been strictly prohibited in all artistic centers in the Middle Ages. When an allusion to the Divine presence was important to the scene, as in the depiction of Moses receiving the Tablets of the Law, God's hand alone was depicted. In one notable exception, the *Kaufmann Mishneh Torah* (Library of the Hungarian Academy of Sciences, Budapest, Ms. Kaufmann A77), a complete personification of God was initially portrayed, undoubtedly by a Christian artist who was unaware of the Jewish restrictions. The image was then concealed by a representation of Mount Sinai which was painted over the forbidden form.

Jews were not permitted to belong to the craft guilds, and not much is known about Jewish illuminators. Colophons providing information about the scribe sometimes mentioned the vocalizer but rarely referred to the artist. There are some notable exceptions, particularly in the *Cervera Bible* (Biblioteca Nacional, Lisbon, Ms. Hebr. 72) from 1300 and the *Kennicott Bible* (Bodleian Library, Oxford, Ms. Kennicott 1), which was inspired by it in 1476. In both of these manuscripts from Spain, a full page is devoted to the artist's colophon, in which his name is written in large zoomorphic and anthropomorphic letters. Unfortunately there are generally no colophons in Haggadot before the fifteenth century, even on the part of the scribes, so little can be gleaned concerning the artists' identities. The best-known medieval scribe and artist was Joel ben Simeon, who was active in Germany and Italy and is believed to have had a workshop. Of the many manuscripts that have been attributed to him, nine have colophons, and in two of these he stated that he was the illuminator. In one of his manuscripts, in the Library of the Jewish Theological Seminary of America in New York (Mic. No.

8279), Joel ben Simeon specified that he wrote, vocalized, and illustrated the Haggadah, which he completed in 1454.

In most cases the motifs that were depicted in Hebrew manuscripts did not differ significantly from those found in works of art in general. Some representations were based on midrashic sources, but these depictions appear in Christian manuscripts as well. Pictorial Jewish sources were not necessarily needed by Christian illuminators because aggadic literature was already known to the Church Fathers. Some subjects, especially eschatological images, do have a specifically Jewish nature. As Joseph Gutmann has pointed out in numerous studies, different regions expressed the desire for the coming of the Messianic era in different ways. In Spanish Bibles, depictions of the sanctuary implements conveyed the desire that the Temple in Jerusalem be built once again. Ashkenazic Bibles and prayerbooks included representations of the battle between the Leviathan and Behemoth and the subsequent feast of the righteous. The Talmud (*Baba Batra* 74b) recounts that at the end of time the enormous fish and the mythical beast will engage in a battle unto death. The righteous will then feast on the flesh of these two animals while seated under a tent formed from the skin of the Leviathan. In the fifteenth century a new eschatological motif was depicted in German and Italian Haggadot; the

Sanctuary implements from a northern Spanish or Provençal Bible of 1301, including (clockwise from upper right) the golden incense altar, two silver trumpets, a horn, pots for ashes, basins for the blood of sacrifices, scrapers for removing ashes, flesh hooks, a firepan for hot coals, the laver and its stand, and the altar of burnt offering.

Royal Library, Copenhagen, Cod. Hebr. II [Ex. no. 8]

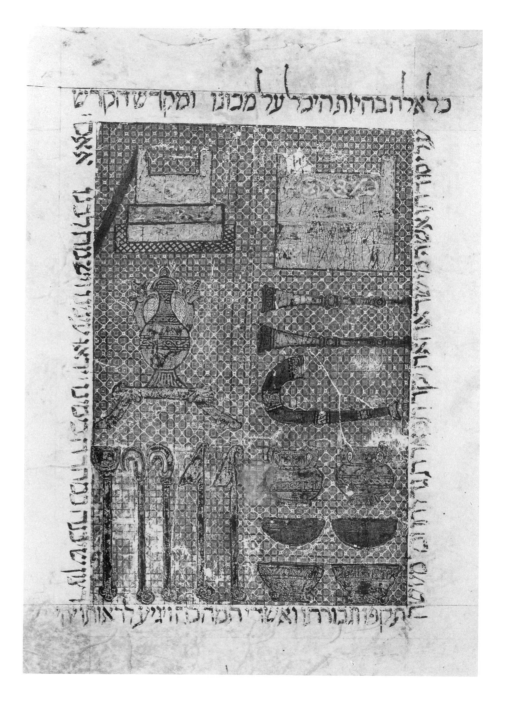

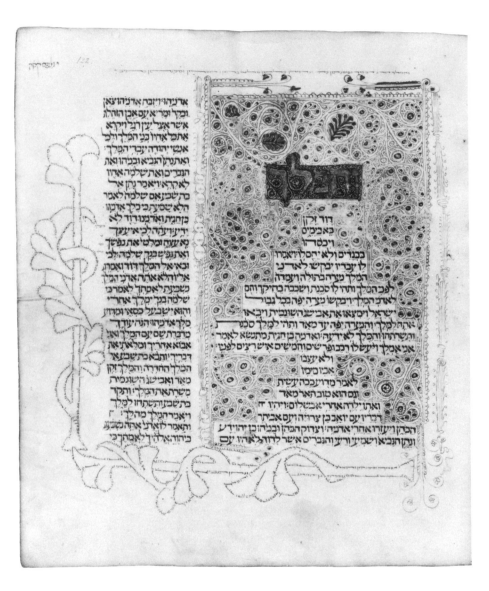

The opening of First Kings in a Hebrew Bible from Spain, 1460–80. The entire first word, veha-Melekh (translated as "Now King"), is set apart in a decorated panel. In the lower and left-hand margins is the Masorah in micrography, forming a plant-like frame.
Royal Library, Copenhagen, Cod. Hebr. V [Ex. no. 11]

figure of Elijah or the Messiah was portrayed riding on a donkey.

Of the many types of medieval Hebrew books that were decorated, the manuscripts most frequently illuminated were Bibles, prayerbooks, and Haggadot. Other texts found worthy of ornamentation include rabbinic writings, particularly Maimonides' *Mishneh Torah* and to a lesser degree his *Moreh Nevukhim*, Jacob ben Asher's *Arba'ah Turim*, Rashi's commentary on the Bible, medical and astronomical treatises, and Isaac ibn Sahulah's book of animal fables entitled *Meshal ha-Kadmoni*. The type of decoration found in these works varied enormously from simple scribal designs to lavish illuminations. Decorations could be pure ornamentation or carefully depicted text illustrations. As was typical of medieval manuscripts in general, the illuminations at times occupied a full page, or part of a page, and at other times appeared in the margins. Unlike the practice in Christian manuscripts, however, the initial letter was rarely a major field for decoration. As Hebrew does not have capital letters, usually the entire word at the beginning of a text, rather than the opening letter alone, was painted or illustrated.

Another type of decoration found specifically in Jewish art is micrography, which means, literally, small writing that forms designs. These decorations, which could be either abstract or representational, were made in all regions where Hebrew manuscripts were produced. Frequently, masoretic texts indicating the correct spelling, writing, and reading of the Bible were written in a decorative manner. In some cases the text was incorporated into full-page decorations known as carpet pages, because their abstract designs contained patterns that were similar to those found in rugs. On other occasions the masorator, who was not necessarily the scribe, formed ornamental patterns, or illustrations, from the lines of text at the upper and lower borders of the folios.

The style of the decorations of medieval manuscripts varied greatly depending upon where the books were produced. No distinctive Jewish style ever developed; Jewish artists painted in whatever manner was prevalent in the region where they worked. It might be a reflection of the traditional taste of Jewish patrons, but the illuminators of Hebrew manuscripts often tended to be conservative and sometimes continued to paint in a style long after it had ceased to be fashionable. This phenomenon is exemplified in the *Kennicott Bible,* which reflects not only the imagery but also the style of the *Cervera Bible* of more than a century and a half before. In Italy as well, the style of Joel ben Simeon continued to be used late into the fifteenth century, and appears in the *Rothschild Maḥzor* from Florence, 1492 (The Library of the Jewish Theological Seminary of America, New York, Mic. No. 8892), alongside illuminations executed in the latest Renaissance style.

An example of a picture in micrography of Aaron dressing the lamps (Exodus 30:7) in a Pentateuch from Germany, 1294/95. Bibliothèque Nationale, Paris, Ms. Hebr. 5 [Ex. no. 21]

The region from which the earliest decorated Hebrew manuscripts are extant is the Islamic East, particularly ninth- to thirteenth-century Palestine and Egypt, and fifteenth-century Yemen. Stylistically and programmatically the manuscripts are similar to others produced in this part of the world; in fact, the decorations often reflect those found in copies of the Koran. An example of this type of ornamentation exists in the small copy of the *parashah* of *Shelaḥ-lekha* (Jewish National and University Library, Jerusalem, Ms. Heb. 8° 2238) where both the palmette motifs in the margins of the text, and the full-page designs at the beginning and end of the manuscript, which possibly echo the decoration of the book's binding, are typical of other Islamic manuscripts of the period.

Most of the decorated writings from this region are Bibles, but some other texts were adorned as well. Children's primers are extant in which the large display letters of the alphabet are filled in with different colors. In one noteworthy example (University Library, Cambridge, T-S. K5.13) a menorah is depicted opposite the beginning of the alphabet. This motif, as well as other sanctuary implements, is sometimes represented in Bible manuscripts. The designs are often nonfigural, however, in keeping with the artistic practices in the Islamic milieu in which they were created.

Around the end of the fourteenth century, manuscript illumination flourished in the Sephardic region of Spain, and in southern France. Large, meticulously written Bibles were

A carpet page from a Pentateuch produced in Spain around 1460.
Royal Library, Copenhagen, Cod. Hebr. VII, volume 1 [Ex. no. 24]

often decorated, either with the abstract designs reminiscent of those found in the Hebrew Bibles from the Islamic East, or with text illustrations. The many ornamental carpet pages formed of symmetrical interlaced patterns and geometrical designs, in a Bible written in Burgos in 1260 (Jewish National and University Library, Jerusalem, Ms. Heb. 4° 790), still reflect the influence of Islamic art. The decorative leaves were placed at the beginning and end of the manuscript, and before the Prophets, Hagiographa, and Psalms. The designs are often micrographic, with background areas illuminated in different colors. The figural representations decorating the signs at the beginning of the text's divisions into *parashot* and *sidrot* function as realistic text illustrations.

The decoration of the *Cervera Bible,* on the other hand, shows new developments in Bible design. Text illustrations play a more significant role, either as full-page images, like the Prophet Zechariah's vision of the menorah between two olive trees, or as scenes for the opening of books. Before the text of the Book of Jonah begins, for example, the protagonist is shown being thrown into the mouth of a huge fish. Full-page decorations are no longer true carpet pages, but form an architectural framework for the texts at the beginning and end of the manuscripts. As was commonly the case in these Bibles, the scribe indicated his identity and the date of the manuscript, although in the *Cervera Bible,* as was mentioned above, a full page was devoted to the artist's colophon as well.

The stylized depiction of the matzah, the unleavened bread eaten at Passover, in the Kaufmann Haggadah *(Spain, fourteenth century).*
Library of the Hungarian Academy of Sciences, Budapest, Ms. Kaufmann A422 [Ex. no. 36]

קמג

מעל זה כחא

עֲמֵק אוּרְמַיָה   שׁ בַּתֹ שַׁבְּתוֹן לְקִימָה
שׁ וְרִשׁ וְעָנַת סִימֵיהּ   שׁ רִים יַחַד לְצִיּוּמָה
בּ עָה מַטוּ יִסְרוֹהִיהּ   בּ טְחָה בְּחֵזוּ מִסְרוֹהִיהּ
בּ סֵהֲקָעה יָדוּתֵיהּ   בּ בָּפֵל לְהַשְׁעִין יְדוֹהִיהּ
הּ מְנֵהּ פָּעַל יְבוּרִים   הּ מַיֹ הֶמָה הַיְצָרִים
הּ רוּפָקַהֹת לָעֵינוּרִים   הּ בֵּל לָהּ אֵפֵל לָצָרִים
שׁ תְלֵי יָגְבֵיהֹ אַרְבַּע   שׁ אַג סֵפֵר הַמַרְבַּע
שׁ יַע פֹּנֵעִית אַרְבַּע   שׁ עֵה יַרְחַם לְיֹבֵּעַ
בּ יַסְֹתָהּ בְּמַהֲלַךְ הַמַּיִם בּ מַיְסַר לְהוּמֵי חֲדוּמִים
בּ יָרְדְּי דַּרִיח כְּתָמִים בּ אֲבָּס אוּרֵיב וְֹהֻמִים

A fourteenth-century folio Maḥzor from Germany showing a piyyut or liturgical hymn for the additional service of the Day of Atonement. The initial word, Shoshan, *means "lily" and was understood in the Middle Ages to represent the Jewish people. The four letters which make it up are decorated with grotesque figures.*

Staatsbibliothek Preussischer Kulturbesitz, Orientabteilung, Berlin (West), Ms. or. fol. 388 [Ex. no. 60]

It is not in the Bibles, but in the luxurious copies of the Haggadah which were made for private family use, that biblical cycles were depicted. The *Rylands Spanish Haggadah* (John Rylands University Library, Manchester, Ms. 6), for example, begins with biblical illustrations on full pages which were usually divided into two registers. The cycle commenced with the scene of Moses and the Burning Bush and concluded with the crossing of the Red Sea. Likewise, the *Kaufmann Haggadah* (Library of the Hungarian Academy of Sciences, Budapest, Ms. Kaufmann A422), whose folios were for many years not in their proper sequence, contains a biblical cycle which begins with the discovery of Moses in the casket and ends with the song and dance of Miriam after the crossing of the Red Sea. As was usually the case, both of these fourteenth-century manuscripts contain illustrations for the text of the Haggadah and show contemporary preparations for Passover.

An outstanding example of manuscript illumination from the fourteenth century is found in the *Copenhagen Moreh Nevukhim*. The beginning of each of the three sections of the text is decorated with a framed miniature. The first shows two scenes that were commonly portrayed in non-Hebrew medieval manuscripts: the scribe presenting his patron with a copy of his book, and a teacher instructing his pupils. The second part shows a group of scientists, and the third, mentioned above, contains a representation of the four creatures of Ezekiel's vision. The illuminator was able to illustrate parts of the text itself, by literally representing individual words like "leg" and "man."

With its fine brushwork and lush foliate borders of brilliant colors, a copy of Maimonides' *Mishneh Torah* from 1472 (British Library, London, Harley Ms. 5698/5699) is one of the highlights of the fifteenth-century Portuguese school of illumination. It belongs to a group of Sephardic manuscripts that were decorated in a recently developed Renaissance manner. This type of manuscript illumination came to an abrupt end in this region with the expulsion of the Jews from Spain in 1492 and from Portugal in 1496. It was, however, transported to Italy where it continued to flourish.

In the Ashkenazic world, large Bibles with elaborate micrographic decorations were common. The *Ebermannstadt Pentateuch* (The Royal Library, Copenhagen, Cod. Hebr. XI) displays a sophisticated use of micrography in the ornate decorations which surround the opening words of the Five Books. Text illustrations like the depiction of the ram caught in the thicket in the *Duke of Sussex Bible* (British Library, London, Add. Ms. 15282) were formed in micrography, using the words of the Masorah. This manuscript also contains brilliant full-page illuminations for the opening The Books of the Bible. The decorations in the *Ambrosian Bible,* although generally smaller in scale, include historiated initial word panels containing biblical scenes.

Haggadot were also frequently illustrated, although unlike their Sephardic counterparts, full-page representations were rare. Biblical scenes

Page of a Maḥzor produced in Northern Italy in the fifteenth century. The text is rendered in square and semi-cursive letters, both of which scripts are markedly Ashkenazic, while the filigree decoration has Sephardic features.

Staatsbibliothek Preussischer Kulturbesitz, Orientabteilung, Berlin (West), Ms. or. quart. 361 [Ex. no. 63]

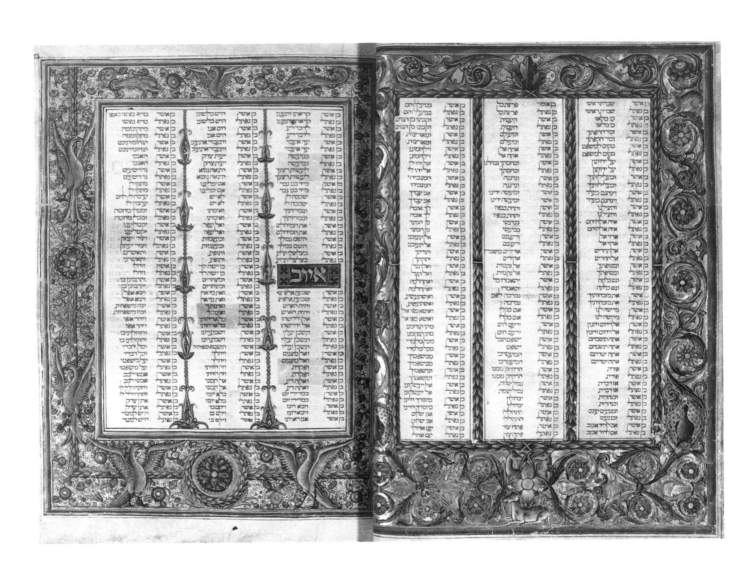

were incorporated into the text, rather than appearing as separate cycles, and illustrations were usually placed in the margins of the text. The scenes of preparation for Passover, illustrations for the text—including the traditional representations of the four sons, the matzah, and maror—images portraying the biblical events alluded to in the closing piyyutim, and eschatological depictions became somewhat standardized. One outstanding exception is found in the fifteenth-century *Darmstadt Haggadah,* which is populated with numerous female figures. None of the traditional representations is depicted.

Oversize Maḥzorim, prayerbooks containing the complete cycle of liturgical readings for the entire year, were frequently illustrated. A traditional iconography developed in which specific readings were usually

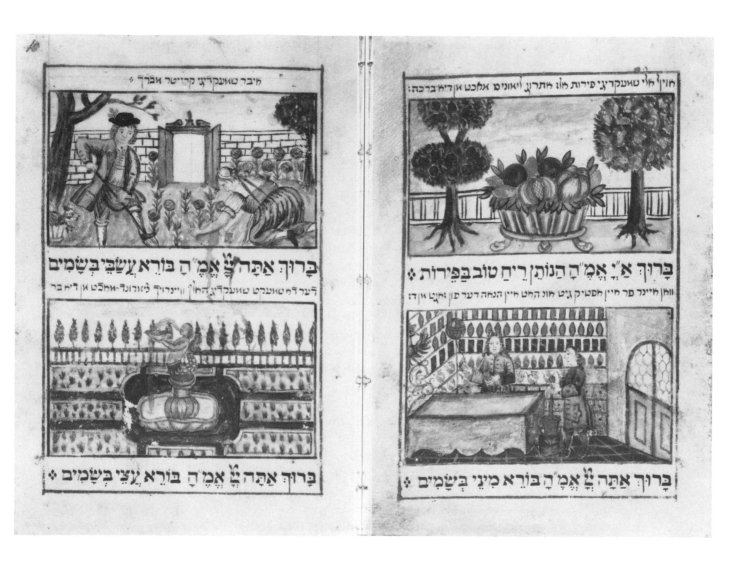

adorned with the same scene. For example, in both the *Hammelburg Mahzor* of 1348 (Hessische Landes- und Hochschulbibliothek, Darmstadt, Cod. Or. 13) and in the *Tripartite Mahzor,* the piyyutim for the Sabbath before the beginning of the month of Nissan are decorated with a crescent moon and a star, and the reading for the morning of the first day of Shavuot is illustrated by the scene of Moses receiving the Tablets of the Law. In both manuscripts, the

Prayer for Dew, which is recited on the first day of Passover, is accompanied by the signs of the zodiac, although in the *Tripartite Mahzor* the corresponding Labors of the Months are also depicted. These motifs, borrowed from Christian imagery, were frequently represented in manuscripts of the Book of Hours and often adorned the facades of Gothic cathedrals.

Seder Birkat ha-Mazon, an illustrated compilation of blessings to be recited on various occasions (Nikolsburg, Moravia, now Mikulov, Czechoslovakia, 1728). The blessings on these pages are for the fragrance of fruit, perfumes, fragrant herbs, and fragrant wood.
Royal Library, Copenhagen, Cod. Hebr. XXXII [Ex. no. 81]

Italian manuscript decorations, like the scripts that were used to write their texts, sometimes included distinctly Ashkenazic and Sephardic features. This is not surprising considering that a scribe like Joel ben Simeon, who came from Germany, continued to work there as well as in Italy. The style he used for manuscripts produced in both countries was basically the same. Similarly, the *Aberdeen Bible* (Aberdeen University Library, Ms. 23), which was written in Naples in 1493 or 1494, was executed by a scribe who apparently had been expelled from Spain; the handwriting, illumination, and micrographic designs are all in the Sephardic tradition.

Fifteenth-century manuscript illumination in Italy is often considered the apex of this art form, and many Hebrew books were of the same caliber as those produced for Christians. That the Italian artistic vocabulary was used in Hebrew works is readily apparent in elements like the naked putti who inhabit the pages of the *Rothschild Maḥzor* and of Joseph Albo's *Sefer ha-'Ikarim* (Accademia dei Concordi, Rovigo, Ms. Silvestriana 220).

The illustrations from the Italian manuscripts provide a wealth of information concerning contemporary Jewish life. In a copy of the *Mishneh Torah* which is today divided between the Biblioteca Apostolica Vaticana (Cod. Rossiana 498) and a private collection in New York, each book begins with an illustration that is represented as a fifteenth-century scene. This is a very different approach from the one found in most Ashkenazic versions, where usually the only illustrations were diagrams of the Temple as described by Maimonides.

One of the most informative pictorial sources for fifteenth-century Italian customs is found in a palm-size prayerbook in Princeton (Princeton University Library, Garrett Ms. 26). As Erwin Panofsky wrote, in it is depicted religious life "from the cradle to the grave." Included in these depictions are scenes of birth, circumcision, the redemption of the firstborn, an engagement and marriage, the interpretation of dreams, prayers and repentance, death and burial. This manuscript and other related works in libraries throughout the world provide a wealth of knowledge concerning Jewish practices in Italy.

By the end of the fifteenth century, the production of printed books began to eclipse that of illuminated manuscripts. In subsequent centuries, with the exception of a revival in eighteenth-century Central Europe, painted codices were generally no longer made. Manuscript illumination did continue, however, in decorated scrolls of the Book of Esther and in marriage contracts, a tradition that is still practiced today.

4 MENAHEM SCHMELZER

The Hebrew Manuscript as Source for the Study of History and Literature

THE MENTION of a Hebrew manuscript often conjures the image of an object relevant only to select *cognoscenti* or highly trained specialists. In reality, most Hebrew manuscripts, books written by hand (*libri manuscripti*) in Hebrew characters, are ready and eager to yield the manifold information contained among their leaves. After all, Hebrew manuscripts were read and studied by ordinary people, not only by scholars, during the time before printed books (*libri impressi*) were made and sometimes even after the invention of printing.

Hebrew manuscripts can teach us a great deal about the reading and study habits of each generation in the various Jewish communities and about the authority and popularity of certain works. Of course, they are equally important because they often preserve significant unpublished religious, literary, historical, philosophical, and scientific texts. Furthermore, manuscripts may serve as objects of study in themselves, as artifacts and physical remnants of the culture in which they were created. As such, manuscripts teach us about Hebrew scribal traditions, book

manufacturing, and aesthetic tastes, as well as offering genealogical and biographical facts concerning the scribes and owners by whom and for whom they were written.

Our principal and primary access to the study of Hebrew manuscripts is provided by the numerous catalogs of public and private collections of Hebrew manuscripts to be found in Europe, Israel, and America. Rather complete lists of these catalogs may be found in Shlomo Shunami's *Bibliography of Jewish Bibliographies* (1965 and supplement in 1975) and in Aron Freimann's *Union Catalog of Hebrew Manuscripts and Their Location* (volume 1, 1973). Needless to say, the quality of the various catalogs is uneven; some are extremely careful, detailed, and scholarly, while others display opposite characteristics.

The pioneering project of the Institute of Microfilmed Hebrew Manuscripts at the Jewish National and University Library in Jerusalem was initiated in 1950 by David Ben-Gurion and has as its goal "to systematically collect microfilms of Hebrew manuscripts scattered in libraries and collections throughout the world, catalogue the manuscripts and make them available to readers who come to the Institute." This goal has been substantially achieved, and at present records relating to

well over forty thousand Hebrew manuscripts and countless fragments are at the service of Jewish scholarship.

Despite this progress, there is still no textbook that provides solid, comprehensive, up-to-date information on Hebrew manuscripts and the various aspects of their study. The last guide to the subject is Moritz Steinschneider's *Vorlesungen über die Kunde hebräischer Handschriften* (1897; with supplementary notes by A. M. Habermann and in a Hebrew translation, 1965).

For one, albeit extremely significant area of Hebrew manuscript study, we have now at our disposal the fundamental work by Malachi Beit-Arié, *Hebrew Codicology* (1976). Thanks to Beit-Arié's book we are able to supply some statistical information on the early centuries of medieval Hebrew manuscripts. The oldest known dated Hebrew manuscript was written in Tiberias, in 895 C.E., and it contains a portion of the Bible. Although there are undated fragments that may be older, their existence does not alter the basic situation, which is that there is a huge gap of centuries separating the Dead Sea Scrolls from the appearance of the earliest medieval Hebrew manu-

The Coburg Pentateuch *(Coburg, 1395).*
The illustration at the end of Leviticus shows
a teacher and his pupil. The teacher is bran-
dishing a whip. Before the pupil is Hillel's
maxim "What is hateful to you, do not to
your neighbor: [that is the whole Torah,]
while the rest is commentary thereof" (Talmud, Shabbat 31a).
By permission of The British Library, London,
Add. Ms. 19776 [Ex. no. 23]

scripts. The rabbinic inclination against writing down rabbinic and liturgical texts may partially explain this phenomenon, but it does not explain the lack of surviving copies of the Bible from that period. Even after the ninth century, Hebrew manuscripts remain very scarce. In Beit-Arié's words: "Of some 2700 extant dated Hebrew manuscripts until 1540,* 6 dated codices from the tenth century, 8 from the eleventh century and 22 from the twelfth century are known to us" (*Hebrew Codicology*, p. 11). These figures are in sharp contrast with the large number of Latin and Greek manuscripts that are extant from the fifth century onward.

Some change in this respect may be expected once the approximately two hundred thousand fragments of the Cairo Geniza are thoroughly researched. The Cairo Geniza, a treasure trove of manuscript leaves written in Hebrew characters, was discovered in an old synagogue in Fostat, near Cairo, toward the end of the nineteenth century. The Geniza owes its existence to the traditionally respectful attitude of Jews toward the written Hebrew word, even after the book or document that carries the Hebrew script has become worn out or otherwise outlived its usefulness. The contents of the Geniza represent the literary as well as economic and social creativity and activity of the Jewish community in the Mediterra-

nean era, covering a period of many centuries. The Geniza fragments are now scattered in the libraries of the world, the largest collection of them being held by the Cambridge University Library in England. Despite the great advances in Geniza research, there is still hope that further systematic study will shed light on Hebrew manuscript scholarship, especially in the earlier medieval period.

If we now turn our attention to the broad subject areas within collections of Hebrew manuscripts, we arrive at widely varying situations.

First, let us look at manuscripts of the Hebrew Bible. There are extant hundreds, if not thousands, of medieval and later Hebrew Bible manuscripts. Given the care taken with the transmission of a sacred text, one expects and finds few significant textual variants among them. On the other hand, these manuscripts have great scholarly importance for the study of Hebrew orthography, pronunciation, systems of vocalization of Hebrew, cantillation, and the entire range of the so-called masoretic literature that deals with scribal instructions and the rules for the transmission of the text. Some Bible codices, especially the older ones, were considered in their times as models by scribes who used them for copying other Bibles with as much care and exactitude as possible. That some of the manuscripts are richly illuminated adds to their significance. The recent reproduction in facsimile editions of some of the finest codices, for example, the *Aleppo, Damascus,* and *Kennicott Bibles,* allows even the

nonspecialist to enjoy the beauty and antiquity of these monuments of the Jewish heritage.

Arabic and Aramaic as well as other versions of the Hebrew Bible are found in large numbers among Hebrew manuscripts. These reflect local traditions and serve as research materials for linguists and historians of Bible exegesis.

Works of Bible commentators of all ages are richly represented in this group. They may be divided into two categories: copies of classic commentaries that are also found in many printed editions, such as the works of Rashi, Abraham ibn Ezra, and Naḥmanides, and texts that are preserved only in manuscripts. In both categories one may discover important elements for the critical understanding of the long history of Jewish Bible interpretation.

Let us look at two works as examples: the Pentateuch commentary of Rashi and that of his grandson, Samuel ben Meir (the *Rashbam*). Rashi's commentary has been the staple of elementary education for Jewish children throughout the centuries and it has also been an extremely popular text for lay adults. As a result, throughout the Jewish diaspora, in the east and in the west, in Spain and in Germany, in Yemen and in Italy, numerous manuscripts of this beloved work were written, containing local variants. Although attempts have been made to collate large numbers of manuscripts and printed editions in order to present the scholar with the various traditions of the Rashi text, the classification of all available manuscripts according to

*These manuscripts, with palaeographical and codicological descriptions and representative reproductions, are now in the process of being published by the Comité de Paléographie Hébraïque, a joint Israeli-French project. Several volumes have already appeared.

families of tradition is still a *desideratum.* Accordingly, here it is not so much individual manuscripts, but rather the totality of all the sources, that are valuable for their contribution to an understanding of the history of the transmission of this standard text. On the other hand, if someone were to discover in our day a hitherto unknown manuscript of the Pentateuch commentary by Samuel ben Meir, high expectations would arise, for the commentary by Rashi's grandson is available in only a very few manuscripts, some poorly preserved. Thus, any new material would be eagerly explored for a better understanding of and insights into the mind of the commentator who, in contrast to most medieval Jewish Bible exegetes, radically adhered to the so-called simple meaning of the Bible. It is interesting to note that the first edition of this work was not published until 1705, when the greatest Jewish bibliophile of all time, Rabbi David Oppenheim, printed it on the basis of a defective manuscript that he had discovered in the geniza of the synagogue of Worms. The fates of these two works could serve as models for the evaluation of the intellectual and perhaps even religious preferences and tastes of generations of Jewish students and readers.

When we turn to manuscripts of the Talmud we find that they are of utmost scarcity. The medieval Church regarded the Talmud as the source and symbol of what it considered to be the perfidy of the Jews. As a result, the Talmud became a constant target and victim of persecution, defamation, censorship,

The Shulḥan ʿArukh *(The Set Table) by Joseph Caro, printed in Venice, 1564–65, during its author's lifetime. Although many were opposed to this code of Jewish law when it appeared, claiming that it reflected only Sephardic practice, it was augmented by the Ashkenazic scholar Moses Isserles and came to occupy a position of great authority. The three crowns are the printer's device of Alvise Bragadini.*
NYPL, Jewish Division [Ex. no. 122]

confiscation, and bookburning. The relationship between the number of surviving copies of the Talmud and that of the Bible can best be illustrated by pointing out that in the catalog of the outstanding collection of Hebrew manuscripts at the British Library are listed 161 manuscripts of the Bible and its translations, while the collection includes only five fragmentary Talmud manuscripts. At the Bibliothèque Nationale in Paris the ratio is 132:0.

The situation is not as bleak in the field of commentaries to the Talmud, Midrashim, halakic codes, and responsa. These works, although related to and dependent on the Talmud, survived in large numbers of manuscripts, and their study yields valuable insights in many areas of Jewish studies. Some highly important texts have been discovered and published only relatively recently, for example, the now popular commentary to the Talmud by Menahem Meiri (Provence, thirteenth century) which was edited for the first time on the basis of manuscripts at the Palatine Library in Parma. The large number of extant manuscripts of the halakic codes *Sefer Mitsvot Gadol (SeMaG)* by Moses of Coucy (France, thirteenth century) and of the *Sefer Mitsvot Katan (SeMaK)* by Isaac of Corbeil (late thirteenth century) indicate that these works were much more popular in the Middle Ages than in later times, when the *Shulḥan ʿArukh,* the authoritative code by Joseph Caro (sixteenth century), began to be published in an almost unending stream of printed editions. Because the first edition of the *Shulḥan ʿArukh* was printed in

1564–65, in the lifetime of its author, any eventual manuscript of the work, except for a most unlikely autograph, would be almost redundant and of little significance. Responsa manuscripts are frequently of great usefulness for not only the halakic but also the historical materials they contain.

The intensive institutional and individual efforts that are being diligently devoted to the publication of rabbinic texts from manuscripts contribute significantly to our understanding of personalities and trends in the history of rabbinic literature.

Liturgical manuscripts are perhaps the most colorful representatives of Hebrew manuscripts. In the words of Shalom Spiegel, "the standard prayers, the oldest nucleus of the liturgy, always and everywhere became the center of Jewish worship, a bond of union despite geographic dispersal . . . [while] new compositions, called *piyyut,* or poetry, constitute . . . an ever changing and restless element in the Jewish liturgy" (*The Jews, Their History, Culture, and Religion,* ed. L. Finkelstein, 3rd ed., 1960, p. 866). The extant manuscripts faithfully reflect this description. From all the countries of the Jewish diaspora and from all ages, manuscript prayerbooks for local usage provide us with a wealth of information about the history of the standard prayers but even more about the immense literature of religious poetry. Among the multitudes of piyyutim one finds many by the great Hebrew poets of the Middle Ages such as Judah ha-Levi, but also large numbers of liturgical compositions by local talent. Although the

A liturgical hymn associated with the special Torah portion Shekalim (Exodus 30:11–16), read on the Sabbath preceding the second day of the month of Adar, in a German Maḥzor of the thirteenth or fourteenth century. Württembergische Landesbibliothek, Stuttgart, Cod. Or. Fol. 42 [Ex. no. 56]

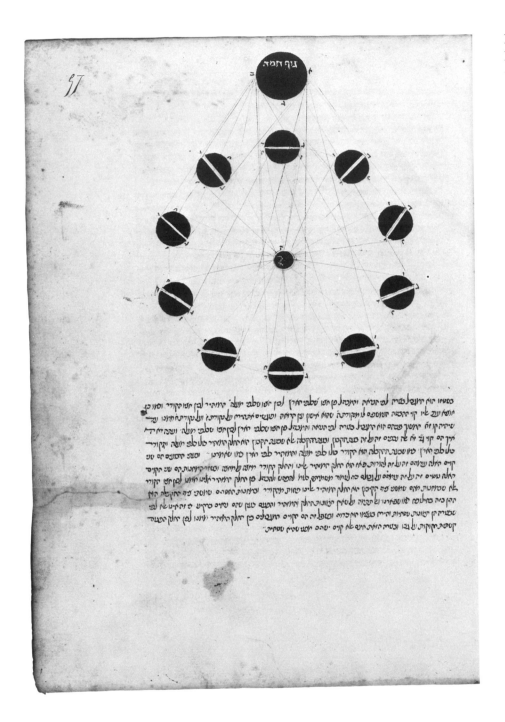

Yesod 'Olam, *a work on astronomy by the fourteenth-century Spanish scholar Isaac Israeli, copied in Sicily, 1491. A large moon is shown at various points in its orbit around the* earth, with the sun at some distance. *Bibliothèque Nationale, Paris, Ms. Hebr. 1069* [Ex. no. 48]

literary quality of the poems in the latter category may not be exquisite, they still are important for the study of local tastes and traditions.

Liturgical instructions, frequently in the vernacular—Judeo-French, Judeo-Greek, Judeo-Persian, and, of course, Judeo-Arabic, Yiddish, and Ladino—offer rich research opportunities for linguists and for historians of liturgy. In this group we are also blessed with many beautifully illuminated and decorated codices, as lavish Haggadah and prayerbook manuscripts demonstrate. Prayerbooks of smaller communities often remained in manuscript and accordingly are our only source for their particular liturgy. This was the case with the rite of the small communities of Asti, Fossano, and Moncalvo of Northern Italy (usually referred to by the acronym APAM), of which there are many fine manuscripts but no printed editions.

While liturgical manuscripts display great variety, mainly dictated by the geographic dispersal of the Jews, manuscripts in Jewish thought, philosophy, ethics, mysticism, and homiletics reflect the vast differences of interest conditioned by the changing intellectual preoccupation among the Jews during their long history. In the Middle Ages, up to approximately the fifteenth century, the works of Aristotle, accompanied by the commentaries of Averroës, in Hebrew translation, dominated the field. Large collections of these works are preserved on the shelves of the great libraries of the world, and they are studied for what they contribute to the general, not only Jewish, history of medieval philosophy.

The classic works of Jewish philosophers and ethicists, Bahya, Maimonides, Albo, and others, are available in many manuscripts. Interestingly, some codices containing Maimonides' *Guide to the Perplexed* are richly illuminated, for example, the *Copenhagen Codex*.

Toward the fourteenth century, manuscripts containing mystical works began to appear. The sixteenth and seventeenth centuries produced more and more manuscripts in this field. The majority of these texts of the Kabbalah remained in manuscript form until recent centuries. There was reluctance among the leaders of the Jewish community to allow wide circulation for esoteric, mystical writings and, accordingly, many kabbalistic works were copied only privately. The popular *Ets Ḥayyim* by the famous sixteenth-century kabbalist Ḥayyim Vital was not printed until the end of the eighteenth century, when many handwritten copies of it were produced in Europe and in North Africa.

It should be pointed out that there were other reasons as well for the continued use of handwritten books at a time when printing was widespread. In distant places, for example, Yemen, the art of printing was never practiced and the rich and ancient literature of Yemenite Jews was transmitted in manuscript form from generation to generation. This explains why, among Yemenite manuscripts, there are many of late vintage, some even from the twentieth century. When such manuscripts contain standard texts their significance for scholarship or even as collectors' items is minimal. On

Symbols for magical writing in Sefer ha-Razim (The Book of Secrets), an early work of Jewish mystical literature, copied as part of a collection of mystical works in Greece, 1468.

*NYPL, Jewish Division, **P (formerly Sassoon, no. 56) [Ex. no. 50]*

Sefer 'Ivronot, *a work on the calendar with discs used for calculations, copied at Bingen am Rhein, Germany, in 1651.*

Staatsbibliothek Preussischer Kulturbesitz, Orient-abteilung, Berlin (West), Ms. or. oct. 3150 [Ex. no. 49]

the other hand, they often preserve older traditions. Only individual examination will determine a given manuscript's importance, if any.

Alongside well-known works of Jewish philosophy and ethics, one finds many manuscript collections of homiletical materials. These must be judged individually and considered frequently as no more than private notebooks. Works on medicine and the sciences, especially astronomy, a subject which was important beyond its intrinsic merit for calendar calculation, are common among the older libraries of Hebrew manuscripts. These include the works of

Greek, Latin, and Arabic physicians, mathematicians, and scientists in Hebrew translation. As in philosophy, Jews played a prominent role in the Middle Ages as translators of the classical and Arabic scientific heritage; thanks to their activity, works by Galen, Hippocrates, Euclid, Ptolemy, Avicenna, and others are preserved in Hebrew versions. Toward the beginning of modern times these works became all but obsolete and were rarely copied or reprinted; historians of the sciences

A Mohel Book (London, 1826). A mohel is a ritual circumciser. Such a book contains pertinent Jewish law, the order of service for a ritual circumcision, and, often, a record of actual circumcisions performed. The illustration depicts a circumcision feast. Note the Dickensian top hats of four of the participants.
Collection of Richard D. Levy [Ex. no. 77]

must therefore rely mainly on medieval manuscripts.

Manuscripts also contain diverse materials of a belletristic nature. Poems, both secular and religious, stories, folktales, dramatic works, parodies, etc., in Hebrew, or in the vernacular but in Hebrew characters, constitute a large segment of Hebrew manuscript collections, especially those assembled more recently. Many of these works were intended for private or local use, and the works of even famous poets were rarely collected in complete manuscripts and survive in fragmentary sources, often only among the leaves of the Cairo Geniza.

There are, of course, other groups of manuscripts of great importance. Karaite manuscripts, some older ones in a mixture of Hebrew and Arabic characters, Hebrew dictionaries and grammars, polemical works that were composed for the frequent disputations between Jews and Christians or Muslims, all provide materials for the interested scholar. Manuscripts of the record books of the various Jewish communities and societies, containing minutes, by-laws, and personal and financial records, were by nature intended for local use and were preserved in community, society, or family archives. With the destruction of old Jewish communities, the surviving, scattered examples of this type of document assumed a highly important place in libraries of Hebrew manuscripts. These handwritten records became the primary source for the study of the political, economic, and social history of the Jews throughout the ages. Furthermore,

they serve as a mine of genealogical and biographical information. Since some of these sources require expertise in many disciplines as well as familiarity with languages and many types of script, relatively few have been published in full scholarly editions. Thus, a great deal of painstaking, systematic work still awaits the attention of the competent historian.

SINCE the Holocaust, the appreciation of Hebrew manuscripts as testimony to the spiritual and historical greatness of destroyed Jewish life has assumed new dimensions. The overwhelming loss of Jewish treasures during the Third Reich has made the survivor generation much more conscious of the need for the preservation and exploration of what remains. The dramatic upsurge in Jewish studies, in Israel and in the United States, has led many scholars to the study and publication of Hebrew manuscripts. Through the ready availability of modern technology, microfilming, computerization, and the growth of the reprint industry, scholars have built upon the advances that had already been achieved. Progress will undoubtedly continue, and still-hidden treasures preserved among the leaves of Hebrew manuscripts will come to light: to enrich, to instruct, and to add to our understanding of the Jewish heritage.

5 JOSEPH GUTMANN

Forming the Great Collections

ALTHOUGH the written word has always been stressed in Judaism, the attitude toward illustrations in books varies greatly. On the one hand, the distinguished thirteenth-century German rabbi, Meir ben Baruch of Rothenburg, saw no objection to animals and bird figures in contemporary Hebrew prayerbooks. On the other hand, the fourteenth- and fifteenth-century German Rabbi Jacob ben Moses ha-Levi Moelln strongly objected to finely decorated prayerbooks that were handed to him while he was officiating at High Holy Day synagogal services.

Profiat Duran, the Spanish Jewish scholar of the fourteenth and fifteenth centuries, observed:

One should always contemplate beautiful books with splendid decorations, fine calligraphy, parchment and bindings. The contemplation of pleasing forms, beautiful images and drawings broadens and stimulates the mind and strengthens its faculties. I want to adorn the Holy Books [for] this matter is worthy and obligatory, and call attention to the beauty, splendor and aesthetic quality to be found in them. As God wanted to beautify His Holy Place with gold, silver, jewels and precious stones so [should it] be properly done with His Holy Books. [*Ma'aseh Efod*, 19]

Jewish scholars who compiled catalogs in the nineteenth century paid scant attention to the illuminations in Hebrew manuscripts, and it was only at the turn of the present century that they began to be studied. Even Christian medieval miniatures were not highly valued until about 1850. Manuscript illuminations were dismissed as "rude monkish drawings which reflected the barbarity of the age."

The three greatest collections of Hebrew manuscripts, especially illuminated manuscripts, are undoubtedly those of the British Library in London, the Bodleian Library in Oxford, and the Biblioteca Palatina in Parma.

The richest of these, of approximately seventy-five illuminated manuscripts, is that of the British Library, which began with the bequests of Jewish as well as non-Jewish donors. The first Earl of Oxford, Robert Harley (1661–1724), a Whig and Governor of the South Sea Company, and Sir Hans Sloane (1660–1753), a wealthy physician, were among the early benefactors. Another was the broker and *gabbai* of Bevis Mark's synagogue, Solomon da Costa Athias (1690–1769), who bequeathed manuscripts to the British Library with the following letter:

Thus saith Solomon, son of the humble, pious and honored Isaac da Costa, surnamed Athias, late of the City of Amsterdam, deceased, one of the people called Jews which are scattered among the nations and from among that part of the captives of Jerusalem which settled in Spain. I have dwelt 54 years and upwards, with security, advantage and ease of mind in this renowned metropolis, eminent above all others for the number, valor, freedom, commerce, knowledge, ingenuity, politeness and humility of its inhabitants . . . whereas a most stately monument hath been lately erected and endowed by the wisdom and munificence of the British legislature . . . an house abounding in books, old and new, written and printed, and in the choicest curiosities both natural and artificial, with intent to preserve the same to succeeding generations in benefit to the people of these nations and of the whole earth . . . as a small token of my esteem, love, reverence and gratitude, to this magnanimous nation and as a thanksgiving offering in part, for the generous protection and numberless blessings which I enjoyed under it.

Another major acquisition was the library of the Duke of Sussex (1774–1843), the sixth son of King George III. In 1823 King George IV presented the library started by George III, who had bought the collection of Joseph Smith, the British consul in Venice. Some finely illuminated He-

*A south German Pentateuch, ca. 1300, from
the collection of the Duke of Sussex. Shown
is the beginning of the Book of Numbers, with
four figures in chain mail holding banners representing the four leading tribes of Israel
camped around the Tabernacle, clockwise from
top: Judah (a lion), Reuben (an eagle),
Ephraim (a bull), Dan (a serpent).*
By permission of The British Library, London,
Add. Ms. 15282 [Ex. no. 22]

brew manuscripts are to be found in these contributions.

In 1865 the collection of Joseph Almanzi (1801–1860), a noted linguist and Hebrew poet, was added. It was this acquisition in particular that placed the British Library's collection in the forefront of outstanding Judaica collections. Many of Almanzi's books had been acquired from Rabbi Ḥayyim Joseph David Azulai (1724–1807), a well-known bibliographer and talmudist. In 1882, M. W. Shapira (1830–1884), a Polish convert to Christianity who had settled in Jerusalem, sold to the British Museum a choice collection of Karaite and Yemenite manuscripts. A colorful character, he was also a missionary and a notorious dealer in spurious antiquities. A large part of the collection of Dr. Moses Gaster, *hakham* of the Sephardic community of London and principal of Lady Montefiore College, which contains some fine illuminated Hebrew manuscripts, was purchased in 1924.

The Bodleian Library in Oxford is another repository of outstanding illuminated Hebrew manuscripts, a key portion of which consists of the library of David ben Abraham Oppenheim (or Oppenheimer) (1664–1736), acquired in 1829. Oppenheim was a leading rabbi, liturgist, and bibliophile who had inherited a sizable fortune. When he became Chief Rabbi of Prague in 1702, he left his extensive library with his father-in-law in Hanover, since he feared that the Holy Office might confiscate his books. After his death the library passed from member to member of the Oppenheim family, eventually being pawned with a senator in Hamburg and stored away in twenty-eight cases. To facilitate its sale, special catalogs were printed, but the various attempts to sell the library were unsuccessful. Although the Oppenheim collection was valued at 22,000 English pounds by the noted philosopher Moses Mendelssohn, this library of some 780 Hebrew manuscripts was finally obtained by the Bodleian Library for the trifling sum of 2,000 English pounds. Another major acquisition, in 1853, was the library of Rabbi Isaac Samuel Reggio (1784–1855), a prominent Austrian-Italian scholar. A prolific writer, he was also the founder of the Rabbinical College at Padua. A significant collection of some 860 Hebrew manuscripts was purchased in 1848 from the Hamburg bibliophile Heimann Joseph Michael (1792–1846). In 1869 the Bodleian Library acquired manuscripts from the collection of Samuel David Luzzatto (1800–1865), a brilliant Italian philologist, poet, and biblical exegete.

Other Hebrew manuscripts in the Bodleian Library came from the collections of William Laud, archbishop of Canterbury; John Selden, an Orientalist and archaeologist; Dr. Edward Pococke, chaplain at Aleppo; Robert Huntington, a seventeenth-century bishop of Raphoe in Ireland; and Matteo Luigi Canonici, an eighteenth-century Italian collector.

The magnificent *Kennicott Bible* of the Bodleian Library, recently reproduced in facsimile, came from

The second volume of the Tripartite Maḥzor (southern Germany, ca. 1320) open to the beginning of the Book of Ruth. The panel shows a harvest scene, in which some figures are portrayed with animal heads.
By permission of The British Library, London, Add. Ms. 22413 [Ex. no. 53]

פרשת   הקדו

ויהי

בִּימֵי שְׁפֹט הַשֹּׁפְטִים וַיְהִי רָעָב בָּאָרֶץ
וַיֵּלֶךְ אִישׁ מִבֵּית לֶחֶם יְהוּדָה לָגוּר בִּשְׂדֵי
מוֹאָב הוּא וְאִשְׁתּוֹ וּשְׁנֵי בָנָיו
וְשֵׁם הָאִישׁ אֱלִימֶלֶךְ וְשֵׁם אִשְׁתּוֹ נָעֳמִי
וְשֵׁם שְׁנֵי בָנָיו מַחְלוֹן וְכִלְיוֹן אֶפְרָתִים
מִבֵּית לֶחֶם יְהוּדָה וַיָּבֹאוּ שְׂדֵי מוֹאָב
וַיִּהְיוּ שָׁם וַיָּמָת אֱלִימֶלֶךְ אִישׁ נָעֳמִי
וַתִּשָּׁאֵר הִיא וּשְׁנֵי בָנֶיהָ וַיִּשְׂאוּ לָהֶם
נָשִׁים מֹאֲבִיּוֹת שֵׁם הָאַחַת עָרְפָּה וְשֵׁם
הַשֵּׁנִית רוּת וַיֵּשְׁבוּ שָׁם כְּעֶשֶׂר שָׁנִים
וַיָּמֻתוּ גַם שְׁנֵיהֶם מַחְלוֹן וְכִלְיוֹן וַתִּשָּׁאֵר
הָאִשָּׁה מִשְּׁנֵי יְלָדֶיהָ וּמֵאִישָׁהּ וַתָּקָם
הִיא וְכַלֹּתֶיהָ וַתָּשָׁב מִשְּׂדֵי מוֹאָב כִּי
שָׁמְעָה בִּשְׂדֵה מוֹאָב כִּי פָקַד יְהוָה אֶת

Dr. Benjamin Kennicott (1718–1783), an English divine and keeper of the Radcliffe Library, who spent a lifetime researching biblical manuscripts. The manuscript, written and illustrated in 1476 in La Coruña in northwest Spain, contains seventy-seven full-page miniatures.

The Biblioteca Palatina in Parma holds an outstanding collection brought together by Giovanni Bernardo de Rossi (1742–1831), a Christian professor of Oriental languages at the University of Parma. Among his 1,430 Hebrew manuscripts were some splendid illuminated books. The De Rossi library was purchased in 1816 and donated to the Biblioteca Palatina by the duchess of Parma, Marie Louise of Austria.

Another fine collection of outstanding illuminated Hebrew manuscripts was that of David Kaufmann (1852–1899), a well-known Hungarian rabbi, professor, and author of some thirty books. Kaufmann acquired most of his books through the purchase in 1895 of the library of Marco Mortara (1815–1894), an Italian rabbi and scholar. His splendid illuminated Hebrew manuscripts came from the purchase of the library of Gabriel Trieste (1784–1860), an Italian merchant and philanthropist. After Kaufmann's death, his valuable collection was donated in 1905 to the Library of the Hungarian Academy of Sciences in Budapest.

David Guenzburg (1857–1910) and Abraham Firkovitch (1786–1874), two Jewish scholars in nineteenth-century Russia, built magnificent collections of illuminated Hebrew manuscripts which are now in the Leningrad Public Library.

Volume I of the Tripartite Maḥzor (southern Germany, ca. 1320), once in the collection of David Kaufmann. This is the beginning of the Song of Songs. King Solomon is depicted in the initial word panel. Before him stand two women with animal heads.
Library of the Hungarian Academy of Sciences, Budapest, Ms. Kaufmann A384 [Ex. no. 52]

Among the early Jewish collectors were Samuel ha-Nagid, the distinguished eleventh-century statesman from Granada, Spain, and Isaac Abravanel, the fifteenth-century Spanish Jewish statesman and scholar, whose son Samuel continued the tradition of his father. The da Pisa and Volterra families in Renaissance Italy had fine collections of Hebrew manuscripts. The Finzi family of fifteenth-century Italy had a library of some two hundred books. In the seventeenth century, Rabbi Manasseh ben Israel of Holland had a collection of Hebrew manuscripts.

Hebrew manuscripts have also been in the collections of non-Jews from the medieval period on. In Augsburg, Germany, Johann Jakob Fugger (1516–1575) had an excellent collection, including the earliest illuminated Hebrew manuscript from Germany. A commentary on the Bible, it was made in the Würzburg region in 1233. After Fugger, who came from the noted banking family, failed in the banking business, his friend Herzog Albrecht V of Bavaria purchased the library and bequeathed it to the Bayerische Staatsbibliothek in Munich. Johann's brother Ulrich (1526–1584) had moved from his native Augsburg to Heidelberg in 1564, taking his extensive library with him. Upon his death, his library, including 175 Hebrew manuscripts, passed to the Palatine Library. When Protestant Heidelberg was captured in 1623 by the troops of Maximilian of Bavaria, the great Palatine Library was given to the pope and thus became the property of the Vatican Library.

In the eighteenth century, Baron Hüpsch of Cologne owned the well-known *Darmstadt Haggadah,* which has twice been reproduced in facsimile and is now in the Hessische Landes- und Hochschulbibliothek in Darmstadt, Germany. This famous manuscript was thought to have been lost during World War II, but was discovered in the German Museum of Leatherwork in Offenbach. Curiously, the Nazis had put the manuscript on display in 1941 because of its finely crafted fifteenth-century leather binding. The public visiting this museum never suspected that a Passover Haggadah lay beneath its leather cover.

The *Sarajevo Haggadah,* also reproduced twice in facsimile, was hidden from the Nazis in 1941 by the director of the Sarajevo National Museum. The *Worms Maḥzor,* illuminated in Germany in 1272, was similarly saved by the director of the Worms Cultural Institute. Since 1957 it has rested in the Jewish National and University Library in Jerusalem.

The Nazis were not the first to covet Hebrew manuscripts. The beautiful illuminated medical treatise *The Canon of Medicine* of Avicenna, now in the Bologna University Library, was one of many Hebrew manuscripts Napoleon carried off to Paris in 1796; along with other Hebrew manuscripts, it was retrieved in 1815.

*Page (slightly enlarged) of a medical work
from the Bibliothèque Nationale. It was copied
in northern Spain or Provence in the first half
of the fifteenth century. The Sephardic script
here shows a very strong Arabic influence.
Bibliothèque Nationale, Paris, Ms. Hebr. 1135
[Ex. no. 73]*

Cardinal Richelieu, King Louis XIV, King Henry IV, and Catherine of Medici in France had collections which included illuminated Hebrew manuscripts; these are now in the Bibliothèque Nationale in Paris.

In England, devout Christians such as Bishop William Bedell had collections that included illuminated Hebrew manuscripts; Bedell's are now in Emmanuel College in Cambridge.

While it is difficult to ascertain the history of ownership of many illuminated Hebrew manuscripts, we do have the testimony of two avid collectors of the nineteenth and twentieth centuries. David Solomon Sassoon (1882–1942), whose family had a mercantile empire that stretched from China to England, was a man of great learning. He tells us that "the study of, and search for, the owners of our manuscripts, may throw light on the wanderings of Hebrew manuscripts from country to country and from continent to continent. Many manuscripts written in Europe came *via* Asia or Africa back to this continent . . . many instances can be adduced of Hebrew manuscripts in Spain finding their way to Bagdad."

Most interesting is the story of the *Farḥi Bible,* one of the most beautiful Catalan manuscripts illuminated in fourteenth-century Spain. Sassoon remarks:

By a mere accident I overheard a conversation between travellers on a boat, whereby I first became aware of the fact that the Farḥi Bible was still available and likely to be sold. My first journey to Aleppo (1913) gave me the opportunity to increase my collection. Through per-

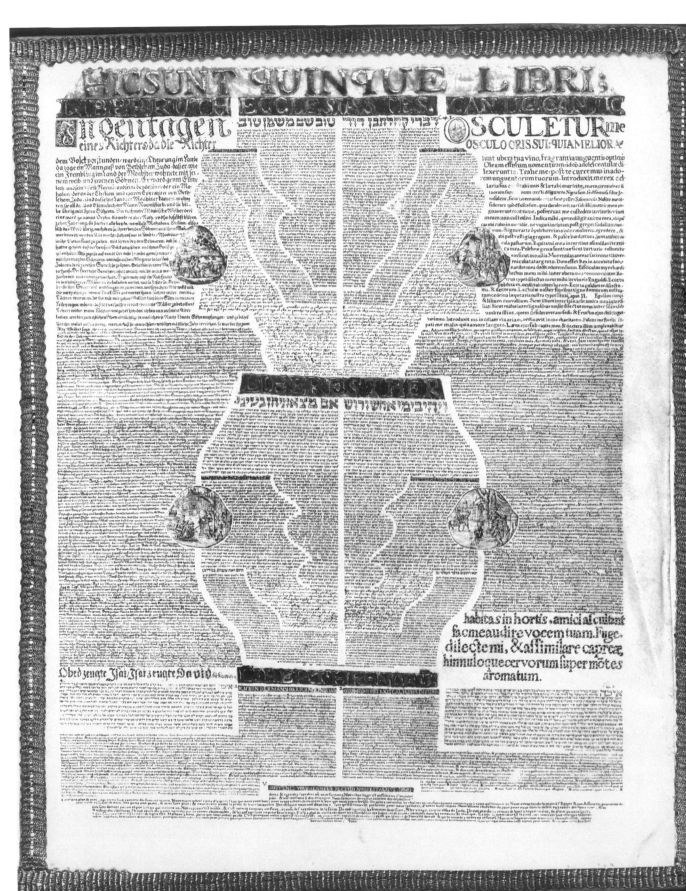

sonal information, obtained twelve years previously, and through references . . . my attention was drawn to the magnificent [*Farḥi Bible*] in the possession of the distinguished Farḥi family, who lived first in Damascus, and later in Aleppo [Ḥayyim Mu'Allim Farḥi (ca. 1750–1820) served as minister to the Pasha of Syria]. Having tried without success for more than a decade to procure that MS. through correspondence, I decided to go in person. [Having] arrived in Aleppo, it was only with the greatest difficulty that I was enabled to have a look at the work of Elisha Crescas, the scribe and illuminator of this [fourteenth-century] Bible. Ultimately [in 1913] I procured the MS.

Sassoon paid 360 English pounds for the manuscript, which is still in the possession of the Sassoon family. At auction today, it would probably bring approximately one million dollars.

Sassoon also informs us of an interesting experience he had on his way from Bombay to England.

The boat on which we travelled weighed anchor at Port Said. Whilst [Sassoon] was waiting there, a local Jewish pedlar boarded the boat with his usual merchandise of beads and feathers. . . . Soon I entered into a conversation with this stall-holder, and to my surprise, I learned that he was the owner of a Hebrew MS. I was anxious to see this book, and we arranged that while he went to fetch it I should sell his goods. After about three hours he returned with a beautifully written Sefardi prayer book for weekdays and the eve of Sabbath, dating most probably from the early fifteenth century, and illuminated throughout with arabesques and other designs. The owner was happy to sell it to me before we left port and was grateful to see how much had been sold at his stall.

Another Jewish collector was Elkan Nathan Adler, an English lawyer, many of whose books were acquired in 1923 by the Jewish Theological Seminary of America. He informs us that in book collecting, "like all hunts, an element of sport enters into it, and one's gambling instincts are undoubtedly stimulated. You must adapt your tactics to the environment in which you find yourself. It is no good to apply the same manoeuvres in attempting to ferret out a rubbish heap in Aleppo that one would employ while treasure-seeking in the ghettos of Northern Italy."

The history of illuminated Hebrew manuscript collections is still largely unexplored. It is hoped that this essay will stimulate further inquiry.

6 MORDECHAI GLATZER

Early Hebrew Printing

HEBREW printing apparently began in Rome around 1470, soon after the appearance of Latin printing in Italy (1462), and quickly spread throughout Italy. In the Iberian peninsula as well, Hebrew printing took its first steps in the fifteenth century, apparently in 1476, shortly after the arrival of Latin printing in Spain (1473). A Hebrew book was quite probably printed in Constantinople in 1493. But Hebrew printing did not spread to other countries until the sixteenth century. Here we shall survey neither all the books printed nor all the printers or printing cities; rather, we shall limit our discussion to selected aspects of the growth of Hebrew printing.

First let us see how Hebrew printing was greeted at its appearance.

If we count all dated Hebrew manuscripts from all countries from the mid-fifteenth century until close to the mid-sixteenth century, the result is rather interesting.[1] From 1451 to 1490 approximately the same number of dated Hebrew manuscripts were produced each decade, totalling 808 manuscripts. From 1491 to 1530 each decade also saw the production of a similar number of manuscripts, but far fewer than in the previous period, totalling only 448 manuscripts. Thus, from the forty years prior to 1490 to those after 1490 there was a dramatic decline

of almost 50 percent in the number of copied Hebrew manuscripts. We see that Hebrew printing began to make its mark on the Hebrew book market just twenty years after it first went into operation. Clearly, in the early years a relatively small number of books were printed, and, as in the Christian world, they were not always well received. However, after the "break-in period," the Jewish community accepted printing without reservation. Within several decades the custom of copying books by hand became limited to certain areas such as Yemen, where books continued to be copied by hand until the nineteenth century because of the land's isolation and distance from the main Jewish centers, or to such types of books as kabbalistic works, which continued to be copied privately because of the esoteric nature of that literature.

We see, therefore, that Hebrew printing was accepted very quickly by the Jewish people, who have always adapted easily to external change.

The novelty of Hebrew printing, wonderment at it, and the attitude toward it are expressed in the writings of the printers and in their need to apologize for their work. In an interesting colophon to Rashi's com-

mentary on the Torah, printed in Zamora (Spain), apparently 1487, the printer wrote a poem: "With the power of the Lord we have finished, to spread the Torah among His people. Behold, it was written without fingers, its form is square, without a ruler, in an absolutely straight line. The paper was placed on the ink, unlike the way [the pen is usually placed on the paper], and the sheet upon the reed." This is a quaint description of the technique of printing, the inked chase, with the paper placed on it, soon to be pressed.

The type used by this printer was engraved by Samuel Ibn Musa,[2] who is so far unmentioned in that capacity in research on Hebrew incunabula,[3] and the typesetter was named Emanuel. In another colophon (to the Tur of Jacob ben Asher, 'Orah Hayyim, Mantua, 1476), the printer, Abraham Conat, calls himself "One who writes with many pens without doing miracles," also apologizing for his work, claiming that it is meant to disseminate Torah among the people.

Before the work of printing was begun, the printer had of course to order Hebrew type. Doubts concerning the proper choice were one of the peculiar problems of Hebrew printing at its inception, bringing about, as we shall see, a true revolution in Hebrew typography.

The beginning of Moses Naḥmanides'
Ḥidushe ha-Torah (Commentary on the
Pentateuch), published at Lisbon in 1489.
This is the second edition of the work. The
first two lines are in square Sephardic letters,
while the rest of the page is in Sephardic semi-
cursive, exhibiting a marked Arabic influence.
The ornamental border had been used previously in books published at Híjar in Spain
and was to be used again in Constantinople in
the early sixteenth century.
NYPL, Jewish Division [Ex. no. 165]

The dispersion of the Jewish people and geopolitical circumstances led to the development of five distinctive regional variants of Hebrew script during the Middle Ages: (1) Oriental, used in the eastern Mediterranean, central Asia, and Yemen; (2) Sephardic, found in the Iberian peninsula, North Africa, Southern Italy, and Sicily; (3) Ashkenazic, used in the northern areas of Eastern and Western Europe; (4) Italian, used in Northern and Central Italy; and (5) Byzantine, used in the countries around the Aegean Sea.

Within each type of script we can distinguish between square and semi-cursive letters; in some regions there was also a true cursive. In Hebrew printing we find square and semi-cursive letters, but no cursive.

Logically, a printer should choose his type font in accordance with the area where he works, and indeed, in Spain and Portugal the first printers (and there were no more, of course, because of the expulsion at the end of the fifteenth century) used square and semi-cursive Sephardic letters. In Eastern Europe as well, in the sixteenth century, the early days of printing there, square and semi-cursive Ashkenazic letters were used.

But what happened in Italy, the cradle of Hebrew printing? In medieval Italy the square alphabet was identical with the Ashkenazic square alphabet, while the semi-cursive script was peculiar to Italy; there are many differences between it and Ashkenazic semi-cursive, though both share certain characteristics. (The Ashkenazi Jews—i.e., the Jews of northern Europe—originally came from Italy, and for that reason, as

Detail showing the first illustrations in a Hebrew printed book from Sefer Mitsvot Gadol *by Moses ben Jacob of Coucy. This is one of the earliest Hebrew printed books extant, one of the group of seven printed in Rome without a date. The entire text is set in square Ashkenazic letters, which preserve features originally associated with the use of a quill for writing.*
NYPL, *Jewish Division* [Ex. no. 162]

well as the geographical proximity, there are more similarities between Italian and Ashkenazic script than between these two and Sephardic or Oriental script, for example.)

The first eight Hebrew books printed in Rome, in approximately 1470 (all are undated), used square Ashkenazic letters like those used in Italy in general; type based on semi-cursive letters had not yet been developed. The books printed by Meshulam Cusi in Piove di Sacco (Northern Italy) in 1475 were also printed using only Ashkenazic square letters. Rashi's commentary on the Torah printed by Isaac Garton, the earliest dated Hebrew book, February 1475, was printed in Reggio di Calabria (Southern Italy) using a Sephardic semi-cursive font, similar to the script used in copying manuscripts in that area, which had been under Spanish political influence for many years.

Maimonides' *Mishneh Torah,* attributed to Rome, ca. 1470, was printed in square Sephardic letters; however, it has not been definitely proven that it comes from Rome, although it was apparently printed before 1480.

Abraham Conat, mentioned above, "who writes with many pens without doing miracles," printed about eight books in Mantua (Northern Italy), starting in 1476 or perhaps earlier. The books he printed did not include the Bible or Talmud, and in fact some were entirely secular. Therefore he chose to use a semi-cursive font. Although he came from

Colophon page of Jacob ben Asher's Arba'ah Turim *(The Four Columns), a code of Jewish law published at Piove di Sacco. This and an edition of Rashi's commentary on the Pentateuch from Reggio di Calabria were both published in 1475 and are the earliest Hebrew printed books to bear a date. As were the earliest Rome imprints, the* Turim *is set entirely in Ashkenazic square letters. The rhymed colophon appears in two columns at the bottom of the page.*

NYPL, *Jewish Division [Ex. no. 137]*

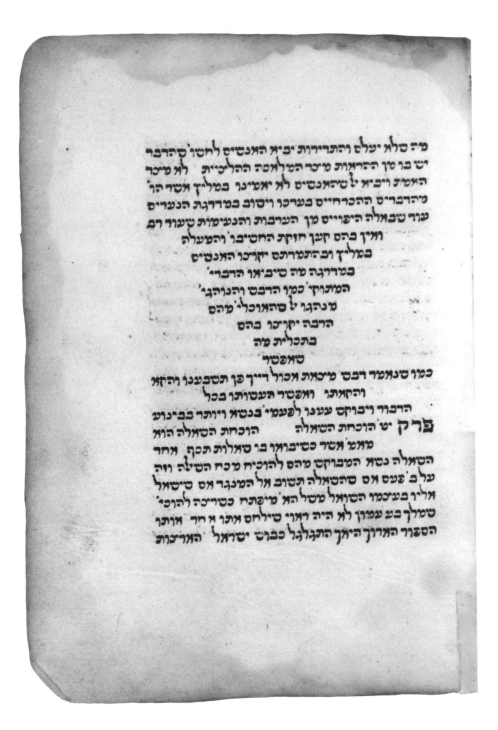

Abraham Conat's Mantua edition of Nofet
Tsufim (The Honeycomb), *a work on rhetoric by Judah ben Jeḥiel, Messer Leon, printed
in an Italian semi-cursive font.*
NYPL, Jewish Division [Ex. no. 141]

Provence, for many years it was assumed that Conat was of Ashkenazic
stock, and that he chose to print in a
style of letter similar to his handwriting, and the letters used in his
printing shop were called "Conat
Letters." However, it has been established beyond any doubt that he had
copied books using Sephardic semi-
cursive letters, unlike the letters he
used for printing, which were regular Italian semi-cursive.[4]

Now we come to the Soncino
family, one of the greatest Hebrew
printing establishments, whose Ashkenazic origins are certain. They
printed in various Italian cities for
many years from 1483 onward,
going beyond Italy to other countries
during the sixteenth century to print
in Constantinople and Salonika; one
member of the family even reached
Egypt and printed there.

The patriarch of the family, R.
Moses of Speyer (thirteenth century),
is mentioned in the Tosaphot. One
of his descendants, R. Moses, lived
in Germany during the fifteenth century, and it is recounted that he held
a dispute in Fürth with the Franciscan monk John of Capistrano and
succeeded in driving him from the
city "with all his forces" (according
to Gershom Soncino, as recorded on
the title page of the last book he
printed). The sons of this Moses
moved to Italy and settled in the
town of Soncino, Northern Italy, in
the mid-fifteenth century. His
grandson Israel Nathan, a distinguished scholar, urged his own son,
Joshua Solomon, to begin printing
Hebrew books. The members of the
family took the name of their native
town, Soncino, where they produced

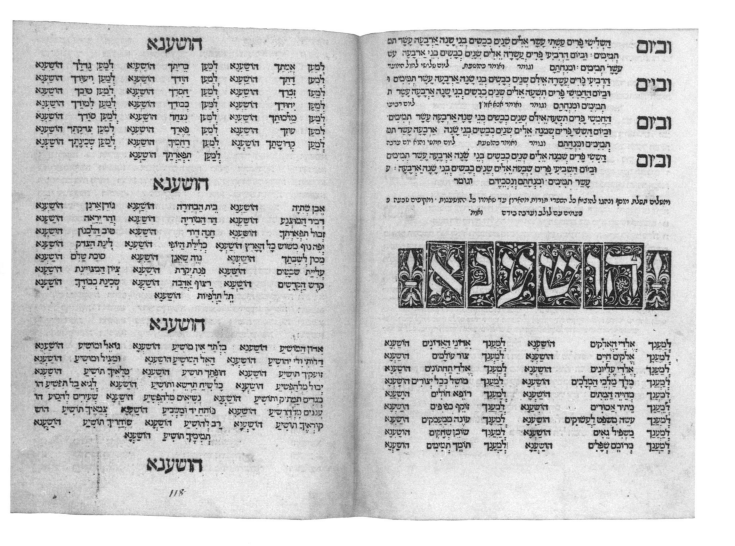

Opening in the first edition of the Maḥzor printed at Soncino and Casalmaggiore by Joshua Solomon Soncino, 1485–86. NYPL, Jewish Division [Ex. no. 151]

their first books. Joshua Solomon's nephew, Gershom Soncino, is the best known of the family for his great diligence and success in printing Hebrew books, although he was often forced to move from place to place.

The Soncino family, like many other German immigrants in Italy, doubtless retained their Ashkenazic handwriting, for we possess a document written by Gershom Soncino himself in an Ashkenazic cursive.[5] Nevertheless, from their very first book, they chose not to print in their Ashkenazic hand. In the tractate *Berakhot* of the Babylonian Talmud, which is both the first printed edition of the Talmud and also Joshua Solomon Soncino's first printed book (1483), he chose to set the text in square Sephardic letters and the commentaries in a Sephardic semi-cursive (only the large initial letters are square Ashkenazic, and they were very soon replaced by Sephardic letters in later printings). The Soncino family's well-developed commercial instincts led to two far-reaching changes in Jewish culture: in the Hebrew letter used in Hebrew books, and in the way the Talmud is studied.

The printing of books in the native Italian letter had quickly ceased in Conat's shop in Mantua, apparently because the local market was insufficient and could not offer a decent profit. Other Hebrew printers at that time, in Ferrara and Bologna, who had produced a few books in which the commentaries were also in an Italian semi-cursive, similarly could not manage to stay in business. The Jewish community in Italy during the Middle Ages was not large in comparison to that of Spain and North Africa, or even of Southern Italy and Sicily, where there was a large Jewish population and where a Sephardic script was used. (It should be recalled that emigrants from Spain had reached Italy before the expulsion, and we know of Sephardic manuscript copyists who used a Sephardic hand in Italy during the Middle Ages.) The Soncino family therefore sought first to reach Southern Italy with their books and then to break through to the more distant centers of Sephardic culture, in North Africa and perhaps even in Spain and Portugal before the expulsion,[6] and to Greece, Turkey, and the eastern Mediterranean, where emigrants from Spain had already arrived. They probably assumed that it would be easier for Italian Jews to get used to Sephardic letters than for

those accustomed to Sephardic letters to accept the Italian or Ashkenazic style; let us remember, of course, that we are speaking of semi-cursive and not of square letters, which could be easily identified and read by Jews anywhere. The intention of the Soncino family to sell and distribute their books outside Italy to the east and even to the west is stated explicitly by Gershom Soncino in his poem at the beginning of Maimonides' *Mishneh Torah* (Soncino, 1490). This was still before the expulsion of the Jews from Spain. In the poem he says to himself:

מהרה חוש וכל קדם וימה מלא בספריך

"Make haste so that East and West may abound with thy books."

At the same time, the original Italian scripts, both the semi-cursive and the cursive, were retained in Italy—in manuscripts, not printed books—into the sixteenth and seventeenth centuries, and even beyond. Thus it is clear from the Hebrew manuscripts in our possession that the local script remained unchanged. It was therefore not Italian custom which brought the Soncino family to choose the Sephardic letter but the reason noted above. Indeed, when the Soncinos printed a book of penitential prayers according to the Ashkenazic rite, intended for Ashkenazim alone, they of course printed it in Ashkenazi letters (the *Seliḥot* of Barco, 1496). The same is true of other books meant only for Ashkenazim, such as Yiddish texts.

This took place at the beginning of Hebrew printing. Later, when the

Table of contents of Sefer Midot (Isny, 1542), one of the earliest Yiddish printed books. The heading at the top of the page and the chapter titles which go down the right side of the page are in Hebrew and are printed in Ashkenazic square letters. The rest of the page is in Yiddish, printed in Ashkenazic semi-cursive letters, often popularly called "Vayber-Taytsh" (Women's Yiddish, Women's Translation).

NYPL, Jewish Division [Ex. no. 158]

סימני הספר

מִדַּת הַגַּאֲוָה

מִדַּת הָעֲנָוָה

מִדַּת הַבּוֹשֶׁת

מִדַּת הָעַזּוּת

מִדַּת הָאַהֲבָה

מִדַּת הַשִּׂנְאָה

מִדַּת הָרַחֲמָנִית

מִדַּת הָאַכְזָרִיּוּת

מִדַּת הַשִּׂמְחָה

מִדַּת הַדְּאָגָה

מִדַּת הַחֲרָטָה

מִדַּת הַכַּעַס

מִדַּת הָרָצוֹן

Soncinos' books increased in number and circulation, their font was imitated by other printers of their time, and especially by those who followed, such as the famous sixteenth-century printer Daniel Bomberg, in Venice, who supplanted them. (Bomberg's being a gentile helped him in obtaining a license to print, while the Soncinos' being Jewish was to their disadvantage, and they were ultimately forced to leave Italy.) Henceforth the Sephardic letter predominated in Hebrew printing without hindrance,[7] spreading to the printers of Eastern Europe as well. They adopted it because of its prevalence in Hebrew books, apparently procuring some type from Italy too. The Sephardic typeface has remained in wide use even in the twentieth century. The Frank-Ruehl letter, for example, which still sets the tone of Hebrew printing, derives from the Sephardic letter of the first Hebrew printing of the Soncinos and Daniel Bomberg. Only in the twentieth century, with the establishment of new centers of Hebrew printing, have typographers added new elements to the Hebrew letter, sometimes imitating medieval manuscripts, including Ashkenazic examples.

At this point we must explain the origin of the term "Rashi script," which refers to the Sephardic semi-cursive typeface used in Hebrew books. Clearly Rashi himself wrote an Ashkenazic script. What, then, is the explanation of this term? It would be absurd to claim that its or-

igin lies in the 1475 Reggio di Calabria edition of Rashi's commentary on the Torah—the oldest dated Hebrew printed book—which was printed in Sephardic semi-cursive letters. There is no reason to assume that that particular edition was more common than the earlier 1470 Rome edition of Rashi's commentary on the Torah, which was printed in *square* Ashkenazic letters. Two editions of Rashi's commentary on the Torah were also printed in Spain in the fifteenth century, one in semi-cursive type and the other in square letters. In general, early editions disappear quickly, and it would be impossible to claim that a single book, the extent of whose circulation is unknown, is the reason for giving that name to the Sephardic semi-cursive script.

The term "Rashi script" originates rather in the editions of the Bible and Talmud beginning with the Soncino editions and those of Bomberg, which were repeatedly reissued, creating a printing *tradition* which remains in force to this day.

In Hebrew manuscripts the text of the Bible is generally written in square letters, while the commentaries are written, even when not within the same book, in semi-cursive letters. The first printed books of course imitated the manuscripts. When the text and the commentary were printed together on the same page (a problem to which we shall return), it was necessary to make a typographical distinction between the two kinds of text. Every Jewish schoolboy, from 1483 on, when he studied the Torah or the Talmud, became accustomed to seeing the text

before him in square characters, while the commentaries—and the major commentary was, of course, that of Rashi—appeared in semi-cursive. We have already noted that from the time of Soncino onward the Sephardic letter was predominant in Hebrew printing. Consequently, "Rashi script" was the name given to the typeface used for the commentaries, Sephardic semi-cursive script, which Jews everywhere became accustomed to seeing in printed books.

Another significant innovation introduced by the Soncino family into Jewish culture was the printing of the Tosaphot (twelfth- and thirteenth-century Ashkenazic talmudic novellae) along with the text of the Talmud and Rashi's commentary. Soon after its composition Rashi's commentary became widespread throughout the Jewish world, accepted as the major commentary on the Talmud. However, the Tosaphot were mainly studied in Germany and France.

The creation of a tradition of printing the Talmud with the commentaries of Rashi and the Tosaphot is, without doubt, attributable, for better or worse, to the Soncino family, and that tradition was later maintained by all Hebrew printers. Their success in selling tractates of the Talmud created a situation in which Sephardic students of Talmud also became accustomed to seeing the commentary of the Tosaphot printed beside the text, so that it gradually became part of the learned tradition of the entire Jewish people during the sixteenth century. The periodic dispute as to which commentator in addition to Rashi should be taught with the Talmud lost its meaning in the face of the consistent traditional format of a printed page of Talmud with Rashi on one side of the column of text and the Tosaphot on the other side.[8]

The greatest of the Soncinos, Gershom, who also printed many books in languages other than Hebrew, described his method of working on the title page of the last book he printed, *Mikhlol* of R. David Kimḥi (Constantinople, 1534)[9] (he died while it was in press, and his son Eliezer finished the job): "I searched out and found books that had been blocked off and sealed up for an age, and I brought them forth to the eye of this sun . . . like the Tosaphot. . . . I went as far as France and Chambery and Genevra [sic], to the rooms where they were born, to benefit the multitude with them, for in Spain and in Italy and in all the lands they were unheard of."

The Soncino family thus endeavored to print unknown books, and in the case of the Tosaphot they joined to the Talmud, which was in demand, a book which was neither well known nor in demand outside of Germany and France, selling them both together.[10] Once again, their commercial instincts and willingness to undertake many efforts brought them success, and contributed to a far-reaching change in the way the Talmud was studied by various Jewish communities.

Another difficult problem confronting the Hebrew printer was how to print a complex text like the Bible or Talmud with commentaries on the same page. It is true that certain Hebrew manuscripts also present the text and commentaries on the same page, as early as the late thirteenth century, for example, the Torah with the Onkelos translation and Rashi's commentary in separate columns. However, scribes could not achieve solutions as neat as those of printers, and one finds many lacunae in manuscripts as a result of a failure to fit the various pieces of text together on a given page. For that reason this format is not very common.[11] The printer, unlike the copyist, can rearrange the type many times until the final printing. Nevertheless, printers made every effort to keep expenses down by not setting a page again and again until the correct balance was achieved between the text and the commentaries, especially when there were several of the latter, as in the Talmud, with Rashi on one side of the column and the Tosaphot on the other.

Let us hear a printer himself discussing his work. In 1484 Gabriel Strassburg, the proofreader of the tractate *Beẓah,* the second tractate printed by Joshua Solomon Soncino, wrote about the difficulty of printing and its many problems, the inability of the printers to manage everything involved with printing by themselves, and how, for that reason, he had been invited to prepare "a book, to make a copy of it . . . to make

. . . a model of the Gemara and the commentary [Rashi] and the Tosaphot and the Mordecai." He did so, saying, "I proofread them in the *model copy,*" and then, "after the workmen copied the Gemara from that model and the commentary and the Tosaphot and the aforementioned Mordecai and engraved it in book form [i.e., printed it], with 'Piske Tosaphot' and [Maimonides'] commentary on the Mishnah, which they copied themselves [!], they brought the entire printed book to me, and I was pleased as though I had found a great treasure."

That is to say, before the printing itself, a special worker sat and planned the layout of the Talmud. He copied from the various manuscripts, proofread the text, and prepared a special model copy of the text with the commentaries around it. However, such easier texts as Maimonides' commentary on the Mishnah (twelfth century) or "Piske Tosaphot" (an anonymous brief summary of the conclusions of the Tosaphot regarding the Halaka, attributed to R. Asher ben Jeḥi'el or to his son, R. Jacob, thirteenth–fourteenth century), which are not printed on the same page as the text of the Talmud, could be directly set in type by the printers themselves, without a model copy.[12]

Now that we have seen several aspects of the work of Hebrew printing at its inception, and the far-reaching cultural innovations which it brought, in conclusion let us quote the blessing and praise of printing written by the first Ashkenazi He-

brew historiographer, R. David
Gans, in his *Tsemaḥ David,* written
in Prague, 1592 (edited by M.
Breuer, Jerusalem, 1983, p. 369):
"Blessed be He who favors man with
knowledge and teaches humans understanding, who amplified His
grace with a great invention, one
that is useful for all inhabitants of
the world, there is none beside it,
and nothing can equal it in all the
wisdom and cleverness from the day
when God created man on the
earth."

Notes

1 The Hebrew Paleography Project in Jerusalem has listed and described all dated Hebrew
manuscripts from the Middle Ages until 1540.
Given that most manuscripts contain no indication of the date and place of writing, the
dated manuscripts constitute only a representative sample (approximately 5 percent) of all
Hebrew manuscripts to that date.

2 I hope to speak at greater length of him
elsewhere.

3 That is the meaning of the word *tsiyer* in
this colophon, like the use of the same root in
the colophon of Rashi's commentary on the
Torah, Guadalajara (Spain), 1476. See Y.
Sonne, *Kiryat Sefer* 14 (1937–38): 372–373.

4 See M. Beit-Arié, "ha-Zikah she-beyn
Bikure ha-Defus ha-'Ivri le-veyn Kitve ha-
Yad," in *Essays and Studies in Librarianship Presented to Curt David Wormann* (Jerusalem,
1975), Hebrew part, pp. 30, 113.

5 See A. Z. Schwarz, "Eine Verkaufs-
bestaetigung des Geršom Soncino," *Soncino
Blaetter* I (1925): 14–15.

6 See R. N. N. Rabinowitz, *Ma'amar 'al Hadpasat ha-Talmud,* ed. A. M. Habermann (Jerusalem, 1952), p. 15. On the sixteenth-century
Hebrew book trade, see Z. Baruchson,
"Yedi'ot 'al ha-mishar be-sefarim 'ivriyim
beyn Italiyah veha-imperiyah ha-'Otomanit
ba-me'ah ha-t"z," *Mi-Mizraḥ umi-Ma'arav* 5
(1986): 53–57.

7 See Beit-Arié (above, n. 4), p. 31.

8 See E. E. Urbach, *Ba'ale ha-Tosaphot,* 4th
ed. (Jerusalem, 1980), pp. 30, 585.

9 Reference is to the folio edition, not to the
octavo edition of Gershom Soncino, of the
same book in the same place, in 1533.

10 It is true that Gershom refers explicitly to a
certain collection of Tosaphot; however, the
very fact that he has chosen to print this particular collection, rather than the better-known
ones, in at least some of the tractates of the
Talmud and to circulate it corroborates my argument. See Urbach, above, n. 8.

11 The layout of the Masorah, in Hebrew
Bible manuscripts of as early as the tenth century, is entirely different from the layout of
text and commentaries. See my article on the
Aleppo Codex, in *Sefunot,* 1988 (in press),

Chapter 11. On the root of the layout of a text
and commentaries on the same page, see
Christopher De Hamel, *Glossed Books of the
Bible and the Origins of the Paris Booktrade*
(Woodbridge, Suffolk; Dover, N.H., 1984).

12 The proofreader also mentions the preparation of a model copy of the "Mordecai" (the
novellae and halakic decisions of R. Mordecai
ben R. Hillel Ashkenazi, thirteenth century).
However, the "Mordecai" is not printed on the
same page as the text of the Talmud, but at
the end of the volume, separately. Why, then,
did he need a model copy? The proofreader
emphasized two aspects of preparing the
model copy: correcting the text and determining the correct layout of the pages. The proofreading of the Talmud was a difficult task,
which only a learned scholar could undertake,
and even he was liable to err. As for the
"Mordecai," it is known to exist in various
versions and widely different copies. Therefore, in this case as well, it was necessary to
prepare a special "model copy" to determine
the text before printing. We thus learn, inci-
dentally, from the words of the proofreader,
about the condition of the text of the "Mordecai," the proper editing of which is still a
matter of scholarly discussion.

7 MOSHE N. ROSENFELD

The Development of Hebrew Printing in the Sixteenth and Seventeenth Centuries

THE WORLD of the Jewish book is one of never-ending fascination. Every volume represents a mirror of Jewish life through the generations, relating to us tales of fates, fortunes, laws, and learning.

In early days, a scholar could rely only on manuscripts. If his means allowed for the extraordinary expense, these would be written to order for him by a professional scribe. Otherwise he had to depend on the generosity of collectors, who would sometimes grant access to their precious libraries. The art of printing with movable type marked the beginning of a new era for academics. No other single invention has so advanced the status of humankind as the process of printing from movable type. The tedious copying of letters by stylus or quill gave way to printing a full page or more at a time.

Hebrew printing was initially limited to Italy and the Iberian peninsula (these beginnings are discussed elsewhere in this volume), and not one Hebrew book is known to have been printed in Germany before the year 1500, although the invention of printing is generally accepted to have occurred there. However, production in northern Europe soon overtook both in numbers and in scope the earlier Italian, Spanish, and Portuguese output. This was due in part to the expulsion of Jews from Spain and Portugal, which put an end to such illustrious printing centers as Guadalajara and Híjar (Ixar) and the Portuguese cities of Lisbon, Leiria, and Faro. But even in the more liberal states of Italy, many Hebrew printing centers—Brescia, Reggio di Calabria, Barco, Piove di Sacco, and Casalmaggiore, to name but a few— achieved only temporary fame and existence, and even Soncino faded forever as a center of Hebrew printing before the end of the fifteenth century.

Other Italian towns were also centers of Jewish life, and printing flourished in the sixteenth century in such places as Rome (1518), Bologna (1537), Trino (1525), Mantua (1513), Ferrara, Cremona, Riva di Trento, Verona (1594), Sabionetta (1551), and, most active of all, Venice (1515). Many important Bibles, liturgies, and responsa as well as Talmud editions emerged from the presses of such master printers as Daniel Bomberg, Abraham Usque, Vincenzo Conti, and Juan de Gara. They excelled in their work, and the enduring quality of the ink and paper they used has ensured that although rare and sometimes unique, fine examples of their productions are still to be found in outstanding condition. Without doubt, the prince of all the printers was the non-Jew Daniel Bomberg, who in his quest for both excellence of material and perfection of production spared neither effort nor money to secure the most significant manuscripts and the finest craftsmen. His establishment in Venice issued a constant stream of highly important works from about 1516 to 1549, including the first complete and uniform edition of the Talmud. The superiority of his work and the high technical ability of his staff are attested by the fact that his layout and physical arrangement of the Talmud have essentially endured and have been retained to this day for all editions.

By producing books in the Moroccan city of Fez, Jewish refugees can lay claim to being the first printers on the continent of Africa. This activity, dating from 1516, included a number of Talmud tractates, with type brought from Lisbon. The enterprise would have been successful for a longer period, but "the long arm of the wicked Spanish authori-

ties cut off the supply of paper" (*Abudarham,* Fez, December 1521), thus terminating the printing venture of Samuel and his son Isaac, after a mere six years of activity.

Meanwhile, gentile printers north of the Alps had discovered the existence of Hebrew type. Some modest attempts to incorporate Hebrew text are known in printed works originating in Strasbourg (1504), Paris (1508), Augsburg (1509), Basel (1516), Lyon (1520), and London (1524).

For central and northern Europe, Gershom ben Solomon ha-Kohen is recognized as the first Jewish printer. Supported by a number of wealthy individuals, he began printing in Prague toward the end of 1512. His first work was a prayerbook, and he continued almost exclusively with liturgies and the like, supplying Germany and Poland. His assistant, Ḥayyim Schwarz (Shaḥor), soon became a master printer in his own right and adopting the mode of his Italian counterparts, the Soncinos, he wandered across Europe, carrying his tools of trade and setting up his press in a number of towns including Oels in Silesia (1530), Augsburg (1532), Ichenhausen (1544), and Heddernheim (1546).

He finally moved eastward again, having attempted and failed to gain a foothold in Italy. In Lublin, through his son Isaac, he became the forerunner of all Jewish printers there. Kalonymus ben Mordecai Jaffe, who had married into his family, continued the printshop into the seventeenth century. Earlier, there was Jewish printing in the city of Cracow, through the offices of the

מוגה

קהלת יעקב

[Hebrew title page text within decorative border]

הדור אתם ראו תורה טוב לכו משה
מרטה קהלת יעקב סכרו הככם
הטלם כמהרר משה נלאכטי כלו
והוא ביאור כחמר על מנלת
קהלת אשר היו דבריו סותרי זה
את זה והוא כטוב טעמו וכמוקנ
טיו העטיד הדבר על בוריו
והכין טעמו על מכוננ ומלבד זה
הכיח על כל כסוק וכסוק דכרי
הזותר והתקונים הכחמדים מזהב
ומפ͏ז רב הטליא לעטות :

יסודותו בהררי קדש

צפת תוכב שבגליל העליון קרית מלך רכ היא היום תחת
ממשלת ארונינו המלך סולטן מארד יר͏ה :

נדפם בכית הנדיר ונעלה בכ͏ר לאברהם אשכנזי יטו   על ידי אליעזר בכהר ינקק זל
כתחזקק   כיוס יוס נ͏ כ͏ה לחשון   סכת כ͏ קר͏וכה יסועתי לבא אכיר :

One of the first Hebrew books printed in the Land of Israel, a sample of the work of Eliezer ben Isaac Ashkenazi: Kehilat Ya'akov, the Book of Ecclesiastes, with the kabbalistic commentary of Moses Galante (Safed, 1577–78).

NYPL, Jewish Division [Ex. no. 110]

Halicz brothers, who were active there about 1534. Their works are the first known Yiddish imprints, and as such mark an important milestone in printing history. They opened the floodgates to an ever-increasing quantity of material aimed at the less knowledgeable population, who avidly sought these works of biblical text, customs, Talmud stories, and the like, with the popular Yiddish translations.

Some Hebrew books are also recorded from the Polish villages of Konskawola and Bistrowitz, to which places the printers hastily moved on the outbreak of plague in Lublin. Many of the rarest imprints hail from these presses. Although printed in the thousands for the masses, they survive in single copies only.

Another fascinating character, Eliezer ben Isaac Ashkenazi, also came from Prague. We can trace his press to a number of cities in countries as far apart as Turkey and Palestine, as a few rare works survive with imprints of Lublin (1558–73), Konskawola (1562), Constantinople (1574–76 and 1586), and Safed (1577–79 and 1587). His gallant attempt to establish himself on holy soil has brought this printer renown. To commemorate the 400th anniversary of his establishing the first press of any kind in the Holy Land, the Israeli postal authority issued in 1977 a stamp depicting the title page of one of his Safed imprints.

It is ironic that after various attempts to remove the Jewish presence from most Germanic lands in this period, there was a growing demand for Jewish works generated by the increased interest of humanists and

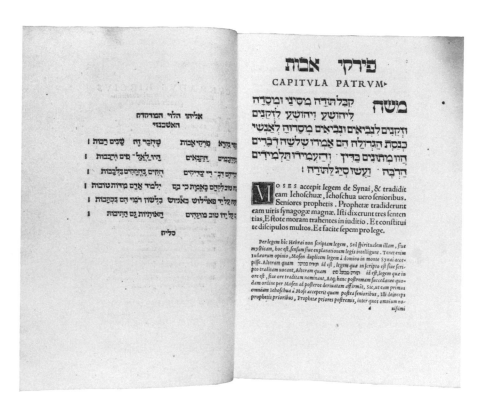

Pirke Avot (The Chapters of the Fathers), published by Paul Fagius (Isny, 1541). On the left is a Hebrew rhyme by Elijah Levita, on the right, the beginning of the tractate in Hebrew, followed by a Latin translation by Fagius. The Ashkenazic square Hebrew letters are printed with vowel points.
NYPL, Jewish Division [Ex. no. 159]

academics, who needed Hebrew sources for their studies. This resulted in an upsurge of works with Hebrew texts from presses at Pforzheim, Tübingen, Cologne, Wittenberg, and elsewhere. While some volumes contain only an occasional Hebrew phrase, others are virtually entirely in Hebrew, and it is obvious that Jews participated in the printing. This was evidently the case in the city of Isny, where a renowned Jewish scholar was involved in the establishment of the first (and only) press there. Elijah Levita, commonly called Elya Bokher, cooperated with Paul Fagius to found a printshop there in 1541, and by 1542, when the press moved to nearby Constance, nearly twenty scholarly works had been published.

Fagius continued issuing Hebrew and Yiddish texts without the help of Levita until 1544, although his output was greatly reduced. He is of special interest to English scholars since, because of his Lutheran allegiance, Fagius was forced to flee for his life. He found refuge in England, and settled as Hebrew Lecturer in Cambridge, where he died soon thereafter. Even in death he found no peace. Upon Queen Mary's accession in 1553, she quickly rescinded the religious liberties which had been introduced by her father, Henry VIII. Fagius' bones were disinterred and publicly burned together with his printed works. Happily, his reputation and honor were soon restored by Mary's successor, Elizabeth I, who formally reinstated the erstwhile printer of Isny by "declaration" on February 6, 1559. Many British colleges still have copies of his Hebrew-

Latin works from that early period, but his Yiddish editions are extremely scarce.

Switzerland, too, figures in the annals of early Jewish printing, for two of the most beautifully printed works of the first half of the sixteenth century came from a press in Zürich. The rarest Yiddish edition of Josephus was published there in 1546, embellished with specially created exquisite woodcuts. For this work, and for an ethical tract entitled *Sefer ha-Yir'ah,* a special font was cut, which renders the Yiddish text in beautiful letters of exceptional clarity.

In contrast to this short-lived venture in Zürich, the Hebrew publication of the Book of Psalms in Basel in 1516 heralded the successful start of three hundred years of continuous printing there. The presses of Froben, Petri, Münster, and others issued many important Hebrew and Yiddish works comprising grammars, codes, liturgies, ethics, and also a set of the Talmud. All their books are distinguished for their quality and elegance. The diligence of the Swiss printers guaranteed to customers high standards of text and presentation.

Following the publication of a Yiddish book of Psalms in Zürich in 1558, Eliezer ben Naphtali Herz Treves and Joseph ben Naphtali were forced to move across the border to Germany to Thiengen, where their press issued six distinguished works in 1560. This output included the famous prayerbook *Mal'ah ha-Arets*

From Elijah Levita's Hebrew grammar, Pirke Eliyahu, *published with a Latin translation at Basel by J. Froben in 1527.*
NYPL, *Jewish Division [Ex. no. 147]*

De'ah, commonly called *Siddur Rabbi Herz,* with a kabbalistic commentary, still used and recently reprinted.

A reference in one of the most virulently anti-Semitic works of the seventeenth century reveals the determination of the small number of Jews in Germany to furnish themselves with suitable liturgical works, at a time when no Jewish printer was active in the country. The story is a fascinating one, and though the research of this author has revealed new aspects of the publication of a Maḥzor in the Bavarian village of Thannhausen, it is probable that the full drama surrounding its emergence has still to be unearthed. What is known is that Rabbi Isaac Mazia (the name Mazia being apparently abbreviated from *Mi-Zera' Yehudim Anusim,* i.e., of Marrano origin), partnered by Simon Levi of Guenzburg, surreptitiously hired the gentile press of Adam Berg of Munich and published a Maḥzor and a *Zultot* (supplementary festival prayers). The ornamental title page names as assistants Stefan Schurmann and Peter Geisler, both non-Jews, and dates the *Zultot* 1594.

The apostate Samuel Friedrich Brenz, in his book *Juedischer Abgestreiffter Schlangenbalg (Jewish Snakesbrood Unveiled),* published in 1614, refers to this short-lived printing activity—"they printed their blasphemies without shame"—and gleefully records the closing of the press and the destruction of all remaining copies of the books. We can recognize the fears of Rabbi Mazia by the way the work has been laid out. For those texts whose translations might possibly be misinterpreted as blasphemy and anti-Christian sentiment, blanks have been left, for owners to fill in the omissions by hand.

The authorities discovered the unlawful printing in July 1594, and though his partner escaped, Rabbi Mazia was imprisoned and his complete production confiscated. In preparation for a trial, the still uncompleted Maḥzor was sent to the University of Ingolstadt for examination by experts. In October 1594 Rabbi Mazia was still under arrest; only after prolonged pleading was he finally granted bail against a high surety and the Jewish oath to the court. He courageously made a formal request for permission to complete the printing of his Maḥzor. His plea was refused and finally, in August 1597, he was fined and released. Fifteen hundred copies of the uncompleted Maḥzor were destroyed. As late as 1604 we find Adam Berg still fighting for the return of his impounded press. The censor's copy found its way from Ingolstadt via Landshut to Munich, where it was long thought to be a unique copy; four others are now known to exist, one of them in the Bodleian Library, Oxford.

During the seventeenth century there was further expansion of the areas of Hebrew printing activity. An attempt to print Hebrew books in Damascus (Syria) failed in 1605. Rabbi Josiah Pinto had commissioned the Veronese printer Abraham ben Mattathiah of the Batsheva fam-

ily and his partners to publish his *Kesef Nivḥar*. "This book has cost me blood and sweat to make it perfect," says the author, "but the type is of such poor quality, that I have decided to have the last two parts printed in Venice instead." Indeed, no other Hebrew books were ever printed in Damascus.

After the second half of the seventeenth century, the Italian printshops of Cremona and Ferrara closed down, and Venice and Mantua were reduced to secondary importance as printing centers. The author of the Mishnah commentary *Kaf Naḥat*, Rabbi Jedediah ben Isaac Gabbai, established himself in the city of Leghorn in 1649, utilizing typographic material from Bragadin, the former Venetian printer. This foundation was the start of an illustrious three-hundred-year history of printing there.

In Poland, activity at Cracow and Lublin continued until the Chmielnicki uprising in 1648. This pogrom caused immeasurable hardship, following which it took two hundred years for the Jewish press to reestablish itself in that country.

Holland emerged as the great guardian of the Jewish press in the seventeenth century, and Amsterdam established itself as a major center for works of enduring quality and stylish production. The prosperity of the country, which was engaged in worldwide trade, created the wherewithal for the fine productions issued from the famous presses of Manasseh ben Israel, Athias, Benveniste, and Phoebus. We find, for the first time, deluxe editions of Bibles and prayerbooks offered alongside the ordinary

Left: Title page of the second and most important of the editions of the Hebrew Bible prepared by Manasseh ben Israel (Amsterdam, 1635).
NYPL, Jewish Division [Ex. no. 108]

Above: Page of Shabbethai ben Joseph Bass's bibliographic work Sifte Yeshenim *(Amsterdam, 1679/80).*
NYPL, Jewish Division [Ex. no. 101]

versions, to satisfy the demands of the wealthy merchants of the period. The printers ignored prevailing styles and created new typefaces, which became in time an example for the rest of Europe. For more than another century, we find on numerous title pages of printers outside Holland claims that their books have been printed in "Amsterdam letters," testifying to the supremacy of the new Dutch typography. Their print quality was superb, and the use of copper plates to create picturesque title pages was an innovation which gave added beauty to their works.

At this time, the first Hebrew bibliographies emerged. The initiative was taken by Giulio Bartolocci with his four-volume pioneer catalog, *Bibliotheca Magna Rabbinica*. Rabbi Shabbethai ben Joseph Bass produced in 1679/80 the first listing in Hebrew, called *Sifte Yeshenim*. Another scholar, Johann Christoph Wolf, published his four-volume *Bibliotheca Hebraea* between 1715 and 1733. These catalogs are still of assistance today in tracing vanished editions.

Toward the end of the seventeenth century the famous German printing centers of Sulzbach and Fürth competed successfully with Amsterdam. Well over one thousand different Jewish publications are now recorded for the city of Fürth, where activity continued into the nineteenth century.

Throughout the centuries, Jews have been persecuted and expelled from their countries of residence. When they escaped bodily harm, spiritual persecution was inflicted upon them. Hebrew books and manuscripts were confiscated and burned, and but for the diligence and determination of printers, the fate of the People of the Book might well have been a different one.

In recognition of printers and of their efforts to perpetuate our love of learning, Rabbi Joseph Teomim in the introduction to his work *Pri Megadim* (Frankfurt on the Oder, 1785) writes: "Come and let us hail the printers, for if it was not for the art of printing in these difficult times, the Torah would have been forgotten from Israel. Praised be their efforts through the help of the Lord."

The tribute is as valid today as when it was first penned.

8 DAVID B. RUDERMAN

The Hebrew Book in a Christian World

WHEN François Tissard, the French humanist, entered the synagogue of Ferrara, Italy, at the beginning of the sixteenth century, his eyes riveted instantly on a precious Hebrew scroll of the Pentateuch. Having come to the synagogue in search of the mysteries of Jewish culture, he was thrilled to discover this ancient Jewish book. Nevertheless, his enthusiasm was dampened considerably by the spectacle of a Jewish congregation engaged in prayer, standing before the modestly decorated ark in which the priceless manuscript was stored. This house of worship was no more than a plain building with empty benches. A group of males, old and young alike, stood wrapped in "strange" prayer shawls chattering in what sounded like bizarre and primitive noises. Judged by the aesthetic standards of the medieval Church, this synagogue seemed like "a den of iniquities" to Tissard, and thus he wrote: "One might hear one man howling, another braying, and another bellowing; such a cacophony of discordant sounds do they make! Weighing this with the rest of their rites, I was almost brought to nausea."[1]

That a learned Christian scholar could be so enchanted by a Jewish text but so nauseated by living, breathing Jews is actually less paradoxical than it first might appear in the context of the often complex relationships between Christians and their Jewish minority in Europe. While, on the one hand, Christianity ultimately was based on a Hebrew book, the sacred record of its divine revelation, it had on the other hand defined its own identity against the background of a conscious rejection and supersession of the Jewish bearers of that revelation. It was therefore conceivable for certain Christians to familiarize themselves with the literal meaning of the *Hebraica veritas* and freely utilize Jewish exegetical writings on the Bible, while openly detesting Jews or even denying their right to collective existence. Viewed from this vantage point, it might be theoretically possible, for the purposes of this essay, to treat the history of Hebrew books in a Christian world, distinct and disembodied from their authors, without considering directly the history of Jews who composed, studied, and immersed themselves in these works. Of course, ultimately, no such differentiation is possible. The Christian reader who perused a Jewish book became acquainted with a universe of Jewish signs and associations, an experience which on some level eventually led him to encounter the distinct reality of actual human be-

ings who created such products of the mind and the heart. So, for Peter of Blois, writing in the twelfth century, the link was obvious: "Even today the Jews are to be allowed to live, because they are our enslaved book-bearers (*capsarii*), as they carry around the prophets and the law of Moses for the assertion of our faith. Not only in their books but also in their faces do we read of the passion of Christ."[2] In the final analysis, a study of Christian attitudes to Jewish books must eventually address the question of how such attitudes affected Christian perceptions of the Jews themselves.

PRIOR TO the late fifteenth century, one might generally categorize the range of Christian reactions to Jewish writings—the Hebrew Bible and the extensive corpus of post-biblical Jewish exegetical, legal, homiletical, philosophical, and mystical works—in the following way. Some Christians came to Jewish literature as a natural extension of their intense involvement with the biblical text itself and because of their own quest to fathom the ancient origins of Christian teaching. Others dismissed as worthless the entire body of rabbinic literature, even considered its existence diabolical and heretical, constituting a gross violation of the divine order in which the Jewish minority would be tolerated in a Christian world. Still others viewed Jewish books as an opportunity for Christians to proselytize Jews, to argue that certain rabbinic teachings allude to Christian truths, thus encouraging Jews to approach the baptismal font through the agency of their own sacred writings. Of course, from their perspective, such "truths" were often encrusted in the dung of useless and even blasphemous Jewish utterances. Jewish texts accordingly were to be used with extreme caution. Jewish blasphemies were to be zealously extirpated; those texts which remained and could be used to illuminate the message of Christianity to stubborn and backsliding Jews were to be highlighted and singled out for Jewish instruction.[3]

Prior to the twelfth century, Christian scholars' access to Jewish learning was generally limited to what they could glean from the classic works of Philo or Josephus or from the biblical commentaries of Jerome and Origen. With the rapid dissemination of the biblical commentaries of Rashi as well as those of some of his students (especially Joseph Kara, Samuel ben Meir, and Joseph Bekhor Shor) by the twelfth century, certain Christian scholars quickly discovered these indispensable aids in their own "scientific" search to recover the literal and simple meaning of the biblical text. Motivated by a desire to penetrate the sense of the original language of the Bible beyond what was offered in the standard patristic commentaries, certain exegetes attempted to study Hebrew with the help of contemporary Jews or apostates. Christian

commentators stemming especially from the abbey of St. Victor in Paris—Hugh of St. Victor, his student, Andrew, and the latter's student, Herbert of Bosham—familiarized themselves with rabbinic learning to an unprecedented degree, quoted the rabbis directly in their biblical commentaries, and even deemed them authoritative in establishing the literal meaning of the text. No doubt these intellectual excursions into the cultural world of post-biblical Jews were accompanied by a certain degree of reticence in agreeing "too much" with the Jewish positions. In fact, to judge from the disproportionate amount of polemical and apologetic material found in Jewish exegesis of the period, this renewed Christian interest in Jewish learning ultimately may have exacerbated religious controversy between Jews and Christians rather than diminished it.[4]

Another important font of postbiblical Jewish learning among learned Christians from the twelfth century on was the growing philosophical and scientific corpus of medieval Hebrew writing. This included the Hebrew translations and interpretations of medieval Arabic texts, as well as the philosophic and scientific writing of Maimonides, Ibn Ezra, Abraham Bar Ḥiyyah (Savasorda), Gersonides, and others. Maimonides' *Guide to the Perplexed* was especially valued by scholastic philosophers attempting to fuse the Aristotelian physics with Christian faith.[5] Thus, by the twelfth century, certain Christian thinkers had tasted significant dosages of either Jewish literalist biblical exegesis or writings on physics and metaphysics, and in both cases were favorably affected.

Growing familiarity with Jewish texts could also engender marked animosity and contempt. The more Christian scholars acquainted themselves with rabbinic writing, the more they were forced to realize that today's Jew was hardly identical with his "Old Testament" counterpart. As long as Judaism was identifiable with biblical religion, medieval Jews were legitimately entitled to a theological place in the divine order of things. According to St. Augustine's well-known formulation, since the Jews had killed Christ, they deserved death, but like Cain who murdered his brother, Abel, they were not to die but rather were doomed to wander the earth as witnesses to the ultimate truth of Christianity. When Christ returned, they finally would acknowledge their error, convert to Christianity, or be condemned to final damnation. Augustine's position emerged as a kind of unwritten contract used to define the theological and subsequently the social place of Jews within Christian society through the twelfth century.

When Pope Gregory IX denounced the Talmud, which subsequently led to its public incineration in Paris in 1242, he introduced a radically different approach in relating to post-biblical Jewish texts and in defining the place of Judaism in Christian so-

Diagram of a lunar eclipse from Abraham bar Hiyya's twelfth-century astronomical work Tsurat ha-Arets *or* Sphaera Mundi. *Alongside the Hebrew text is the Latin translation by Erasmus Oswald Schreckenfuchs. Published in Basel by H. Petrus, 1546. NYPL, Jewish Division [Ex. no. 88]*

ciety. The pope had adopted his new position through the strong encouragement of a Jewish apostate named Nicholas Donin, who had approached him with a list of explicit charges against rabbinic Judaism and subsequently engaged in a bitter disputation with the rabbi of Paris, Jehiel ben Joseph. Donin forcefully articulated the new ideology which served to justify the burning of the talmudic tomes. Having intimate familiarity with rabbinic writing, Donin appreciated better than most Christians that the religion of medieval Jewry was the result of a radical transformation from that of the ancient Israelites. When Augustine justified the preservation of the Jews, he had in mind only their life under the "old law" set forth in "the Old Testament." But the Jews of Donin's day had substituted and supplanted that law with a new one, as the Talmud amply testified, and by so doing, they had vitiated their right to Christian protection. Talmudic Judaism was not simply further evidence of Jewish blindness; it constituted no less than a willful heresy since the Jews had actually violated Mosaic law. And to make matters worse, claimed Donin, the Talmud contained numerous examples of passages blaspheming the fundamental principles of the Christian faith. According to such logic, the Talmud had to be destroyed and the Jews deserved the punishment befitting heretics.[6] The legacy of this aggressive view of Gregory and Donin was not circumscribed to the thirteenth century. In 1553 the Roman Holy Office, guided by Cardinal Caraffa, the Grand-Inquisitor who was to become

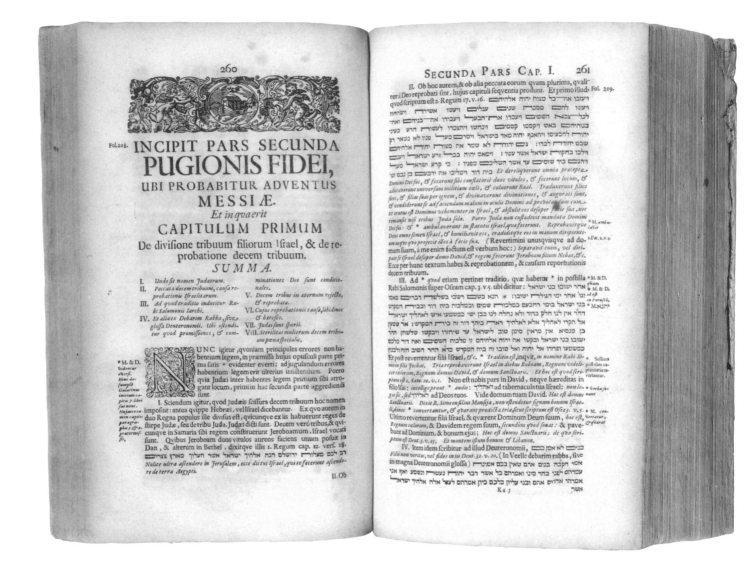

Pope Paul IV, and with the approval of Pope Julius III, ordered the public burning of the Talmud for reasons not unlike those expressed in the thirteenth century.[7]

By the second half of the thirteenth century, the Christian assault on the Jewish book had shifted to the Iberian peninsula and to the missionizing activities of a group of Dominicans associated with the school of Raymond de Penaforte. Their approach no longer favored the utter holocaust of all post-biblical Jewish writing as advocated by Donin; neither did it call for the unrestrained use of rabbinic materials to elucidate Christian exegesis characteristic of the Victorines. Its leading spokesmen were apostates like Donin, men fully conversant with Jewish literature and well prepared to exploit their knowledge to the detriment of Judaism. Among the most prominent of these new Christian readers of Jewish texts was Pablo Christiani, the Christian polemicist at the public disputation of Barcelona in 1263, and Raymundus Martini, the author of the *Pugio Fidei,* the most exhaustive examination of rabbinic literature compiled by a Christian up to that time (the work was completed in 1278). Their approach was to manipulate rabbinic literature in such a way as to expose its anti-Christian bias on the one hand, and simultaneously to reveal its clear Christological message, on the other. These men agreed with Donin that rabbinic texts often blasphemed the Christian religion, had to be read with utmost caution, and were often deserving of censure. At the same time, they recognized in these texts an extraordinary oppor-

tunity for inculcating Christian doctrines among Jews. By combing the vast rabbinic literature, especially nonlegal, homiletical materials, by reading passages out of context, and often by perverting their original meaning, they claimed to discern the truly "genuine and authentic" traditions of post-biblical Judaism. Talmudic discourses were now to be adduced as proof-passages and as witnesses of the true Christian faith. As such, they constituted a formidable weapon in the arsenal of Christian polemics against Judaism and in missionizing among Jews. Like Donin's approach, this position represented a dramatic reversal of Augustinian toleration of Jews and Judaism. Rather than leaving the Jews to their own devices until the second coming of Christ, these friars advocated an activist stance of direct verbal confrontation and harassment leading to the aggressive proselytization of Jews. Familiar with Jewish texts, driven by their own self-hatred, and acting out of a burning passion to promote themselves within the Church, these Christian neophytes fully exploited their previous background and impressive ingenuity with Jewish texts through their highly publicized adversarial roles.[8]

Martini's collection of Christian *testimonia* had already utilized kabbalistic discourses in addition to rabbinic homilies. His approach was followed by those of Abner of Burgos of the fourteenth century and Pedro de la Cavalleria of the fif-

teenth, both of whom were especially skillful in locating particularly obscure and ambiguous passages in Jewish literature and implanting them with Christian meaning. By the fifteenth century, other Christian readers of Jewish texts boldly expanded such activity to include the fabrication of newly composed homiletic and kabbalistic collections, written in Hebrew and Aramaic, cleverly designed to preserve the style and outward appearance of authentic Jewish writings. The most notorious of these authors was Paulus de Heredia who wrote in Spain prior to the expulsion of the Jews and whose works circulated widely in Italy. Such apostates as Paulus Ricchius and Petrus Galatinus of the sixteenth century similarly utilized rabbinic and kabbalistic materials, both real and invented, for missionizing purposes.[9]

As early as the end of the fifteenth century, however, two significant changes in the cultural landscape of European Christendom were to affect profoundly the Christian involvement with the Hebrew book. The first was the influence of the Renaissance and the Reformation on Christian Hebraic scholarship; the second was the invention of the printing press and its revolutionary impact on the production and dissemination of Hebraica.

The most prominent Renaissance figure to approach Hebrew books in a way radically different from that of earlier Christian scholars was Pico della Mirandola in the late fifteenth century. Out of a mutually stimulating interaction and prolonged study of Jewish texts between Pico and his associates and a number of contemporary Jews, one of the most unusual and obscure currents in the intellectual history of the Renaissance, the Christian Kabbalah, emerged. With the assistance of his Jewish tutors as well as others who converted to Christianity, Pico studied Hebrew texts while assembling a most impressive collection of Jewish exegetical, homiletical, and philosophic writing translated from the Hebrew into Latin. But his first passion was the mystical legacy of the Jews, to which he devoted his primary energies.

That Pico and his Florentine colleagues shared with earlier Christian students of Jewish literature a sincere devotion to missionary activity among Jews need not be doubted, but this fact alone would not explain sufficiently their extraordinary passion for unraveling the mysteries of arcane Jewish texts. Their attraction can best be understood by placing it in the broader context of Florentine Neoplatonism. From an intense exposure to the thought of Marsilio Ficino, the leading Neoplatonist of Florence, they derived the vital concept of *prisca theologia,* or ancient theology. Ficino had maintained that a single truth pervades all historical periods and that a direct line of thinking can be traced back to Plato through a succession of pagan writers. By identifying and translating the primary writings of these authors, Ficino came to appreciate that underlying the external differences between each of them and between

the sacred writings of Christianity was to be found a unity and harmony of religious insight, a basic core of universal truth. This genealogy of knowledge from Plato back through pagan sources eventually led to the era of the Hebrew Bible and the Mosaic tradition. By universalizing all religious knowledge, Ficino and Pico fashioned an open and more tolerant version of Christianity; in searching for the source of universal truth in ancient cultural and religious settings distant from their own, they came to appreciate the centrality and priority of Hebrew culture in Western civilization.

While ancient theology led Pico's circle back to the beginnings of Jewish civilization, their concept of poetic theology facilitated a concentration on the Kabbalah. They believed that the ancient pagan religions had concealed their sacred truths through a kind of "hieroglyphic" imagery of myths and fables designed to attract the attention of their following while safeguarding their esoteric character by not divulging their divine secrets. Moses had similarly addressed the Hebrews in veiled language, and only the kabbalists were capable of deciphering it. For Pico and his associates, the Kabbalah was the key to lay bare the secrets of Judaism, to reconcile them with the mysteries of other religions and cultures, and thus to universalize them. Through the Kabbalah, the essential differences between Judaism and Christianity would be eradicated: "Taken together, there is absolutely no controversy between ourselves and the Hebrews on any matter, with regard to which they cannot be refuted and

gainsaid out of the kabbalistic books, so that there will not even be a corner left in which they may hide themselves."[10]

Pico and his circle were fascinated by the Kabbalah for two additional reasons. The humanist tradition had sensitized them to the importance of language in understanding the inherent character of any culture. In the study of the Kabbalah, they discovered a cultivated sense of the meaning of language as a vehicle for penetrating deeply the underlying significance of human experience. By correctly deciphering the words and letters of "the holy language," they hoped to restore a means of direct communication with God Himself. Furthermore, the Kabbalah also represented power, a higher form of licit magic establishing a direct link between heaven and earth whereby human beings could capture the divine effluvia in order to transform themselves into divine beings.

Thus Jewish learning in general and the Kabbalah in particular had real meaning for Pico and subsequently for a surprising number of other Christians in later centuries, in the broader context of their syncretistic thought and their religious quest as Christians. In the hands of Pico and similarly minded Christian scholars, the Kabbalah was soon estranged from its original cultural and spiritual source in Judaism and instead confronted a new mixture of radically different associations and meanings blended together from pagan and Christian modes of think-

Johann Reuchlin's De Arte Cabalistica *(Hagenau, 1517) showing instances of the Tetragrammaton in the Hebrew Psalms. NYPL, Rare Books and Manuscripts Division [Ex. no. 177]*

DE ARTE CABALISTICA

Rabi Akiba procedůt de throno gloriæ dei, Sed ne quis uana supstitiõe ductus putet ab angelis omnia humanę mortalitati cœlitus conferri ac nõ poti⁹ per angelos ab ipsa dei maiestate, oĩa fieri etiam in angelis, ut in Da niele Nabuchadnezer chaldaice testař וּכְמִצְבְיֵה עָבֵד בְּחֵיל שְׁמַיָּא וְדָאֲרֵי אַרְעָא .i.Et secundů uoluntatē suam facit in exer citu cœli & habitatoribus terræ. Ideo receperůt Cabalæi de libro psalmo rum pias orõnes ad deum septuaginta duobus uersibus habendas, q̃rum unusquisq̃ nomen Tetragrammaton cũ noĩe angeli ex lxxii. cõtinet, uno haud ab re excepto q principium Geneseos indicat, eleuant aũt q̃tum fieri potest aĩos suos istis uersibus ad deum, fortiter ascendendo de angelo ad angelum. Et semp inter laudes dei tot & tantas ab altera ad alterã in subli me tēdendo. Ad illud eos iuuãt angeli, ut relicta seculari sollicitudine pro captu suo uehant in deũ, ceu leuissima pluma tenuissimi spiritus adiumēto ad sublimia cœlestiacq̃ sustolliř. Videte & audite orõnem uersuum cũ te tragrammato & angelis, utrůcq̃ eم̃ uobis tã digito q̃ uoce monstrabo sic.

וְאַתָּה יְהוָֹה מָגֵן בַּעֲדִי כְּבוֹדִי וּמֵרִים רֹאשִׁי
וְאַתָּה יְהוָֹה אַל תִּרְחָק אֱיָלוּתִי לְעֶזְרָתִי חוּשָׁה
אוֹמַר לַיהוָה מַחְסִי וּמְצוּדָתִי אֱלֹהַי אֶבְטַח בּוֹ
שׁוּבָה יְהוָה חַלְּצָה נַפְשִׁי הוֹשִׁיעֵנִי לְמַעַן חַסְדֶּךָ
דָּרַשְׁתִּי אֶת יְהוָה וְעָנָנִי וּמִכָּל מְגוּרוֹתַי הִצִּילַנִי
זַמְּרוּ לַיהוָה יֹשֵׁב צִיּוֹן הַגִּידוּ בָעַמִּים עֲלִילוֹתָיו
רַחוּם וְחַנּוּן יְהוָה אֶרֶךְ אַפַּיִם וְרַב חָסֶד
בֹּאוּ נִשְׁתַּחֲוֶה וְנִכְרָעָה נִבְרְכָה לִפְנֵי יְהוָה עֹשֵׂנוּ
זְכוֹר רַחֲמֶיךָ יְהוָה וַחֲסָדֶיךָ כִּי מֵעוֹלָם הֵמָּה
יְהִי חַסְדְּךָ יְהוָה עָלֵינוּ כַּאֲשֶׁר יִחַלְנוּ לָךְ
כִּי יְהוָה צוּרִי וְרָרוּם אֱלֹהֵי יִשְׁעִי
לָמָה יְהוָה תַּעֲמֹד בְּרָחוֹק תַּעֲלִים לְעִתּוֹת בַּצָּרָה
הָרִיעוּ לַיהוָה כָּל הָאָרֶץ פִּצְחוּ וְרַנְּנוּ וְזַמֵּרוּ
וִיהִי יְהוָה מִשְׂגָּב לַדָּךְ מִשְׂגָּב לְעִתּוֹת בַּצָּרָה
וִיהִי יְהוָה לִי לְמִשְׂגָּב וֵאלֹהַי לְצוּר מַחְסִי
יְהוָה אֱלֹהַי יִשַּׁעְתִּי בַיּוֹם צָעַקְתִּי בַלַּיְלָה נֶגְדֶּךָ
יְהוָה אֲרֹנֵינוּ מָה אַדִּיר שִׁמְךָ בְּכָל הָאָרֶץ
שָׁפְטֵנִי בְצִדְקָתְךָ יְהוָה אֱלֹהָי וְאַל יִשְׂמְחוּ לִי
קוֹל קָרָאתִי יְהוָה וַיַּעַט אֵלַי וַיִּשְׁמַע שַׁוְעָתִי
וּבְשֵׁם יְהוָה אֶקְרָא אָנָּא יְהוָה מַלְּטָה נַפְשִׁי

ing. The Jewish Kabbalah, having lost its Jewish identity, was literally recast into a Christian one.

Pico subsequently became the pioneer figure in the dramatic re-evaluation of Jewish literature and the gradual penetration of contemporary Jewish thought into European culture. His Christianization of kabbalistic techniques and his amalgamation of Renaissance magic and Jewish mysticism, while officially condemned by the Church, were enthusiastically received by a notable number of Christian thinkers in Italy, France, Germany, and England well into the eighteenth century. The Christian Kabbalah through Pico left its mark on Renaissance culture through its integration with Neoplatonism; it also influenced both the Catholic and the Protestant Reformations through its impact on such thinkers as Egidio of Viterbo, Francesco Giorgio, Cornelius Agrippa, and especially Johann Reuchlin.[11]

After Pico, Reuchlin was the most prominent Christian scholar to master Hebrew sources and to utilize them in revitalizing Christian theology. In *De Arte Cabalistica,* first published in 1517, Reuchlin followed Pico in considering the Kabbalah as a higher and theologically licit form of magic, a source of divine revelation equivalent ultimately to the highest truths of Neoplatonic and Pythagorean philosophy. Reuchlin's commitment to Jewish studies aroused the antagonism of some of his contemporaries in Reformation Germany, especially the Dominicans of Cologne who had initiated a bitter campaign to ban the reading of Hebrew

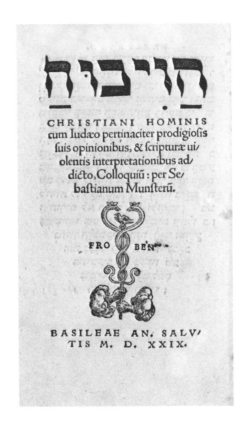

ha-Vikuaḥ, *a disputation of a Christian with a Jew by the Christian Hebraist Sebastian Münster (Basel, 1529).*
NYPL, Jewish Division [Ex. no. 163]

books. Reuchlin's well-reasoned responses to the extreme accusations of a Jewish apostate named Johann Pfefferkorn drew him unwittingly into a bitter and acrimonious debate over the value of Jewish learning for Christians and the place of Judaism within Christian society.[12]

But Reuchlin was hardly alone in his appropriation of Hebrew learning for Christian reform. Other Protestant thinkers in the first half of the sixteenth century focused on the more conventional sources of Jewish knowledge beyond the study of the Kabbalah. In their return to the biblical roots of Christianity, they were attracted especially to comprehending the literal sense of Scripture, so they mastered biblical Hebrew, and explored rabbinic learning out of a profound need for Christian self-understanding and a yearning for spiritual revival. Some, like Paul Fagius and Sebastian Münster, published Hebrew grammars, examined Jewish rites and customs, and explored the Pharisaic content of Jesus' teaching. Others, like Michael Servetus, even used Hebrew sources to offer a radical critique of Trinitarian Christianity.[13]

These intellectual and religious transformations of the Renaissance and Reformation went hand in hand with the dissemination of Jewish learning through the printing press. Elizabeth Eisenstein, among others, has perspicaciously examined the impact of printing on both these cultural movements.[14] The reception of the Hebrew printed book in Christian society constitutes one fascinating part of this larger story, for printing was critically important in exposing a sizable Christian readership to the classics of Judaic learning to a degree unprecedented in the history of Christian Hebraism.

The first Hebrew books were printed in the last quarter of the fifteenth century. By the next century, hundreds of classic works were being set in type by publishers first in Italy, then in the Ottoman empire, and eventually in northern Europe, even in areas uninhabited by Jews. The great publishers during the first stage of Hebrew printing included Gershom Soncino, heir of a family of Jewish printers who originated in Germany, and Daniel Bomberg, a Christian from Antwerp who settled in Venice and systematically published all the major works of rabbinic scholarship. Bomberg's crowning achievements were a grand edition of the Bible with its major rabbinic commentaries as well as the first complete edition of both the Babylonian and Palestinian Talmuds. Because of the pressing need for literary competence in setting and proofreading these texts, the Christian Bomberg collaborated with a number of learned Jews, some of whom were eventually baptized. Bomberg's pattern of operation, especially the dimension of Jewish-Christian cooperation, was emulated elsewhere in Europe, especially in cities like Basel, Leiden, and Amsterdam. Some presses specialized in Hebraica designed especially for Christian readers, publishing Hebrew and polyglot Bibles, grammars, and even works designed for missionizing among Jews.[15]

The beginning of the Mishnah tractate Pe'ah (Corner of the Field) *from the first complete edition of the Babylonian Talmud, produced by Daniel Bomberg in Venice, 1520–23. NYPL, Jewish Division [Ex. no. 183]*

Ḥinukh, hoc est Catechesis, *a catechism by*
John Calvin (Leiden, 1591) in Hebrew,
Latin, and Greek.
NYPL, *Jewish Division* [Ex. no. 121]

The final result of this massive infusion of Hebrew works into the literary world of Christian learning was the emergence of a group of distinguished Christian scholars who significantly advanced the Christian study of biblical and post-biblical Judaism. Among the outstanding students of the Hebrew Bible and rabbinics in the seventeenth century were Johannes Buxtorf I and his son, Johannes Buxtorf II, Jean Plantavit, Edward Pococke, J. C. Wagenseil, and John Lightfoot. One of the most significant by-products of these advances in Hebraic learning was the translation of Hebrew works into Latin and other European languages. The Buxtorfs, for example, produced translations of some of the classic philosophic texts of medieval Judaism, including those of Maimonides and Halevi; J. C. Wagenseil published both the original Hebrew and Latin translations of a series of Jewish anti-Christian polemical works; and Christian Knorr von Rosenroth compiled a vast compendium of kabbalistic texts which he called the *Kabbala Denudata,* making available to interested Christian readers the most extensive collection ever available in one place.[16]

Not all of the works produced by this new erudite breed of Christian scholars were complimentary to Jews and Judaism. Jewish writers soon came to realize the power of the printed text as a tool in repudiating the negative image of Judaism among certain contemporary Christian writers. By the seventeenth century, such Jewish writers as Simone Luzzatto, Manasseh ben Israel, and Leon of Modena began to counter the unattractive image of their religion and culture in their own compositions composed in European languages. This literature of Jewish apologetics sought to correct the crude stereotypes of Jewish culture by presenting Jews in a more favorable light and to address a wider Christian audience uneducated in the Hebrew language.[17] As Jews began to write more frequently in European languages, and as they and Christian scholars made Jewish civilization more accessible to non-Hebrew readers through their writings, the learning of the rabbis previously hidden within the covers of Hebrew books was increasingly publicized and demystified for ever-larger numbers of literate Christians living in modern Europe.

OF COURSE these new post-fifteenth-century transformations did not obliterate or supplant completely the previously formulated negative approaches to Hebrew books discussed above. As we have mentioned, the Talmud was burned in Italy in the middle of the sixteenth century despite the new intellectual and spiritual trends of the era, and despite the newly discovered interest by Christian publishers in printing Judaica. An elaborate procedure of Church censorship of Hebrew books was zealously maintained from the sixteenth century on, while other clerics, especially apostates, continued to pursue their missionary campaigns against Jews by crudely exploiting rabbinic and kabbalistic

materials.[18] In view of this legacy, we are prompted to return to the critical question posed at the beginning of this essay: Did increased Christian enthusiasm and familiarity with Hebrew writing engender a greater appreciation of Jews living in Christian society? Jeremy Cohen has recently attempted to answer this question with a resounding "no" with respect to the twelfth and thirteenth centuries. He writes:

It is instructive that in the period of the most intense Christian study of Judaica new polemics undermined the security of European Jewry. . . . In the high medieval academy, increased study of a minority viewpoint led not to greater toleration but to greater bifurcation between the circumscribed value of such an outlook and its despised protagonists. . . . As Scholasticism facilitated an understanding of his [the Jew's] books, it nearly eliminated his theologically grounded utility in European Christendom.[19]

And what of the later centuries? One can easily locate examples of Christian students of Hebrew books who learned to appreciate some of the positive qualities of Judaism and even of Jews themselves. François Tissard, the aforementioned French humanist, developed an open and respectful relationship with his Jewish instructor. Johann Reuchlin was even capable of publicly praising a Jew, albeit a fictional one, in the opening of Book II of his *De Arte Cabalistica*. But Reuchlin was no friend of the Jews, as Heiko Oberman has recently demonstrated.[20] And on a larger scale, no one could seriously argue that the Renaissance or Reformation left any significant positive impact on the social, political, or economic status of Jews living in Western Europe. Nor did the mere circulation of Hebrew books in European libraries and bookshops alter in any appreciable way the majority's treatment of Europe's Jewish minority.

Perhaps the most dramatic example of a Christian scholar's displaying extraordinary familiarity with Jewish books and blatant intolerance of Jews is the case of Johann Andreas Eisenmenger. In his *Entdecktes Judenthum* published in two volumes of some 2,120 pages in 1711 and again in 1741 with a 1700 imprint date, Eisenmenger displayed an impressive command of Jewish sources, quoting over two hundred Jewish texts. Notwithstanding such vast erudition, Eisenmenger painted a most derogatory and inflammatory portrait of Jewish religion and society. His prejudices against Jews were not affected one iota by his substantial knowledge of Jewish texts.[21]

Nevertheless, Jews on the threshold of the modern era persisted in the facile belief that increased literacy about Judaism among Christians would lead to greater toleration and appreciation of the Jews in European society. When Solomon Ibn Verga of the sixteenth century wrote that he had never met an intelligent person who hated Jews, he was articulating a standard assumption of Jewish intellectuals for centuries to come.[22] There is something absurdly naive and chillingly tragic about Heinrich Graetz's unswerving devotion to writing a massive Jewish history in order to educate nineteenth-century German society about its past and present treatment of its Jews in the midst of the swelling anti-Semitism within his society![23] To a twentieth-century observer with the hindsight of the destruction of European Jews, Ibn Verga's assumption about the relationship between scholarship and toleration now appears hopelessly unrealistic.

Yet Jews continue to write their books, Christians continue to read them, and the extent of publication of Judaica in recent decades in the United States, in Europe, and in Israel exceeds all previous expectations. Whether, in the long run, Jewish learning makes people more tolerant of Jews or not, many educated Jews and Christians alike persist in believing that books do make a difference, if not in transforming social realities, at least in pointing to ideals and possibilities still unrealized yet earnestly pursued.

Notes

1 The whole incident is described in D. Ruderman, *The World of a Renaissance Jew: The Life and Thought of Abraham ben Mordecai Farissol* (Cincinnati, 1981), pp. 98–106.

2 Peter of Blois, *Contra perfidiam Judaeorum,* trans. J. Cohen in "Scholarship and Intolerance in the Medieval Academy: The Study and Evaluation of Judaism in European Christendom," *American Historical Review* 91 (1986): 599.

3 See the useful summary of R. Loewe in his entry on "Hebraists, Christian," in *Encyclopaedia Judaica* (Jerusalem, 1971), 8:9–71.

4 All this is admirably discussed by B. Smalley, *The Study of the Bible in the Middle Ages,* 3rd ed. (Oxford, 1983). See also H. Hailperin, *Rashi and the Christian Scholars* (Pittsburgh, 1963).

5 See J. Guttmann, "Der Einfluss der maimonidischen Philosophie auf des christliche Abendland," *Moses ben Maimon: Sein Leben, seine Werke und sein Einfluss,* ed. W. Bacher, M. Brann, and D. Simonsen, 2 vols. (Leipzig, 1914; reprint, Hildesheim, 1971), 1:135–230.

6 This is all discussed with ample documentation in J. Cohen, *The Friars and the Jews: The Evolution of Medieval Anti-Judaism* (Ithaca, N.Y., 1982); see also A. Funkenstein, "Basic Types of Christian Anti-Jewish Polemics in the Later Middle Ages," *Viator* 2 (1971): 373–382.

7 See K. Stow, "The Burning of the Talmud in 1553, in the Light of Sixteenth Century Catholic Attitudes toward the Talmud," *Bibliothèque d'Humanisme et Renaissance* 34 (1972): 435–459.

8 See the works cited in note 6 above.

9 On these apostates and their relationship to the later Christian Kabbalah, see G. Scholem, "Zur Geschichte der Anfänge der Christlichen Kabbala," *Essays Presented to Leo Baeck* (London, 1954), pp. 158–193.

10 Pico della Mirandola, *Oratio,* trans. E. Forbes in *The Renaissance Philosophy of Man,* ed. E. Cassirer, P. O. Kristeller, and J. H. Randall (Chicago, 1948), pp. 282–283.

11 For a more detailed discussion of Pico and Christian Kabbalah with extensive bibliographical references, see D. Ruderman, "The Italian Renaissance and Jewish Thought," *Renaissance Humanism: Foundations, Forms and Legacy,* ed. A. Rabil, Jr., Vol. 1 (Philadelphia, 1988), pp. 382–433.

12 The Reuchlin-Pfefferkorn debate is fully discussed by S. W. Baron, *A Social and Religious History of the Jews* (New York and London, 1969), 13:182–191.

13 The most recent treatment of Christian Hebraism in the Reformation period is that of J. Freedman, *The Most Ancient Testimony: Sixteenth-Century Christian-Hebraica in the Age of Renaissance Nostalgia* (Athens, Ohio, 1983).

14 E. Eisenstein, *The Printing Press as an Agent of Change,* 2 vols. (Cambridge, 1979).

15 The bibliography on Jewish printing is extensive. See the general surveys of D. W. Amram, *The Makers of Hebrew Books in Italy* (Philadelphia, 1909; reprint, 1963); J. Bloch, "Venetian Printers of Hebrew Books," *Bulletin of The New York Public Library* 36 (1932): 71–92.

16 Christian Hebraism in the seventeenth century is briefly summarized with additional bibliography in R. Loewe's essay cited above, n. 3.

17 See, for example, M. Cohen, "Leone da Modena's Riti: A Seventeenth Century Plea for Toleration of Jews," *Jewish Social Studies* 34 (1972): 287–321.

18 These measures are generally surveyed in K. Stow, *Catholic Thought and Papal Jewry Policy* (New York, 1977).

19 J. Cohen, "Scholarship and Intolerance" (cited in n. 2), pp. 612–613.

20 See the succinct summary of his recent book in B. Cooperman, ed., *Jewish Thought in the Sixteenth Century* (Cambridge, Mass., 1983), pp. 326–364, entitled "Three Sixteenth-Century Attitudes to Judaism: Reuchlin, Erasmus, and Luther."

21 See J. Katz, *From Prejudice to Destruction: Anti-Semitism, 1700–1933* (Cambridge, Mass., and London, 1980), pp. 13–22.

22 This passage from his Hebrew work, *Shevet Yehudah,* is translated in M. Meyer, *Ideas of Jewish History* (New York, 1974), p. 112.

23 See I. Schorsch, "Ideology and History in the Age of Emancipation," in Heinrich Graetz, *The Structure of Jewish History and Other Essays* (New York, 1975), pp. 1–62.

9 MICHAEL W. GRUNBERGER

Publishing and the Rise of Modern Hebrew Literature

THE beginnings of modern Hebrew literature may be traced to the appearance of *ha-Me'asef,* a Haskalah (or enlightenment) journal published in Königsburg and Berlin from 1783 to 1811. The seeds of the Jewish Enlightenment—sown in Germany, Italy, and Holland—spread eastward, first to Galicia, and finally to Russia by the middle of the nineteenth century. In this, its East European manifestation, a fundamental change occurred in both the nature and the quantity of the literature published—a change made possible by the active role played by the Hebrew literary intelligentsia in the production and distribution of the new literature.

It is not, however, immediately apparent that the nineteenth century represents a watershed in the history of the Hebrew book. After all, Hebrew books were among the first printed anywhere, and the early printers functioned both as publishers and booksellers—initiating, producing, selling, and often financing the books issued from their presses.

And yet, a substantive change did occur beginning in the mid-nineteenth century: for the first time there appeared in Hebrew a diverse national literature, complete with poetry, fiction, children's literature, literary criticism, and translations from the classics. Several factors contributed to the success of this great literary awakening. Of special significance was the close link between the emerging Zionist ideology and the literature which sustained it. Fueling the emerging nationalism were historical novels recalling the days of biblical glory; poetry expressing the anguish and despair born of generations of exile; and a body of critical literature pointing unremittingly toward a spiritual and cultural rebirth. The two—the literature and the ideology—marched in step, sustaining and nurturing one another.

What distinguished the new author/publisher of Hebrew from his predecessor, the printer/craftsman, was not only the subject matter issuing from his publishing house, but also his view of the publisher's role in the intellectual life of the Jewish people. In contrast to the early printers and their relatively passive role, the new publisher saw himself as a cultural catalyst, improving the intellectual life of his people while at the same time helping to develop and sustain a cadre of talented authors writing in Hebrew.

This essay explores the historical context of Hebrew publishing—including a review of some early methods used to publish and disseminate Hebrew books—and then focuses on late nineteenth-century Hebrew publishing and its contribution to the growth of modern Hebrew literature.

SINCE its invention, the craft of printing has been characterized as *melekhet ha-kodesh,* or "holy work." Yet the early printers and their successors could hardly escape the business of publishing. Printing was (and still is) a capital-intensive enterprise, requiring significant advance outlays of funds for equipment, supplies, and labor. How the early printers of Hebrew financed their operations is a complex and as yet largely unexplored topic. In this essay, we will examine this area only insofar as it sheds light on our main interest: the late nineteenth-century literary awakening and the pioneer Hebrew publishers who sustained it.

For the early printers, the initiative to print a title could come from a variety of sources. If it was a standard text—biblical, liturgical, or rabbinic—the decision to publish was often based on a conjecture by the printer as to what would sell. The

Title page of ha-Me'asef *(Koenigsberg, 1784).*
NYPL, Jewish Division [Ex. no. 156]

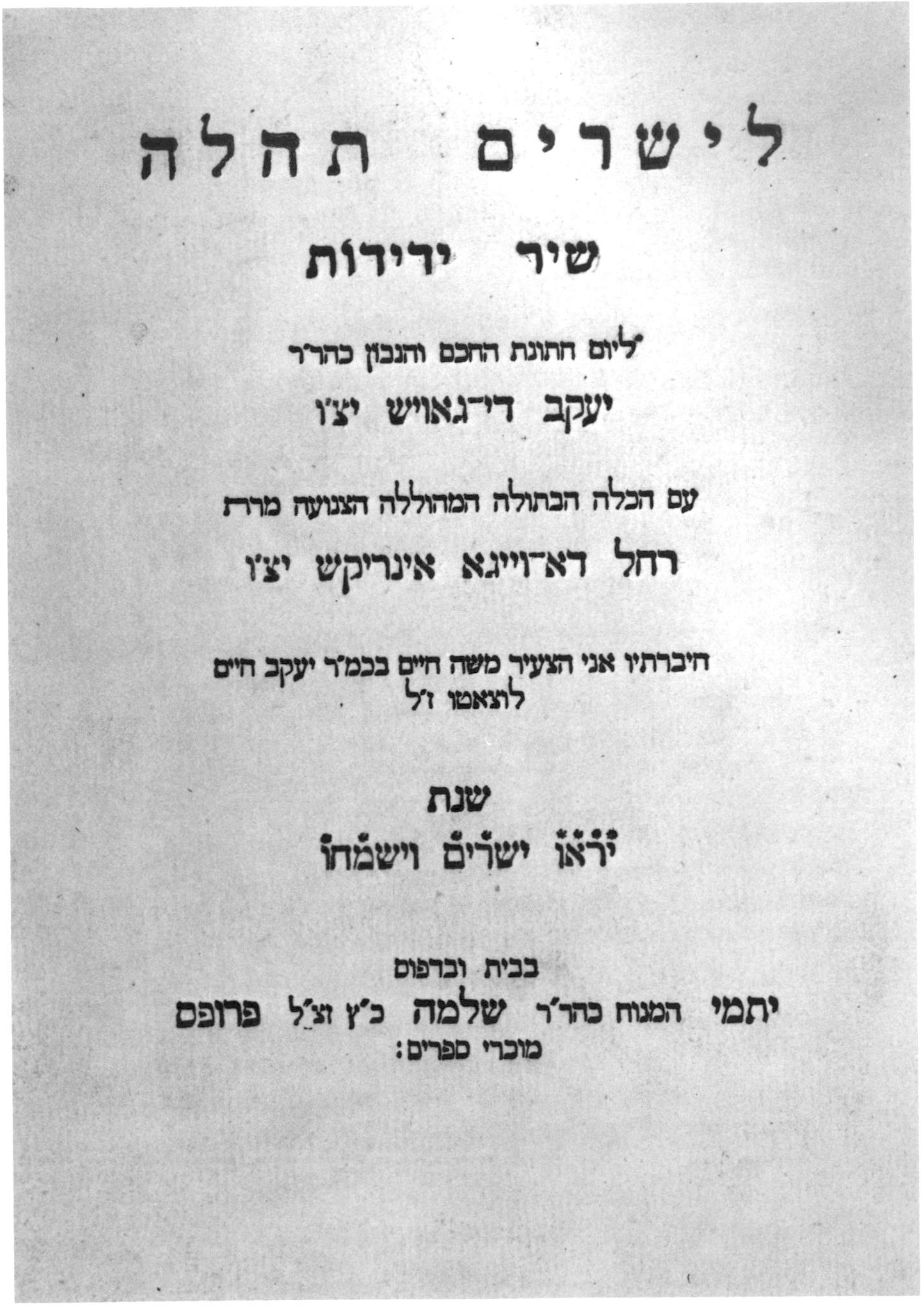

ליש רים ת ה ל ה

שיר ידידות

ליום חתונת החכם והנבון כהר"ר

יעקב די־גאויש יצ"ו

עם הכלה הבתולה המהוללה הצנועה מרת

רחל דא־וייגא אינריקש יצ"ו

חיברתיו אני הצעיר משה חיים בכמ"ר יעקב חיים
לוצאטו ז"ל

שנת

ירֿאֿוֹ ישרֿים וישֿמֿחוֹ

בבית ובדפוס

יתמי המנוח כהר"ר שלמה כ"ץ זצ"ל פרופס
מוכרי ספרים:

La-Yesharim Tehilah *(Praise to the Upright)*, *an allegorical play by Moses Ḥayyim
Luzzatto published in honor of the marriage
of Jacob de Chaves and Rachel da Veiga
Henriques (Amsterdam, 1743). Some critics
consider modern Hebrew literature to have begun with Luzzatto's poetry.*
NYPL, *Jewish Division [Ex. no. 150]*

risks in this case would be assumed by the printer and/or his backer(s), and a variety of methods of financing could be adopted—the most effective combined both advance financing and distribution.

In sixteenth-century Constantinople, for example, fascicles of books were distributed in the synagogue at the Sabbath service and paid for after sundown; cash raised in this manner was then used to finance subsequent fascicles.[1] In certain situations, the printer was able to attract a backer or patron to invest in a certain title or group of titles. Both Manasseh ben Israel and Manuel Benveniste, seventeenth-century Amsterdam's most important printers, succeeded in attracting financial backers for many of the books issued from their presses. Interestingly, many of these backers were wealthy non-Jews who viewed the publishing of Hebrew religious texts as a potentially profitable enterprise.[2] Of course, if the printer was himself wealthy, he did not need to look for outside support. Daniel Bomberg, a native of Antwerp, gained the exclusive privilege to publish Hebrew books in Venice in the first half of the sixteenth century. His wealth—he was said to have invested more than four million ducats in his printing operation—enabled him to undertake long-term, expensive projects such as publishing the first rabbinic Bible (1516–17) and the first complete editions of both Talmuds (1520–23). He could also afford to be patient and stockpile unsold titles while waiting for demand to catch up with his inventory.

The printer, however, rarely was willing to assume the financial risk of printing an unknown author's book. In such a case, the author himself was expected to raise the money needed to cover the costs of printing. In arrangements similar to the ones worked out with today's "vanity presses," an author would pay a printer for a specified number of copies that the author would then undertake to sell himself.

By far the most popular way for an author to raise money was through the sale of advance subscriptions. For Hebrew books, the phenomenon of subscriptions seems to have originated in the last quarter of the eighteenth century. In Berl Kagan's classic work on Hebrew book subscriptions, *Sefer ha-Prenumerantn,* more than 350,000 subscribers are listed—a figure that attests to the system's acceptance as well as to its efficacy. Kagan estimated that a more complete listing would have included an additional 150,000 subscribers.[3]

Prenumerantn were generally gathered by an author—sometimes by his agent—in travels through the cities and towns of a particular region. If possible, an author secured a written endorsement from a renowned rabbi—whose letter was then used to gather additional endorsements. Armed with approbations and perhaps accompanied by one or two prominent members of the community, the author would then set out to collect the individual subscriptions for inclusion in the book's *prenumerantn* list.

An interesting variation occurred in nineteenth-century Amsterdam, with the announced sale of subscriptions to *Ahavat David,* a proposed encyclopedic work by the Haskalah poet David Franco Mendes.[4] The subscription announcement spelled out the cost for each subscription, as well as the 10 percent commission that would be paid to individuals who sold multiple copies of the encyclopedia. Subscribers could pay out in installments, with each payment due on delivery of a section of the printed book. The subscription offer was set to expire on Rosh Hashanah, 5561 (September 20, 1800), and printing would begin immediately on receipt of three hundred subscriptions. Since *Ahavat David* was never published, the required number of subscriptions, in all likelihood, was not secured.

In the hands of a skillful publisher, sale by subscription was a valuable market-research tool, especially useful when complex, long-term, and expensive projects were being planned. The publisher could use the response to his offering to explore a project's feasibility, determine its costs, and calculate the number of copies needed to meet the expected demand. In 1880 the "Widow and Brothers Romm Press" in Vilna announced its intention to publish a new edition of the Talmud—later known as the *Vilna Shas*—and offered advance subscriptions to the public. S. Feigensohn, director of the firm, recounts in his memoir of the Romm Press that as soon as the new edition was announced, subscribers descended "like locusts" to sign up. Forewarned, Romm prepared for the extraordinary demand: a year later, 22,000 copies of the first volume of this landmark edition were printed—and sold. The project, completed in 1886, was both a financial and critical success for the publisher.[5]

Primarily known for the religious texts it issued, the Vilna firm of the "Widow and Brothers Romm Press" also played a central role in the publishing of Haskalah literature. To it goes the distinction of having printed the first modern Hebrew novel: *Ahavat Tsiyon,* by Abraham Mapu (Vilna, 1853); entering into the first author/publisher contract (between Romm and the Yiddish writer I. M. Dick); and publishing the first Hebrew "best-seller": Kalman Schulmann's serial translation of Eugène Sue's *Les Mystères de Paris* (Vilna, 1858–60), which sold 2,000 copies, purportedly earning Schulmann 1,000 rubles.[6]

Though *Ahavat Tsiyon* and Mapu's second novel, *'Ayit Tsavu'a* (Vilna, 1857), were printed by Romm, Mapu himself financed and distributed both books. He paid Romm a fee per printed sheet to set the type, print, proofread, and bind 1,200 copies of *Ahavat Tsiyon* and 2,000 of *'Ayit Tsavu'a*. Despite *Ahavat Tsiyon'*s apparent popularity—during Mapu's lifetime it reached readers as far away as the United States and Egypt—it took four years to sell out the first edition.[7] *'Ayit Tsavu'a* fared even worse. In May 1857, he wrote to his friend Y. Mandelstamm:

My books—that the new generation loves very much but doesn't buy! Only 30 [copies of *'Ayit Tsavu'a*] are found in that great metropolis of Vilna and they suffice for all the city's enlightened. Such is the reward for all my efforts!

Title page of the second edition of Mapu's Ahavat Tsiyon (Love of Zion, *translated as* Amnon: Prince and Peasant *and as* The Shepherd Prince*), published at the press of Joseph Reuben ben Menaḥem Romm (Vilna, 1864).*
NYPL, Jewish Division [Ex. no. 154]

Later that week, he wrote to his brother Mattityahu: "Until now I have distributed only 600 [copies of *'Ayit Tsavu'a*]. . . . But what can I do? As yet I haven't shipped any to Kremenitz, Odessa, or Kishinev. . . ."[8] By the end of 1857, Mapu reported that he had sold only 800 copies.[9]

To reduce his printing costs, Mapu actively explored the possibility of publishing the second volume of *'Ayit Tsavu'a* and his third novel, *Ḥozei Ḥezyonot,* outside of Russia. Mapu's petition to the authorities for an exemption from the duty on imported books was denied after Re'uven Romm voiced strong objections. Romm argued that Mapu had been well treated by the firm; that Romm's printing rates were reasonable and not at all excessive; that credit had even been extended to Mapu; and that an exception made in this case would open the floodgates for other tax-free imports of Hebrew books.[10]

In addition to Vilna, an early center for the publishing of Haskalah literature was the city of Vienna. With restrictions placed on publishing by Jews, early Haskalah literature was published primarily by non-Jews such as Anton von Schmid (1775–1855). Schmid was so grateful to the Jewish community for their support that he donated all the Hebrew books published by his firm to the Viennese Jewish community for their library. Published in Vienna were a number of important Haskalah journals, including Peretz Smolenskin's *Ha-Shaḥar* (1868–84), *Kerem Ḥemed* (1833–56), and *Bikure ha-'Itim* (1821–31).

Despite the very real obstacles standing in the way of nineteenth-century Hebrew writers, there was a slow increase in the number of titles published and a steady growth in the number of readers. The composition of this new literature—the writers it includes and their respective place within the literature—is still the subject of much disagreement and discussion. Yet we may infer its quantitative dimensions using Abraham Ya'ari's bibliography of modern Hebrew literature, which lists approximately four thousand titles. Citing works published between 1729 and 1926, he divided the literature into the following categories: poetry (31 percent), fiction (31 percent), children's literature (27 percent), drama (7 percent), and literary criticism (4 percent).[11] While the new literature appeared in tens of European cities, by the last decades of the nineteenth century and the first decade of the twentieth, Hebrew publishing was concentrated in the cities of Warsaw, Vilna, and Odessa, reflecting both the vitality of each city's respective Jewish intelligentsia and a loosening of governmental restrictions on Hebrew publishing.

If we examine the publishing of narrative fiction in four European cities and Palestine from 1850 through 1919 (see table), we note a gradual increase in publishing from 1850 through 1879, with the peak of book production occurring in the 1890s. By 1910, the Eastern European center began its decline and was gradually replaced by the growing center in Palestine.

Warsaw, as the publishing "capital" of modern Hebrew literature,

PUBLISHING OF FICTION[12]

	Odessa	Warsaw	Vilna	Vienna	Palestine	Total
1850–59	—	—	5	1	—	6
1860–69	9	7	11	4	—	31
1870–79	2	21	7	12	2	44
1880–89	4	69	14	10	—	97
1890–99	9	128	13	1	3	154
1900–09	10	69	18	—	50	147
1910–19	10	33	5	2	21	71
	44	327	73	30	76	550

was closely identified with the activities and energies of one man: Abraham Leib Shalkovich (1867–1921), better known by his pen name, Ben-Avigdor. He began as a writer in Warsaw, and several pieces of his literary criticism appeared in the Hebrew press of the day. An innovator who claimed credit for inaugurating a "new direction" in Hebrew literature, his enduring legacy rests with his publishing endeavors rather than with his literary creations. Ben-Avigdor's goal as a publisher was twofold: to create a readership that looked to the Hebrew word for inspiration and to develop a cadre of skilled writers to produce a worthy literary corpus. The publisher's role would be as an interlocutor between the two.

Ben-Avigdor's credo was explicitly stated in a manifesto published in 1891 that was included in the first book to bear the Ben-Avigdor imprint—his own *Leah Mokheret Dagim*. As Ben-Avigdor saw it:

. . . the material situation of our literature is very deficient. The number of those who know Hebrew is very small and, of these, the ones who know other languages consider it beneath their dignity to read Hebrew books written by Hebrew writers. Whenever possible, they satisfy their spiritual hunger by reading books in other languages. . . .[13]

Even those who could read Hebrew books, he continued, viewed them as a luxury, preferring to spend money on trivialities instead. Consequently, the few books that were published were not read. With so few purchasers of Hebrew books, it was no wonder that there were no professional Hebrew writers—only writer/shopkeepers, writer/merchants, writer/teachers, writer/matchmakers, and so on. This situation, according to Ben-Avigdor, forced the best writers to abandon Hebrew in favor of other languages, while Hebrew retained only second-rate authors. To his own question: "What is the cure for this condition?" Ben-Avigdor answered:

If we [can] create a Hebrew audience, a public that reads Hebrew books and buys them, the material situation of the writer will improve. And once literature rewards its workers—not only with praises, speeches, and telegrams of congratulations on anniversaries, and with eulogies and elegies after they die—but with tangible rewards, then the spiritual situation of our literature will improve as well and our literature will truly become a national literature.[14]

The opportunity to put his credo into action came when the Bene Mosheh—a secret society founded in Odessa in 1889 whose spiritual leader was Ahad Ha'am (Asher Ginsberg)—began a program to publish books advocating the spiritual rebirth of the Jewish people. Their plan was to publish a series of inexpensive booklets in Warsaw and distribute them through the regional Bene Mosheh chapters. Three titles (one of which was seized by the censor)—two in Russian and one in Hebrew—were published in this fashion. But since the Bene Mosheh themselves never numbered more than two hundred, the books went unsold and the enterprise was abandoned.[15]

It was at this point that Ben-Avigdor, secretary of the Warsaw chapter of the Bene Mosheh, decided to try his hand at publishing. In 1891, he issued the *Sifrei Agurah* or "Penny Books" over his own imprint and mainly with his own funds—though some of the booklets were surely sponsored by wealthy patrons.[16] The first title published was his own *Leah Mokheret Dagim;* it was followed by five other pamphlets. He then joined with Eliezer Kaplan—also of the Warsaw Bene Mosheh—to issue the forty remaining pamphlets in the series. The *Sifrei Agurah* were a rousing success and were widely distributed. Their subject matter—unidealized depictions of everyday Jewish life—was new, and the language was simple and relatively unadorned.

The success of these small booklets convinced the Bene Mosheh and Ben-Avigdor of the feasibility of a more ambitious undertaking: the founding of a conventional publishing house that would publish the treasures of Hebrew literature—old as well as new. Ahiasaf was founded in 1893 with Ben-Avigdor at the helm, as its literary editor, bookkeeper, and only salaried employee. In a notice in the first volume of *Luah Ahiasaf,* a calendar and literary annual, the publishers set forth their philosophy:

Upon examining the poverty of our Hebrew literature in all its aspects, we recognize that one of the main factors preventing it from developing as it should is the absence from our midst of well-financed publishers who could pay authors and scholars a just recompense for their labor. . . . [This would enable writers to] work in peace while publishers publish and diligently distribute their work. . . . In general, writers [in other languages] don't get involved in publishing and selling since it involves business and commerce and is outside their ken.[17]

Ben-Avigdor himself left Ahiasaf after three years, finding the ideological guidelines of the Bene Mosheh too constricting for his taste.[18] The publishing firm continued until 1923, issuing, among other things, its annual *Luah Ahiasaf*—containing informative articles and useful lists of recent publications—and *Ha-Shiloah,* pre-revolutionary Russia's leading Hebrew literary journal.

In 1896, with an initial investment of 2,500 rubles, Ben-Avigdor founded Tushiyah in partnership with Y. Romberg, a noted Hebrew lexicographer.[19] The goals Tushiyah set for itself were quite ambitious, seeking to publish original Hebrew literature, translations of the classics into Hebrew, and books on the natural and social sciences. Over the course of two years Ben-Avigdor published two hundred booklets in the *Bibliyotekah 'Ivrit* series, including original works by such important literary figures as H. N. Bialik, S. Tchernichovski, and Z. Schneur, as well as translations from Zola, Nordau, and others. Tushiyah was also a pioneer publisher of children's literature, issuing a highly acclaimed weekly children's magazine, *'Olam Katan,* and a monthly, *ha-Ne'urim,* intended for young adults.

True to his word, Ben-Avigdor worked to improve the financial situation of Hebrew writers. It was reported that in its first four and one-half years, Tushiyah paid out more than 19,150 rubles to Hebrew writers.[20] In 1907 Ben-Avigdor himself boasted that "The stereotype of the author as a 'shnorrer' is no longer with us."[21] But by 1910, with

Tushiyah itself experiencing severe financial difficulties, Ben-Avigdor admitted that publishers could not by themselves save the Hebrew writer. Only the "people," said Ben-Avigdor, could save the starving writers—but the "people" were not yet willing to spend their money on Hebrew books or newspapers.[22]

In 1911, Tushiyah combined with several other small presses to form Merkaz/Tsentral. Despite its initial attempts to undertake a publication program, Merkaz/Tsentral never succeeded in becoming an active publisher. Except for its Aḥisefer branch—founded by Ben-Avigdor in 1913—which issued some eighteen volumes, and the reissue of new editions of old titles from the Tushiyah list, Merkaz/Tsentral was primarily occupied with the distribution of the unsold inventories of its constituent companies.

Tushiyah represented an important first for Hebrew publishing. Its dependence on a keen understanding of the market and the need to develop it, rather than on an ideological foundation, made it a forerunner of the modern-day publisher. But it was also something of an intellectual potpourri, publishing prolifically, with no overall plan. This excessive productivity inevitably resulted in lapses of quality, leading one critic to say of Ben-Avigdor that "he did more to increase than to enrich Hebrew literature."[23]

Yet it would be incorrect to underestimate the extent of Ben-Avigdor's contribution to the growth of modern Hebrew literature. Unlike his predecessors, he commissioned new works, paid out advances to authors,

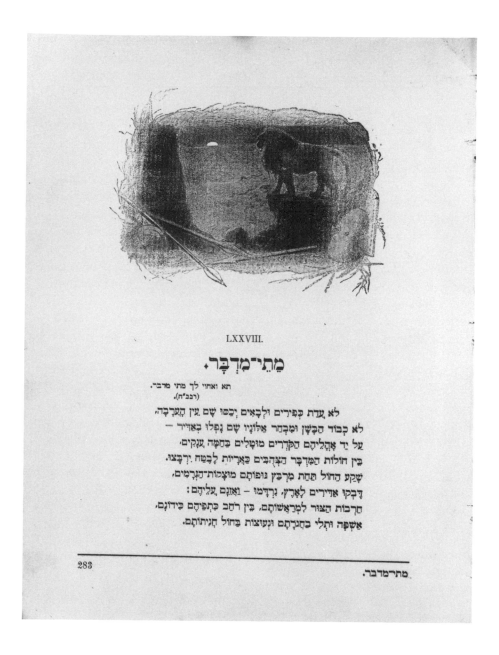

The beginning of Bialik's "Metei-Midbar"
("Dead of the Desert"), from a Cracow,
1907/08 edition of his poems.
NYPL, Jewish Division [Ex. no. 104]

and, in general, worked to sustain a growing circle of professional writers. To build a readership for Hebrew, he published an exceptional variety of materials—ranging from original works to translations; from monographs to journals; and from adult to children's literature. During the course of his thirty-year publishing career, he published or edited virtually the entire roster of Eastern European Hebrew writers. Indeed, a formidable list of more than 250 of the leading authors of the period who were published by Ben-Avigdor was compiled for a festschrift that appeared in 1916, celebrating his twenty-five years in publishing.[24]

With the founding of the Odessan publishing house Moriah, Hebrew publishing came of age. The prime mover behind Moriah was the great Hebrew poet Ḥayyim Naḥman Bialik (1873–1934), who together with authors Y. H. Rawnitzki and S. Ben-Zion (Simḥah Alter Gutmann) founded Moriah in 1901. Rav-Tsa'ir has left us a description of the founding of Moriah:

Bialik spoke loudly of the future profits to all shareholders, because the society was based on shares, 25 rubles per share. The principal partners were the five original founders, two of them "money men"—Levinsky and me—who each put in 1,000 rubles, in notes of course, and the three workers—Bialik, Rawnitzki, and Ben-Zion.[25]

Initially, Moriah concentrated its efforts on producing textbooks, seeing as its primary task the building of a new education based on the sacred Scriptures as well as tradition. In close collaboration, the three partners wrote, edited, and published the highly successful collections of Bible stories *Sipurei Mikra* and *Divrei Nevi'im,* which were intended for children in the traditional "Ḥeder" schools of Eastern Europe. Moriah's edition of Rawnitzki and Bialik's *Sefer ha-Agadah* remains a classic to this day, reprinted many times both as a textbook and in its original format. The partners were especially active editors, sometimes adding whole chapters and sections to the books of outside authors.[26] The works issued by Moriah were selected with care, edited thoroughly, and beautifully presented to the reader. Given the attention and care lavished on each book published, it is not surprising that even in those early years Moriah succeeded in earning a yearly profit of several thousand rubles.

Moriah published vigorously in Russia until the beginning of World War I and began to reemerge after the Revolution with the publication of I. L. Peretz's Hebrew works and the first volume of Gershon Schoffmann's collected works. New editions of the poems of S. Tchernichovski, Z. Schneur, and H. N. Bialik were published during these years as well. In 1921 Bialik left Odessa, stopping in Berlin before settling in Tel Aviv. There, he reestablished Moriah as Dvir, a publishing house that remains active to this day. Bialik's arrival in Tel Aviv in 1924 signaled the emergence of a literary center in Palestine.

The Stybel publishing house was founded in Moscow in 1917 by Abraham Joseph Stybel (1884–1946), a wealthy leather merchant. Stybel's dedication to Hebrew literature was all-consuming and he committed his substantial resources to the building of his publishing house. His first act was to hire noted editor and writer David Frischmann as the principal editor of Stybel. He gave Frischmann carte blanche in literary matters, paid him a princely salary, and, through him, induced the most important Hebrew writers to contribute to the two primary activities of the house: the publication of the literary journal *ha-Tekufah* and the translation of the classics of world literature into Hebrew.

Ha-Tekufah was issued in sizable editions of five thousand, with each volume numbering in the hundreds of pages and containing articles, poems, translations, stories, and dramas by established, as well as new, writers. Concurrently with *ha-Tekufah,* Stybel embarked on a massive program of translating world literature into Hebrew. In just its first year, Stybel published translations of Tolstoy, Wilde, and Turgenev, among others. After the Russian Revolution, Stybel moved first to Warsaw (1919–25) and then to Berlin. Branches of the Stybel firm were established in Tel Aviv (1930–36) and New York (1946–50).

In the immediate aftermath of the Russian Revolution, only 29 of the 188 Hebrew books published were in the disciplines of Hebrew literature or literary criticism.[27] With the help of Maxim Gorky, a small group of Hebrew writers was permitted to leave Russia in 1921. Bialik and Rawnitzki, who were part of this

Cover of the first and only volume of be-Reshit *(In the Beginning), a collection of poetry and prose by Hebrew writers in the Soviet Union, printed in Berlin with a Moscow, Leningrad imprint, 1926.*
NYPL, Jewish Division [Ex. no. 102]

group, left for Berlin, barely escaping with their precious manuscripts. The departure of the Hebrew writers in the wake of the Revolution sounded the death knell for modern Hebrew literature in the Soviet Union; during the first fifty years after the Revolution, fewer than 350 Hebrew titles were published there.[28]

A DECISIVE element in the success of the nineteenth-century literary awakening was the extraordinary involvement of the Hebrew literati in the publishing of the new literature. Their remarkable achievements included the creation of a multifaceted literature in a language not yet "reborn"; the development of a readership that looked to the Hebrew word for intellectual sustenance; and, of special significance, the establishment of a vigorous, effective, and dynamic publishing apparatus that has continued to enrich the spiritual and cultural heritage of contemporary civilization.

Notes

1 See Simhah Assaf, *Be-Oholei Ya'akov* (Jerusalem: Mosad ha-Rav Kook, 1943), p. 19, and Abraham Ya'ari, *Ha-Defus ha-'Ivri be-Kushta* (Jerusalem: Magnes, 1967), pp. 13–14.

2 L. Fuks and R. G. Fuks-Mansfeld, *Hebrew Typography in the Northern Netherlands, 1585–1815,* Part One (Leiden: E. J. Brill, 1984), pp. 99–114 and 146–153; see also the "Index of Financiers," pp. 225–226.

3 Berl Kagan, *Sefer ha-Prenumerantn* (New York: Library of the Jewish Theological Seminary, 1975), p. ix.

4 I am indebted to Mr. Myron M. Weinstein, retired Head of the Library of Congress's Hebraic Section, for calling my attention to a copy of this broadside (Amsterdam: Proops, ca. 1800) held by the Library of Congress. The broadside is reproduced in Joseph Melkman, *David Franco Mendes: A Hebrew Poet* (Jerusalem: Massadah, 1951).

5 Samuel Shraga Feigensohn, "Le-Toldot Defus Romm," in *Yahadut Lita,* Vol. 1 (Tel Aviv: 'Am ha-Sefer, 1959/60), pp. 285 and 288.

6 Abraham Mapu, in a letter to his brother, June 17, 1858, quoted in P. Kon, "Le-Korot Beit ha-Defus shel Romm be-Vilna," in *Kiryat Sefer* 12 (1935/36): 114n.

7 Joseph Klausner, *Toldot ha-Sifrut ha-'Ivrit ha-Hadashah,* Vol. 3 (Jerusalem: Ahiasaf, 1960), p. 297. The continuing popularity of Mapu's *Ahavat Tsiyon* is attested by the many editions of this work—almost twenty—and the translations into Arabic (twice), German, Ladino, Yiddish, Russian, and English. A translation into Judeo-Persian was twice published in Jerusalem (in 1907/8 and 1913 respectively) for a bookdealer in Bukhara.

8 Selections from both letters in Kon, "Le-Korot Beit ha-Defus shel Romm," p. 113n.

9 Abraham Mapu, *Mikhteve Avraham Mapu* (Jerusalem: Mosad Bialik, 1970), pp. 284–285.

10 Ibid., pp. 286–287.

11 Abraham Ya'ari and Ben-Zion Dinur, *Ha-Sifrut ha-Yafah be-'Ivrit* (Jerusalem: Jewish National and University Library, 1927); and supplements by Abraham Ya'ari in *Kiryat Sefer* 6 (1929/30): 119–138 and 277–290; and Israel David Bet-Halevi in *Kiryat Sefer* 7 (1930/31): 282–289.

12 The table includes items from Ya'ari, *Ha-Sifrut,* pp. 125–177, as well as from the supplements to his bibliography; Ya'ari includes in this category translations into Hebrew, but excludes children's literature.

13 Ben-Avigdor's manifesto is reproduced in Menuhah Gilboa, "Ben-Avigdor be-Torat Mevaker," in *Peles: Mehkarim be-Vikoret ha-Sifrut ha-'Ivrit* (Tel Aviv: Tel Aviv University, 1980), pp. 191–194.

14 Ibid., p. 193.

15 Samuel Tchernowitz, *Bene Mosheh u-Tekufatam* (Warsaw: ha-Tsefirah, 1914), pp. 60–62.

16 See, for example, the dedication to "Dem Gönner und Kenner der hebräischen Sprache Herrn Isidor Fuchs" in David Frischmann, *Yizkor!* (Warsaw: Ben-Avigdor, 1891).

17 The prospectus is included in the front matter of *Luah Ahiasaf* 1 (Warsaw, 1893/94): [VII].

18 Shmarya Levin, in *Forward from Exile: The Autobiography of Shmarya Levin* (Philadelphia: Jewish Publication Society, 1967), stated on p. 311: "[Ben-Avigdor] was irked by the restraints we placed on him and finally broke away to found another publishing house, *Toshiah. . . .*"

19 Y. Pogrobinsky, "Toldot ha-Mol"ut ha-'Ivrit," in *Jewish Book Annual* 9 (1950/51): 44 [Hebrew section].

20 [Ezriel Nathan Frenk], "Mikhtavim mi-Varsha," in *ha-Melits,* No. 178 (1900): [1].

21 Abraham Leib Shalkovich [Ben-Avigdor], *Ha-Sifrut ha-'Ivrit ve-'Atidoteha* (New York, 1907), pp. 24–25.

22 Abraham Leib Shalkovich [Ben-Avigdor], *Ha-Sifrut ha-'Ivrit ha-Tse'irah* (Vilna, 1910), pp. 46–47.

23 Levin, *Forward from Exile,* p. 311.

24 In *Ben-Avigdor le-Hag Yovlo* (Warsaw: Va'ad ha-Yovel, 1916), pp. 7–9.

25 Chaim Tchernowitz [Rav Tsa'ir], *Masekhet Zikhronot* (New York: Va'ad ha-Yovel, 1945), p. 119.

26 Fischel Lachower, *Bialik: Hayav ve-Yetsirotav,* Vol. 2 (Tel Aviv: Dvir for Mosad Bialik, 1944), pp. 521–522.

27 *Pirsumim Yehudiyim be-Vrit-ha-Mo'atsot, 1917–1960,* ed. Chone Schmeruk (Jerusalem: Historical Society of Israel, 1961), p. 24.

28 Ibid., pp. 1–41, for a listing of 343 Hebrew items published in the Soviet Union from 1917 to 1960.

10 LEILA AVRIN

The Art of the Hebrew Book in the Twentieth Century

THERE ARE multiple facets to the art of fine printing and the Hebrew book in the twentieth century: new and original Hebrew typography; the influences of the private press movement and the *livre d'artiste*; bibliophile societies and enlightened publishers with high aesthetic standards from the 1920s on; the influence of modern technology and book design on the Hebrew book's appearance; the flowering of Hebrew calligraphy; and the growth of facsimile printing and publishing.

Typography

The most important aspect of twentieth-century Hebrew printing is the introduction of new Hebrew typography. At no earlier time did there exist such a variety of Hebrew faces, let alone ones designed by Jews who saw Hebrew typography as representing a living language. One may look upon this phenomenon as the natural outgrowth of the revival of spoken and literary Hebrew, with its practical need for a greater choice of letters available to both Hebrew printers and readers. Before the twentieth century, Hebrew types had been cut and cast by non-Jews, although their designs may have been inspired or even executed by anonymous Jewish scribes. Until World War II, most Jewish printers in Eastern and Western Europe purchased their typefonts from large foundries, especially in Germany: Stempel and Ludwig & Meyer in Frankfurt am Main, W. Drugulin (from 1850) and Schelter & Gieseke in Leipzig, and Berthold in Berlin. Offizin Haag-Drugulin (the name of the firm after 1927) set type, providing this composition service to European and American printers. Before World War I, the basic styles of type were: Meruba, a square Hebrew face which grew out of the Sephardic hand; a semi-cursive called Rashi; and a running script, Rahut. There were slight variations in the appearance and names of these type families among foundries; for example, Monotype's version of Meruba was called Sonzino, Drugulin's was called Magalith.[1]

These old types were considered inadequate for a number of reasons. Many publishers associated the Meruba faces with ritual texts, especially Bibles and prayerbooks, and, with a new, nonreligious readership in mind, sought a more up-to-date face for secular literature. Type designers rejected the so-called modern-face types in Didot style, with extreme contrasts of thick and thin elements of the letter (called color or shading) and exaggerated serifs, which had been the new faces of the nineteenth century. Meruba was the most legible of these new types, tried and true but, by the twentieth century, dull. Another reason for the rejection of the "modern-face" letter was technological. Press runs were longer, and paper was often of lower quality and was not dampened as it had been in hand-printing. Because type wore down more quickly, hairlines broke. It was no longer practical to produce the extremely shaded letter.

Rafael Frank (1867–1920) was the first Jewish designer to break away from the all-too-available Meruba. Born in Ichenhausen (near Augsburg), Frank supported himself as a schoolteacher and cantor; from 1900 he lived in Leipzig, an important printing and publishing center. Frank also was an accomplished draftsman, applying his talents to Hebrew letter design, and an authority on the history of Hebrew script and typography. While he admired incunabula typography based on the Ashkenazic letter, he objected to its exaggerated Fraktur-like result, brought in with the nineteenth-century Pest-Wiener types, which, like the Didot-based designs, emphasized

מרובע

(Hebrew typeface specimen samples from the Berthold catalog)

H. BERTHOLD AG

Samples of the Meruba typeface from the Berthold catalog.

contrasting main and hairlines.[2] Frank sought a new, dignified letter that would evoke the pleasure of Daniel Bomberg's by avoiding great contrasts in color. The result was Frank-Ruehl. The letter is somewhat dark and bold, narrower than that of Meruba, and thus more economical for the publisher, who could fit more words on the page. In time, Frank-Ruehl, too, became associated with ritual texts, and with Meruba it is still popular for this purpose. Rafael Frank also may have designed the sans serif, unshaded Miriam, for it appears in the 1924 Berthold type catalog along with Frank-Ruehl.[3]

Throughout the printing centuries, there had always been some demand for Hebrew types, primarily by non-Jewish printers as exotic (non-Roman) "Oriental" faces. Bibles and the scholarly writings of Christian Hebraists were printed by non-Jews, who took pride in having Hebrew fonts in their cases along with Greek, Arabic, and Syriac. Non-Jewish typographers who excelled in creating new Hebrew faces in their own day were the great Guillaume Le Bé in the sixteenth century (his types were produced even as late as 1970 by the Nebiolo foundry in Turin), Nicholas Kis and Christoffel van Dijck in the seventeenth century,[4] and Didot in the late eighteenth century. Jewish printer/publishers took advantage of these types, showing no interest in modifying them or in creating new styles. Only in the twentieth century have Jewish designers taken the initiative, or have publishers, printers, and typefounders commissioned or bought new designs from Jewish typographers. This century's most important type designers are Henri Friedlaender, Eliyahu Korén, Ismar David, Franzisca Baruch, Zvi Hausmann, Zvi Narkiss, and Asher Oron.

Henri Friedlaender was born in Lyon in 1904 and was educated in Germany, where the family moved when he was a child. The finishing touch to his training as a compositor was at the Akademie für graphische Künste und Buchgewerbe, from which he received the degree of Master Compositor in 1926. He worked at Klingspor in Offenbach and at Haag-Drugulin in the late 1920s and 1930s. In 1931, a negative response to an inquiry addressed to Offizin Haag-Drugulin from the Schocken publishing house in Berlin, as to whether a modern Hebrew typeface existed, inspired Friedlaender to design one. His early experiments were based on a nineteenth-century megillah which belonged to his mother. In 1932 Friedlaender left Germany for Holland, where he remained in hiding during World War II, all the while working on his letter design.[5] The type was cast by Lettergieterij-Amsterdam in its first size in 1958 as Hadassah, the name of the printing school which Friedlaender had been invited to Jerusalem to head eight years earlier. Intertype, with a license from Lettergieterij-Amsterdam, cast Hadassah Light and Bold, from 1958 to 1966, and eventually made the face available for photocomposition. Hadassah has proved to be the most versatile of twentieth-century Hebrew faces. At first glance, Hadassah

פראנק־ריהל

Samples of Frank-Ruehl type from the Berthold catalog.

appears to consist of horizontals and verticals of even weight, punctuated by strong and firm bracketed serifs rising from the letters' top bars. Only on close inspection does one discern slight contrasts in weight and restrained curves in fourteen of the twenty-two letters. According to Friedlaender, the color is slightly darker than Garamond (Latin) capitals, and there are similar differences in the thickness of lines. Hadassah's display alphabet possesses the dignity of the finest classic Roman inscriptions. Friedlaender has also designed Hebrew types for IBM: Aviv, Hadar, and Shalom. He was awarded the Gutenberg Prize of the city of Mainz in 1971 for outstanding contribution to typography.

Franzisca Baruch (b. 1901) has made a major contribution to the art of Hebrew lettering as both calligrapher and type designer. Her first important commission came from woodcut artist Jakob Steinhardt for his *Haggadah* (1921–22). Baruch's study of medieval Ashkenazic Hebrew manuscripts and the printed *Prague Haggadah* of 1527 inspired the bold script found in the limited edition of the *Steinhardt Haggadah,* reissued during the 1920s, and later woodcut editions of *Jonah* (1953) and *Ruth* (1957), both printed by offset. Baruch's Haggadah script engendered the typeface Stam (the word is an acronym for the Torah scribe), cast by the Berthold foundry and popular in the 1920s and 1930s. Two similar types, Rahel, an open letter, and Ramban, a condensed letter, were cut without Baruch's permission. Franzisca Baruch designed a second Ashkenazic letter for Leo Ary Mayer,

scholar of Islamic art, cast by Enschedé of Haarlem. Later it was manufactured by the Jerusalem Typefoundry, but it was never widely used. Baruch designed another letter, for Salman Schocken (1877–1959), the publisher for whom she worked until her immigration to Palestine in 1933.[6] Schocken-Baruch, inspired by the Sephardic Renaissance types employed by the Soncino family of printers, was cut by Monotype. Franzisca Baruch's types are beautiful to look at, but are not serviceable for long texts.

Ismar David's typeface David is modern in its unshaded, unserifed character, yet it is the most calligraphic of all twentieth-century types. David (b. Breslau, 1910) studied at the School of Arts and Crafts in Berlin-Charlottenburg. Upon winning a lettering competition sponsored by Keren Kayemet (Jewish National Fund) for their Golden Book, David came to Palestine in 1932, where he began his design for a new Hebrew type. Reworked in 1949–50, the matrices in 12-point were produced by Intertype in 1952. David was later available on Photon. There are three styles, Bold, Upright, and Italic. The Jerusalem Typefoundry cast only a display-size David, no longer in existence, for hand-composition. A very small font of David, in 12-point, with just enough type for the opening passages of Genesis, was manufactured by Clark & Way in New York for a multilingual portfolio of Bible passages, *Liber Librorum,* set in type specimens by famous designers and published by Bror Zachrisson in Stockholm in 1957. The elegant David typeface is especially suited to the printing of literature, fine editions, and exhibition catalogs, and is now used frequently in Israel for newspaper supplements.[7]

Eliyahu Korén (originally Korngold, b. 1907) studied graphic art at the City School of Graphic and Applied Art in Nuremburg, where he was a teaching assistant, before immigrating to Palestine in 1933. After heading the graphics department for Keren Kayemet in Jerusalem from 1937 to 1957, Korén founded the house which published the Bible for which he designed his Korén letter. This type was cast in 1957 in 36-point by the French firm of Deberney & Peignot. The type was inspired by thirteenth- to fifteenth-century Sephardic manuscripts; one can see this influence in an intermediate design that was used for printing a small edition of the Book of Jonah, photo-offset from Korén's drawn letters. In the final Korén design, the letters are sharp, almost never rounded, with balanced contrasts, faintly serifed, with its few diagonals always parallel to one another. The beauty of the letter never detracts from its readability. For the Bible, vowel points and other additions to the consonantal text were hand-drawn and applied to the printed page, which was then photographed and printed by offset. The *Korén Bible,* printed by Monson in Jerusalem from 1962 on, with all subsequent editions offset from the original, is one of the masterpieces of Hebrew book design of all time.

Verses from the Song of Songs set in unvocalized sans serif Miriam type from Berthold.

The beginning of Genesis in the Korén *Pentateuch of 1959, in the new typeface developed by Eliyahu Korén. This was a forerunner of the full* Korén Bible, *which appeared in 1962.*
NYPL, *Jewish Division [Ex. no. 116]*

בראשית

א בְּרֵאשִׁית בָּרָא אֱלֹהִים אֵת הַשָּׁמַיִם וְאֵת הָאָרֶץ: וְהָאָרֶץ
הָיְתָה תֹהוּ וָבֹהוּ וְחֹשֶׁךְ עַל־פְּנֵי תְהוֹם וְרוּחַ אֱלֹהִים מְרַחֶפֶת
ג עַל־פְּנֵי הַמָּיִם: וַיֹּאמֶר אֱלֹהִים יְהִי אוֹר וַיְהִי־אוֹר: וַיַּרְא אֱלֹהִים
ה אֶת־הָאוֹר כִּי־טוֹב וַיַּבְדֵּל אֱלֹהִים בֵּין הָאוֹר וּבֵין הַחֹשֶׁךְ: וַיִּקְרָא
אֱלֹהִים לָאוֹר יוֹם וְלַחֹשֶׁךְ קָרָא לָיְלָה וַיְהִי־עֶרֶב וַיְהִי־בֹקֶר יוֹם
אֶחָד:

ו וַיֹּאמֶר אֱלֹהִים יְהִי רָקִיעַ בְּתוֹךְ הַמָּיִם וִיהִי מַבְדִּיל בֵּין מַיִם
ז לָמָיִם: וַיַּעַשׂ אֱלֹהִים אֶת־הָרָקִיעַ וַיַּבְדֵּל בֵּין הַמַּיִם אֲשֶׁר
מִתַּחַת לָרָקִיעַ וּבֵין הַמַּיִם אֲשֶׁר מֵעַל לָרָקִיעַ וַיְהִי־כֵן: וַיִּקְרָא
אֱלֹהִים לָרָקִיעַ שָׁמָיִם וַיְהִי־עֶרֶב וַיְהִי־בֹקֶר יוֹם שֵׁנִי:

ט וַיֹּאמֶר אֱלֹהִים יִקָּווּ הַמַּיִם מִתַּחַת הַשָּׁמַיִם אֶל־מָקוֹם אֶחָד
י וְתֵרָאֶה הַיַּבָּשָׁה וַיְהִי־כֵן: וַיִּקְרָא אֱלֹהִים לַיַּבָּשָׁה אֶרֶץ וּלְמִקְוֵה
יא הַמַּיִם קָרָא יַמִּים וַיַּרְא אֱלֹהִים כִּי־טוֹב: וַיֹּאמֶר אֱלֹהִים תַּדְשֵׁא
הָאָרֶץ דֶּשֶׁא עֵשֶׂב מַזְרִיעַ זֶרַע עֵץ פְּרִי עֹשֶׂה פְּרִי לְמִינוֹ אֲשֶׁר
יב זַרְעוֹ־בוֹ עַל־הָאָרֶץ וַיְהִי־כֵן: וַתּוֹצֵא הָאָרֶץ דֶּשֶׁא עֵשֶׂב מַזְרִיעַ
זֶרַע לְמִינֵהוּ וְעֵץ עֹשֶׂה־פְּרִי אֲשֶׁר זַרְעוֹ־בוֹ לְמִינֵהוּ וַיַּרְא אֱלֹהִים
יג כִּי־טוֹב: וַיְהִי־עֶרֶב וַיְהִי־בֹקֶר יוֹם שְׁלִישִׁי:

יד וַיֹּאמֶר אֱלֹהִים יְהִי מְאֹרֹת בִּרְקִיעַ הַשָּׁמַיִם לְהַבְדִּיל בֵּין הַיּוֹם
טו וּבֵין הַלָּיְלָה וְהָיוּ לְאֹתֹת וּלְמוֹעֲדִים וּלְיָמִים וְשָׁנִים: וְהָיוּ
טז לִמְאוֹרֹת בִּרְקִיעַ הַשָּׁמַיִם לְהָאִיר עַל־הָאָרֶץ וַיְהִי־כֵן: וַיַּעַשׂ
אֱלֹהִים אֶת־שְׁנֵי הַמְּאֹרֹת הַגְּדֹלִים אֶת־הַמָּאוֹר הַגָּדֹל לְמֶמְשֶׁלֶת
הַיּוֹם וְאֶת־הַמָּאוֹר הַקָּטֹן לְמֶמְשֶׁלֶת הַלַּיְלָה וְאֵת הַכּוֹכָבִים:
יז וַיִּתֵּן אֹתָם אֱלֹהִים בִּרְקִיעַ הַשָּׁמַיִם לְהָאִיר עַל־הָאָרֶץ: וְלִמְשֹׁל
בַּיּוֹם וּבַלַּיְלָה וּלְהַבְדִּיל בֵּין הָאוֹר וּבֵין הַחֹשֶׁךְ וַיַּרְא אֱלֹהִים
יט כִּי־טוֹב: וַיְהִי־עֶרֶב וַיְהִי־בֹקֶר יוֹם רְבִיעִי:

כ וַיֹּאמֶר אֱלֹהִים יִשְׁרְצוּ הַמַּיִם שֶׁרֶץ נֶפֶשׁ חַיָּה וְעוֹף יְעוֹפֵף עַל־
כא הָאָרֶץ עַל־פְּנֵי רְקִיעַ הַשָּׁמָיִם: וַיִּבְרָא אֱלֹהִים אֶת־הַתַּנִּינִם

א

Under the Shikmona imprint, Korén published nonritual works which also were carefully designed and produced.[8]

One of the earliest sans serif Hebrew types, after Miriam, was Haim, designed by Jan Le Witt (b. 1907) and George Him (b. 1900), both of whom were born in Poland but later worked as partners in England. Inspired by the Roman sans serif of the Bauhaus, Haim appeared in its first version in 1929. Other outstanding Hebrew types have been designed by Zvi Narkiss (b. 1932), a Tel Aviv graphic artist, whose Narkiss Block and Bold have served as successful display letters. Zvi Narkiss has been extremely active in creating new letters for use as book types, by computers, and for Letraset. Another Israeli graphic designer, Asher Oron (b. 1936), in 1968 designed Oron, which integrates well with the Roman Univers, especially its lower case. It has been produced by Letraset, and is being made available by the designer for computer typesetting. The excellent and successful sans serif Hatsvi, which was inspired by basic Hebrew letter shapes rather than modified Roman, was designed by Zvi (Theo) Hausmann, who died before his type was cast, and was completed and produced by Moshe Spitzer at his Jerusalem Typefoundry, which was established in 1942 by Dr. Spitzer with Heinz Van Cleef to manufacture cast types for hand-composition when the supply from Europe was cut off. A Spanish engraver and punchcutter, Alfonso Ayuso, was brought to Jerusalem for a time to cut and cast type for the foundry.

The Artist's Book

Graphic processes other than letterpress printing have given rise to a genre that is no less important than the typographic book to the art of modern Hebrew printing. From 1900, when Ambroise Vollard in Paris began to commission famous artists to illustrate limited deluxe editions of classical and modern literature, the *livre d'artiste* became a significant aspect of the twentieth-century book. Its impact was eventually felt by Jewish publishers, artists, and patrons. The English private press movement of the late nineteenth century also had an indirect bearing on fine Hebrew printing, by way of the movement's influence on fine commercial printing and book design in England and Germany in the 1920s and 1930s. (The sole difference between "fine printing" and "private printing" is that the latter is theoretically not for profit.) Schocken, the Soncino-Gesellschaft, and Berthold sponsored a few fine editions in Hebrew until the rise of the Nazis brought their endeavors to a halt. It cannot be proven that these publishers had the private press of William Morris and his followers or the *livre d'artiste* in mind; their work may simply have grown out of the ambience in the book world of those two decades, when suddenly there were publishers who cared about paper, typography, design, binding, and book illustration as never before, and when societies and journals devoted to fine printing and book collecting flourished.

The major Hebrew text to take the form of the *livre d'artiste* is the Haggadah, the book read at seder table on the eve of Passover. This artist's book also may be viewed as the revival of the medieval illuminated manuscript, rather than as a continuation of the illustrated printed Haggadah. Two of the early Haggadot were woodcut editions, one by Joseph Budko (Vienna and Berlin: Levitt, 1921), a small, modest book whose text was printed in Meruba, and the *Steinhardt Haggadah,* whose text was reproduced lithographically from Franzisca Baruch's hand-lettering, with woodcut illustrations. By the late 1920s, Haggadot became more elegant. In 1927, the dignified *Offenbacher Haggadah,* designed by Max Dorn and printed by Heinrich Cramer in Offenbach, was published by Siegfried Guggenheim; but its Hebrew lettering, by Berthold Wolpe (b. 1905), was limited to only a few pages. Illustrations were by Fritz Kredel (1900–1973). The *Offenbacher Haggadah* was republished in 1957 in New York and Wiesbaden, with a few new illustrations by Kredel, printed by Max Dorn in Offenbach. More than any other Haggadah, this book was influenced by the style of European fine printing that was inspired by the English and then the German private press movements. While neither Kredel nor Wolpe continued to contribute to the fine Hebrew book specifically, both went on to become major book artists, Kredel as an illustrator in the United States, Wolpe as a designer, calligrapher, and book historian in England.

The Prophet Elijah, illustration by Leonard
Baskin for the Passover Haggadah of the
Central Conference of American Rabbis (New
York, 1974).
NYPL, Jewish Division [Ex. no. 131]

An artistic Haggadah was published in 1930 by the British Soncino Press (unrelated to the Italian Renaissance press of the same name), still a leader in high-quality publications. The *Soncino Haggadah* was printed at Curwen Press, known for its fine work. Its illustrations were by Albert Rutherston (1881–1953), the younger brother of the more famous British impressionist Sir William Rothenstein. The large Hebrew fonts had belonged to the Jewish typefounder Willem Cupy in the eighteenth century, and had passed into the possession of Enschedé en Zonen in Haarlem with the name Groote Kanon Hebreeuws (32-point) in 1769. Enschedé hand-composed the Hebrew text for Soncino.

One sees more of the *livre d'artiste* in the *Szyk Haggadah,* which the artist made between 1932 and 1936, published by Beaconsfield Press in London in 1939. Miniaturist Arthur Szyk (1894–1951) wrote all the Hebrew text by hand, which endows a unified aspect to text and illustration in this luxurious book. Engraved by the Sun Engraving Company and printed on vellum, its 125 copies were bound by Sangorski and Sutcliffe in gold-tooled blue morocco. This Haggadah has been offset printed in Israel in different sizes by Massada Press.

Two other major twentieth-century Jewish artists have been involved in making the artist's book Haggadah: Ben Shahn (1898–1969) and Leonard Baskin (b. 1922). Ben Shahn's *Haggadah* was published by Trianon Press in Paris in 1964. It consisted of collotype and hand-stenciled reproductions of Shahn's 1920 watercolors, with new drawings and hand-lettering, lithographed for this edition of 292 copies. The Hebrew text is Meruba. A low-cost reprint of the original was copublished by Trianon and Little, Brown & Company of Boston in 1965. Ben Shahn's *The Alphabet of Creation,* drawn from the Zohar's legend, includes little Hebrew, but is one of the true fine press books of the century, printed by Joseph Blumenthal's Spiral Press (1954); even the Schocken paperback reprint was well done. Shahn's stylized Hebrew and the drawings resemble those of his Haggadah. Baskin's *Haggadah,* less of an artist's book because there was no high-priced limited edition, was also made for the English reader. But the Hebrew text is there, in Monotype's Peninim, the English firm's version of Frank-Ruehl. Because Baskin was responsible for the design, the popularly priced book was produced with high standards. Baskin's *Five Scrolls* (1984) is stylistically similar.

While both Shahn's and Baskin's Haggadot may represent a publisher's edition of an artist's book which took advantage of a "name" artist, two notable *livres d'artiste* were created independently of publishers. Ya'akov Boussidan's *Haggadah* was made between 1971 and 1976. The story of the Exodus had special meaning to this artist, born in Port Said in 1939. Boussidan's major medium of expression is etching, in both black and white and color, and to date, this is his masterpiece. An edition limited to fifty copies on Barcham Green handmade paper was printed in his own studio in London, with the text first written by hand in a script that combines Ashkenazic and Sephardic characteristics, then transferred to the etching plate photographically. Bindings with relief lettering were made by David Collin, in beige cloth or in a combination of white leather and parchment. The iconography of Boussidan's *Haggadah* is both traditional and new: traditionally Sephardic are images from the Bible grouped before the opening of the text; startling is Boussidan's personal vision of haggadic themes in Abstract Expressionist style. The artist also etched three different editions of the *Song of Solomon,* with Hebrew lettering and English printing reproduced lithographically.

While Boussidan's Haggadah is spontaneous in its imagery, the Haggadah by David Moss (b. 1946) was thoroughly researched. The text of each page was analyzed by the calligrapher for its visual, historic, midrashic, and halakic content, with these delineated by various forms of Hebrew script, colored drawings, and papercuts. This Haggadah, a manuscript on vellum completed by Moss in Jerusalem in 1984, bound and tooled in white leather by Yehuda McClaff, was commissioned by Florida collectors Beatrice and Richard Levy. In 1987 a facsimile edition of five hundred copies was printed by Martino Mardersteig's Stamperia Valdonega in Verona, published by Bet Alpha Editions

(Rochester, New York), and called *A Song of David.* Another maker of artist's books is Tel Aviv miniaturist Renée Koppel, known as Métavel, whose tiny manuscripts are of mystical and midrashic writings and paintings.

Calligraphy

Other calligraphers have made positive contributions to the appearance of the twentieth-century Hebrew book. The revival of Hebrew calligraphy as an art form, as opposed to the scribal Hebrew letter with its continuous history, came at least thirty years later than that of its Latin counterpart. The earliest generation of notable Hebrew calligraphers included Berthold Wolpe; Siegmund Forst (b. Vienna, 1904; in the United States since 1939); Yerachmiel Schechter (b. 1900), a teacher of many of Israel's graphic artists at the Bezalel Academy of Art in Jerusalem for more than four decades; and Franzisca Baruch, who in Israel has designed so many inscriptions in stone and other surfaces that each day the entire country sees her lettering, for example, in the title of the newspaper *Haaretz.* Designers trained by Friedlaender and Schechter employ lettering as part of their everyday work, without considering it "calligraphy." But in the masterful writing of Fred Pauker (1927–1985), the Hebrew letter was transformed into pure art. Other outstanding lettering artists in Israel are Noah Ophir, Malla Carl, Elly Gross, Zvi Narkiss, Hella Hartman, and Eli Preis. Representing the younger generation of calligraphers are Sharon Binder, Yitzhak Pludwinski (also a scribe),

and Debra Walk in Jerusalem, and Jonathan Kremer in Philadelphia. In the United States, the most prominent Hebrew calligraphers are Ismar David, who has lived in New York since 1952, and Lili Cassel Wronker. In each American city, and in several in Europe, there are competent Hebrew calligraphers, too numerous to name.

Publishers and Printers

Few individuals in this century have devoted a lifetime to producing fine Hebrew books, either as publishers, printers, or typographers. Among publishers, the outstanding individual was Dr. Moshe Spitzer (1900–1982). After he received his Ph.D. in Indian studies from the University of Kiel, Spitzer worked first for the Berlin Akademie der Wissenschaften, then for Martin Buber. Next he was employed by the Schocken Publishing Company, initially as a reader, then as an editor, and eventually as manager. It was at Schocken in the 1930s that Spitzer acquired a taste for fine typography, composition, and printing, from the German publisher Lambert Schneider and from Max Malte Müller, who headed the composing room of Jakob Hegner, and with whom Spitzer worked in producing Schocken's Hebrew-German edition of the *Haggadah* (1936). Spitzer's style was that of the subdued, clean book design exemplified by the work of Stanley Morison, Jan Tschichold, Hans Mardersteig, and later of Hans Schmoller (1916–1985), who at that time worked for the S.

דברים
לב.ול.ג

דברים
לג.ול.ד

Page opening containing Deuteronomy 33, the blessing of Moses, in the Ḥumash or Pentateuch published by the Soncino-Gesellschaft der Freunde des jüdischen Buches (Berlin, 1929/30–1932/33). The first two lines and the last two lines of the chapter were printed in red ink (in the reproduction they appear lighter than the rest), and served as a message of encouragement to German Jewry on the eve of the Nazis' rise to power. Together they read: "And this is the blessing, wherewith Moses the man of God blessed the children of Israel before his death. / Happy art thou, O Israel, who is like unto thee? A people saved by the Lord, The shield of thy help, And that is the sword of thy excellency! And thine enemies shall dwindle away before thee; And thou shalt tread upon their high places."
NYPL, Jewish Division [Ex. no. 115]

Scholem Printing Company (founded by Siegfried Scholem, father of historian Gershom Scholem). Spitzer designed and produced five Hebrew books for Schocken, among them early liturgical poems, *Reshuyot le-Ḥatan,* in honor of the wedding of Gershom Schocken (Tel Aviv, 1936, during a visit). In 1939 Spitzer left Germany for Jerusalem, where he soon established his own publishing house, Tarshish Books. One hundred and one books came forth from Tarshish, each in its way a masterpiece of design and execution, despite the poor quality of available materials, particularly paper. Spitzer brought out the best in compositors and printers, who had never before known that there *were* standards of fine printing, and that there was aesthetic value in closely set type. Until 1949 Spitzer also had his own Tarshish typesetting workshop, where a variety of available types were used (among them Drugulin, Schelter-Giesecke, Meruba, and Frank-Ruehl). He relied on many printers, among them Monson, Goldberg, K. Wallach, Weiss, Jerusalem, and Central (of the Ben Zvi family, later to merge with Academic Press to become Ben Zvi Printing Enterprises Ltd.).[9] Many of Spitzer's editions were illustrated by Israel's outstanding artists: Avigdor Arikha, Leopold Krakauer, Tamara Rikman, Jacob Pins, Yigal Tumarkin, and many others. From 1945 to 1960, Spitzer also served as publisher for the Bialik Institute and was director of the publishing department of the World Zionist Organization/Jewish Agency. These bodies, as publishers, continued the high standards of design

Title page of Samuel Joseph Agnon's Maʿaseh Rabi Gadiʾel ha-Tinok *(Tale of the Baby Rabbi Gadiel), issued as a keepsake by the Soncino-Gesellschaft der Freunde des jüdischen Buches (Berlin, 1925).*
NYPL, Jewish Division [Ex. no. 91]

set by Spitzer when special editions were—and still are—issued. Fred Pauker's 1982 *Midrash Yerushalem* is a recent example of the WZO's continuing interest in artistic books. When asked (in 1977) if fine printing existed in Israel, Spitzer's answer was, "No, there is no 'fine' printing, only decent printing."

The person most responsible for good printing active in Israel today is Gideon Stern (b. 1918). Born in Aachen, Stern became interested in the art of the book at age fifteen. Knowing that a university education would be impossible for him in Nazi Germany, he decided upon a printing career, and apprenticed at the S. Scholem Printing Company in Berlin. An early design was for the cover and title page of a bilingual edition of Rachel's *Poems,* printed there by Hans Schmoller. As a Zionist, Stern took a special interest in Hebrew typography, and finally came to Palestine in 1938. He taught at the Hadassah Apprentice School of Printing, and for many years directed the Printing Information Center of the Israel Export Institute; more recently he has been in charge of printing for the publishing department of the Israel Academy of Sciences and Humanities. Like Friedlaender, he has been an adviser to those who are serious about the quality of Hebrew printing.

Jewish bibliophile societies have played a minor role in fine Hebrew printing. From 1924 to 1933, the Soncino-Gesellschaft der Freunde des jüdischen Buches in Berlin issued books, pamphlets, and a journal/

yearbook devoted to Jewish literature and criticism, executed by the best printers of the time. Of some seventy-five publications of the most important Jewish authors and scholars in Europe, nearly all were works in German; seldom did they commission all-Hebrew books. An exception was their Pentateuch (1929/30–1932/33), printed on specially watermarked Van Gelder paper by the Officina Serpentis of E. W. Tieffenbach, with Ashkenazic types designed by Marcus Behmer (1879–1958) that were never used again. Six copies were printed on parchment for special patrons, such as Hermann Meyer, founder of the Soncino-Gesellschaft, and Salman Schocken. A small Hebrew keepsake was made of a story by S. J. Agnon, *Tale of the Baby Rabbi Gadiel* (1925).[10] Similarly, the publications of the Society of Jewish Bibliophiles in Cincinnati (1961 to 1983) exhibited high production standards, but nearly all of the texts were in English, albeit on Jewish subjects. The Israel Bibliophile Society (Yedidei HaSefer), established in Jerusalem in 1979, has the advantage of a Hebrew readership, but its Hebrew-English newsletter (designed by Ariel Vardi, with logo by Fred Pauker) is computer-composed, and the three-column layout, which leads to wide spaces between words, does not do justice to Henri Friedlaender's Hadassah type. The issue which featured the work of Eliyahu Korén unfortunately had to be computer-composed in a Korén imitation, Keter.

The Hebrew private press is still in its infancy, not from lack of interest but from scarcity of metal types for hand-composition. Meruba and Frank-Ruehl seem to be the only fonts available from dealers. Erich and Lili Wronker of Jamaica, New York, operate Ron Press, and occasionally print in Hebrew. Their Hebrew types are the ones originally cast for Ismar David's *Liber Librorum* contribution. David Wishart of Birmingham, England, recently established Hayloft Press and has devoted time to printing contemporary Hebrew poetry. In Detroit, Lynne Avadenka, an accomplished printmaker and letterpress printer, has been creating artist's books which combine Hebrew calligraphy, the printed letter, and art. She cuts templates for letters of her own design, uses wooden Hebrew types, and has recently acquired metal Hebrew type. The books published by Pardes Rimonim, while printed on fine paper, are neither hand-composed nor hand-printed. In the 1960s, Henri Friedlaender produced several fine limited editions in Hebrew at the Hadassah Apprentice School of Printing, among them *Thirteen Poems* by Stefan George, translated by A. Pressman; *Eshet Ḥayil* with an English translation; Solomon Maimon's *Foreword to Moreh Nevukhim*; and M. Claudius' *An Meinen Sohn Johannes,* translated by Dov Sdan.

Facsimiles

One aspect of fine Hebrew publishing is facsimile editions. Until recently, Haggadot, always popular gift books, were the major category of medieval manuscripts to be reproduced by collotype, and now by the newer laser color-printing methods. (The *Leipzig Maḥzor* and the *Kaufmann Mishneh Torah* were no more than color albums of selected pages.) The Bodleian Library's *Kennicott Bible,* a milestone in the facsimile field, was published by Facsimile Editions Ltd. of London (1985); the Israel Museum's *Rothschild Miscellany* will be the next to appear under this imprint. Cyelar Publishing Co. Ltd. produced the *Worms Maḥzor* of the Jewish National and University Library in 1985. The *Darmstadt Haggadah* has been reproduced twice, in 1927–28 and 1971–72; the *Sarajevo Haggadah,* three times (1898, 1963, 1984). "Facsimiles" include works of varying quality, each intended for a specific market; two manuscripts in the British Library exemplify the range in techniques of reproduction, quality, and price—the Sephardic *Golden Haggadah,* Add. Ms. 27210 (1970), and the *Ashkenazi Haggadah,* Add. Ms. 14762 (1985).

WHICH are the most beautiful Hebrew books of the twentieth century? The vellum edition of the Soncino-Gesellschaft's Pentateuch; the *Korén Bible*; the *Szyk Haggadah*;

על הרוחות

ריחיים נאה מאבני גזיה מרובעות, חמישים רגל קומת הבנין, ושלח
מכונה וכלים ואומן אנגלי בקי באותה מלאכה· באו הכלים ליפו
והעלום לירושלים, כל חלק וחלק לעצמו, וארבעה חמשה סבלים טענו
אותם מחמת כבדם, וארבעה חדשים נתעסקו בהבאתם· נבנו הריחיים
ונילנלה הרוח ארבעה זוגות אבנים גדולות· טחנו ועשו קמח· ראו
הערביים ונתקנאו· שכרו זקן אחד לקלל את הריחיים· נתן עיניו
בריחיים ואמר, אני ערב לכם שכשיבואו הגשמים ויבואו הרוחות
יעשו מהן תל עולם· באו הרוחות ובאו הגשמים ולא עשו להן כלום·
ראה הזקן ואמר, מעשה שדים כאן ואין בידי ילוד אשה לעקרו· ואף
הדרווישים הגדולים הסכימו עמו· לא היו שנים מועטות עד שנתקלקלו
שנים שלושה כלים, ולא היה אדם בירושלים לתקנם· כתבו למנטיפיורי
ולא נענה לחם, שכבר נבנו בירושלים ריחיים של קיטור שאינם תלויים
ברוחות· נשתייר אותו בית הריחיים בטל והיה טוחן רוח· אמר בלק
אשכב כאן עד למחר ואנוח קצת מעמלי·

(ב)

נכנס בלק והניח עצמו לישון· שכב במקום שכב כשהרוח מתגלגלת
והולכת וקוראת, דא וילנא דא וילנא, כדרך הרוח המתגלגלת בריחיים
ונדמה שקוראת וילנא וילנא· אמר בלק מה מה שמקשקשת לוילנא
לוילנא, והרי אני מכולל אונגרין· ומיד נהג חשיבות יתירה בעצמו
כאילו היה מקבל חלוקה אונגרית·

היתה שם לילית אחת זקנה, שהכירה את העולם וידעה כל מה שנעשה
תחת כל קורת בית ותחת כל גג· הקישה בכנפיה השחורות ואמרה לו,
אי אתה בלק שכל העולם מתקנא בך בשביל שאתה סמוך על שולחנו של
אותו פרוסי· ואף שריכרד וגגר בעל בית השכר מווירטמברג היה קראה
לו פרוסי, כדרך הערביים שבירושלים שקורין פרוסי לכל גוי גרמני, אמר
לה אני הוא· אמרה לו אפשר שולחנך חסר כלום שבאת לכאן? נתאנח
בלק ואמר לה, שולחני אינו חסר כלום, אבל אני חסר הרבה· אמרה לו
חוט שמיני של ציציותיו ויש שחסר לב בשביל ארבע כנפות, יש שחסר
מה אתה חסר? הביט בלק לכל צדדיו אם אין שומע ביניהם· לחש ואמר,

65

Samuel Joseph Agnon's Kelev Ḥutsot *(A
Stray Dog), designed by Moshe Spitzer, set
in David upright and oblique, with illustrations by Avigdor Arikha (Jerusalem, 1960).
NYPL, Jewish Division [Ex. no. 92]*

Ze'ev Raban's *Megillah*; many of the books Moshe Spitzer designed for Schocken, the Bialik Institute, and his own Tarshish Books, especially Agnon's *Kelev Ḥutsot* (*A Stray Dog*; 1960), with illustrations by Arikha; the Boussidan and Moss Haggadot; a small gem, *Melekhet HaSefer* (*The Making of Books*), printed in 1962 by the Hadassah Apprentice School of Printing under Friedlaender's direction; the aforementioned limited editions Friedlaender produced; the miniature books of Métavel and the original of her *Haggadah of the Angels,* which was reproduced by Schocken (Tel Aviv, 1986); *Krapp's Last Tape* by Samuel Beckett, the last book designed by Dr. Moshe Spitzer for the Bialik Institute, on paper made by hand at the "Uncle Bob Leslie" Paper Mill in Beersheba; and Jonathan Kremer's *Eikhah* (*Lamentations*), a handwritten, letterpress-printed, limited edition (1985).

The typographic Hebrew book appears to some eyes to be colorless, alongside medieval manuscripts. But one must bear in mind that the aesthetics of twentieth-century bookmaking are different from those of the medieval codex. Good printing in this age is clean and invisible, for the printed word must never interfere with the idea that the writer communicates to the reader.

Notes

1 My thanks to Henri Friedlaender and Gideon Stern for providing me with German typefoundry catalogs from the 1930s, and for reading this essay and improving it.

2 Rafael Frank, *Über hebräische Typen und Schriftarten* (Berlin, 1926). This was a publication of the Soncino-Gesellschaft.

3 H. Berthold, Messinglinienfabrik und Schriftgiesserei, A.-G., Berlin, *Berthold. Shriftgiseray un Mesingliniye Fabrikn . . .* (Berlin, 1924). Ruehl was the Leipzig foundry which issued the first type specimen in 1910. Berthold acquired the C. F. Ruehl foundry in 1918, according to John Lane of Reading, England.

4 György Haiman, *Nicholas Kis: A Hungarian Punch-Cutter and Printer, 1650–1702* (Budapest, 1983).

5 Henri Friedlaender, "The Making of Hadassah Hebrew." This article first appeared in German in brochure form as part of a series on book design published in Hamburg in 1967 by Kurt Christians and Richard von Sichowsky for the Bund Deutscher Buchkünstler. It was reprinted in German in 1972 in *Israel-Forum* and appeared in English as a Typophiles Keepsake in 1975, designed by Friedlaender. It was translated into Hebrew for *Ot Hi Le'Olam* (Jerusalem, 1981), pp. 67–89.

6 Gideon Stern and Henri Friedlaender, "People of the Book: Franzisca Baruch," *Israel Bibliophiles Newsletter* 4 (1984): 1–4.

7 The first book to be set in Intertype's David was S. J. Agnon's *Kelev Ḥutsot* (*A Stray Dog*), published by Tarshish Books (Jerusalem, 1960). For *Liber Librorum,* Ismar David supervised the making of the font for hand-typesetting on a Thompson caster, then wrote out a "composition by numbers" to enable Clark & Way to set the Hebrew types. My thanks to Ismar David for this information.

8 Leila Avrin, "People of the Book: Eliyahu Korén," *Israel Bibliophiles Newsletter* 6 (1986): 1–5. Henri Friedlaender calls Korén type "a masterly corrected, invigorated version of the 'modern face' style Hebrew, with clever and daring innovations."

9 Israel Soifer, "The Pioneer Work of Dr. Maurice Spitzer," *Penrose Annual* 63 (1970): 127–142, reprinted in the exhibition catalog *Dr. Moshe Spitzer: Books–Typography–Design* (Jerusalem, 1981), pp. 11–18.

10 A bibliography of the Soncino-Gesellschaft's publications can be found in Abraham Horodisch, "Ein Abenteuer im Geist; die Soncino-Gesellschaft der Freunde des jüdischen Buches," in *Bibliotheca Docet, Festgabe für Carl Wehmer* (Amsterdam, 1963), pp. 186–210, and in "Soncino-Gesellschaft der Freunde des jüdischen Buches, Berlin," in Deutschen Bücherei, Leipzig, *Deutsche Bibliophilie in drei Jahrzehnten* (Leipzig, 1931), pp. 199–210.

II ROBERT SINGERMAN

Between Western Culture and Jewish Tradition: Translations to and from Hebrew

THE CREATIVE role played by the translator in the stimulation and dissemination of ideas is frequently overlooked and seldom acknowledged. Yet, without the services of this unsung cultural intermediary, there would be little or no cross-fertilization across the linguistic barriers that divide nations and alien cultures. The impact of this reciprocal and inherently nourishing tradition of translation on Jewish literature is powerful. It begins in the third century B.C.E., when seventy legendary Palestinian Jews, working independently of one another in separate rooms, produced the seventy identical Greek translations of the Hebrew Bible known as the Septuagint, and continues today in the consistently popular works by such Israeli novelists and poets as Amos Oz, Aharon Appelfeld, A. B. Yehoshua, or Yehuda Amichai which are widely read in English, French, and German translations outside of Israel.

The essayist Zvi Woislawski characterizes translation within the Jewish tradition as having required a "tremendous effort on the part of the nation." He regards it as one of the most effective tactics in the struggle for the continuation of Jewish existence in every age. He continues:

For the world at large the Jew was a source of wonder, a living puzzle in the huge arena of nations, languages and cultures, struggling and fighting among themselves while the Jew was trying to reveal himself, to find a solution to his own riddle. He could never be successful for more than a short while at a time because every new current in the sea of nations caused the emergence of new classes and cultures which, in their turn, stumbled upon the puzzling existence of the Jews: so that each time, we had to start anew the job of translation, giving a new account of ourselves; of our views about the world, about God and man; and in the infrequent moments of calm, of respite from the hard labour of self-interpretation, the children of Israel proceeded to translate the worlds of foreign culture to themselves for their own needs.[1]

Throughout its long and often tortuous history, life in the Jewish diaspora necessitated linguistic accommodations on the part of Jews to their host culture. In Hellenistic times, numerous Jews in Palestine and Egypt adopted Greek. The philosopher Philo and the historian Josephus, for instance, wrote extensively in that language. Rabbinical literature, paradoxically, preserves and incorporates hundreds of Greek

words while at the same time abusing the Jewish assimilationists: "Cursed be a man who rears pigs and cursed be a man who teaches his son Greek wisdom" (Talmud, *Sotah* 49b). Jews living in the Moslem orbit were under the linguistic domination of Arabic, a richly endowed sister language to Hebrew that the illustrious Jewish sages of the Spanish Golden Age (e.g., Solomon Ibn Gabirol, Baḥya ibn Pakuda, Moses Maimonides) employed for their legal, philosophical, and ethical compositions. Even the major grammars of Hebrew by Judah ben David Ḥayyuj (tenth century) and Jonah ibn Janaḥ (990–ca. 1050) were originally composed in vernacular Arabic. It is difficult to doubt the overpowering gravitational pull of Arabic on Jews under Islamic domination in Spain, North Africa, and the Middle East when it is believed that Joseph Ibn Abitur of Spain translated the Talmud into Arabic in the tenth century because Aramaic had lost its 1,200-year status as an international language.[2]

This is not to suggest that Hebrew was ever a dead language. Its everyday liturgical use in the synagogue for prayer and lamentation continued, as did its use for secular and religious poetry. It was widely employed in biblical and talmudic com-

mentaries, communal records, legal
documents, wills, and letters. It may
be said, however, of Jewish bi-
lingualism that Arabic was used primarily for philosophy and belles-
lettres and Hebrew for poetry and religion. "Arabic was the language of
their minds, but Hebrew that of
their hearts."[3]

Throughout the period between
the eleventh and fifteenth centuries,
Jewish translators played a preemi-
nent role in the recovery and transmission of Greek philosophical and
scientific literature from the Arabic
East to the Latin West. Although the
major responsibility for the great intellectual movement of the period in
medicine, mathematics, astronomy
and astrology, and speculative
thought in the form of logic or metaphysics belongs to the Arabs, the
Jews formed a vital link in the process of collaborative transmission to
Europe because of their knowledge of
both Arabic and Spanish and their
long tradition of learning and scholarship. One example, by no means
uncommon, is the translation into
Castilian, in 1256, by Judah ben
Moses ha-Kohen, under the pa-
tronage of King Alfonso X ("El
Sabio"), of Abū al-Ḥasan ʿAlī Ibn
Abī al-Rijāl's astrological treatise,
Kitāb al-bāri ʿfī aḥkām al-nujūm, under
the title *Libro conplido en los iudizios de
las estrellas.* This text was shortly
thereafter translated into Latin (*Liber
in iudiciis astrorum*) by Aegidius de
Thebaldis of Parma and Petrus de
Regio and printed for the first time
in Venice in 1485. Astrology was
shared by the Arabs, Jews, and
Christians as an example of a "common Mediterranean culture." This
text is also known in a Hebrew version and forms yet another link in
the chain of transmission.[4]

This surge of translating activity
cannot be fully appreciated without
further exploration of the collaborative work between Jews and Christians. Moses of Arragel's *Bible of
Alba,* completed in 1430 and deservedly famous for its miniature illuminations, was a commissioned
Castilian translation of the Hebrew
Scriptures. Actually it was the result
of a working partnership between
Rabbi Arragel and Franciscan monks,
the latter adding traditional Christian
exegesis to the former's rabbinic and
midrashic commentaries. Abraham
bar Ḥiyya of Barcelona (d. 1136) assisted Plato of Tivoli in the latter's
translations into Latin of Islamic
writings on geometry, astronomy,
and astrology. Significantly, Plato of
Tivoli also translated Abraham bar
Ḥiyya's *Ḥibbur ha-meshiḥah veha-
tishboret* into Latin in 1145, and this
Liber Embadorum was later consulted
by the mathematician Leonardo
Fibonacci, whose integration of
Greek and Islamic geometry, algebra,
and trigonometry was a "stepping
stone to help lay the basis of the new
European mathematical science."[5]

Not unlike Alfonso X, his learned
Spanish contemporary, Frederick II,
the Holy Roman Emperor and King
of Sicily and Apulia, sponsored Michael Scot's translations from Arabic
to Latin. Active in Toledo as a translator of several of Aristotle's works,
which survived only in Arabic ver-

sions, along with the Arabic commentaries by Averroës, Scot (1175–1234) came to Naples to serve Frederick II as his court astrologer, translator, and sometime alchemist. Together with Jacob Anatoli (1194–1256), a Jewish scholar and physician from Marseilles also in Frederick's employ, Scot may have prepared a very early Latin version of Maimonides' *Moreh Nevukhim* (*Guide to the Perplexed*), a thirteenth-century manuscript now held by the University of Paris. This tantalizing hypothesis, though unproven and challenged, enhances the collaborative aspects of Scot and Anatoli's friendship, characterized by one scholar as "one of the most significant in the history of medieval thought."[6]

Significantly, relatively few original scientific works were written in Hebrew during the twelfth to fifteenth centuries as Judeo-Arabic scholarly activity concentrated on translations of Greek intellectual landmarks (Ptolemy, Plato, Aristotle, Hippocrates, Galen, et al.) at the expense of fresh compositions. As noted by George Sarton, "A large part, we might almost say the largest part, of the intellectual energy in medieval times was spent not in the creation of new intellectual values but in the transmission of older ones."[7] Thus, the fact that the largest number of extant manuscripts (more than fifty) for a Hebrew translation of any book during the Middle Ages is for Averroës' *Middle Commentary* on Aristotle's *Isagoge* offers "confirmation . . . that the works of Averroës, although written in Arabic, found

Kol Melekhet Higayon (*All the Craft of Logic*), *paraphrase of Aristotle's* Organon *by Averroës (Ibn Rushd), the twelfth-century Islamic philosopher who was a contemporary of Maimonides (Riva di Trento, 1559).* NYPL, Jewish Division [Ex. no. 96]

their warmest reception among the Jews." In characterizing Jacob Anatoli's translation of Averroës' *Middle Commentary,* it may be noted that his is an excellent literal and precise translation from the Arabic, preserving even the order and syntax of the original with only occasional misrenderings and inconsistencies.[8]

Some Hebrew translations from Arabic, as in Averroës' *Long Commentary* to Aristotle's *Physics,* are so literal that a word-for-word correspondence can be detected, making it possible even to identify the precise Greek to Arabic translation used by Averroës or, in other instances, to clarify "doubtful or erroneous passages in the underlying Arabic text."[9] Similarly, Arabists have profitably consulted Hebrew translations as in the case of Shem Tob ibn Falaquera's *Reshit ḥokhmah,* a "judaized" text incorporating complete and literal translations of Alfarabi's *Iḥṣā' al-'ulūm* (*Classification of Sciences*) and his *Taḥṣīl al-sa'ādah* (*The Attainment of Happiness*). In the latter instance, Falaquera's Hebrew text predates the oldest extant Arabic manuscript and has been successfully used to establish a critical and authoritative Arabic text.[10]

The Hebrew "translation language" of this time, which used Arabic loan-translations extensively and closely adhered to Arabic semantic patterns and sentence structure, a characteristic even of original Hebrew compositions of the period, is often referred to as "Tibbonian" Hebrew in recognition of the influential Ibn Tibbon family in Provence. Led by Judah ben Saul ibn Tibbon, his son Samuel, Jacob Anatoli (Samuel ben Judah ibn Tibbon's son-in-law), and Jacob ben Machir ibn Tibbon, they produced exact translations of philosophical and grammatical works over five generations. In coining a Hebrew philosophical terminology, the translators were known, however, to misappropriate a Hebrew root whose precise meaning differed from that of the related Arabic root.

Few would deny that the most famous translation of a Jewish work in the medieval period is of Maimonides' *Guide to the Perplexed,* which was composed in Arabic. The Hebrew translation by Samuel ibn Tibbon (ca. 1150–1230) benefitted enormously from an ongoing technical consultation with the author even before Maimonides completed his work. As the author of *Ma'amar yikavu ha-mayim,* Samuel ibn Tibbon is described by Georges Vajda as "no more than [of] mediocre importance," yet as a translator his reputation is secure.[11] Equally fascinating is the astronomer Jacob ben Machir ibn Tibbon's translation of Euclid's *Elements* (ca. 1255), undertaken, in part, to defend the Jews against Christian allegations that the Jews were ignorant of scientific studies.[12]

Other representative and deservedly famous translations include Avicenna's *Kanon;* the printed Hebrew edition of this classic (Naples, 1491) is the largest Hebrew incunabulum and the first medical book printed in Hebrew.[13] In the realm of speculative thought, one can justifiably point to the fifteenth-century court physician and chief

rabbi of Castile, Meir ben Solomon Alguadez, who translated Aristotle's *Ethics* (*Sefer ha-midot*) from the Latin of Boethius into Hebrew (Lemberg, 1877). Best seen as a symbol of the high intellectual attainments of pre-expulsion Spanish Jewry, this relatively unknown scholar-physician-rabbi, despite being burdened with his official duties and service at the king's court,

[made] the work accessible to Jews, who, in practical life, lived up to its principles better than the Greeks, who produced them, or the Christians, who, in the pride of faith and church doctrine, considered themselves above the necessity of conforming to the requirements of morality.[14]

It is also revealing to read al-Ḥarizi's reflections contained in the preface to his translation of Maimonides' Introduction to his *Commentary on the Mishnah,* for in addition to their poetic depiction of translation as a redemptive, even pious act, they also impart the three universal requirements for the translator, which remain true today:

Now, the scholars of all nations agree
That no one may translate a work until
  he know these three:
The essence of the language from whose
  province he will translate
And the essence of the language into
  whose province he will translate
And the essence of the concept whose
  words he is explaining
And with these three strands the rope of
  rhetoric is woven
And this triple stranded twine will not
  quickly break.

And if my heart is empty and bare of the
  Wisdom as an empty vine
And the knowledge too high above me

And to the Three I cometh [sic] not
Then I shall strive with all my might to
  retain the thought and to rebuild the
  edifice,
And this will be an offering on account
  of my errors,
And with only two of the strands will I
  fulfill my task.[15]

Before leaving the medieval period, the judaization of translated texts from the Arabic is worthy of short mention here. At the most basic level, judaization may be no more than the substitution of the word "Torah" or "sefer" for the Islamic scriptural text, the Koran, or the deletion of the Prophet Mohammed's name. This process may be viewed as a cultural defense mechanism or textual form of camouflage whereby the Jewish reader's religious traditions and sensitivities are reinforced. An especially interesting example relates to al-Ghazzali's *Mīzān al-'Amal;* the Hebrew translation of this widely circulated ethical treatise had its Islamic citations from the Koran and hadith literature replaced by biblical and talmudic ones.[16] Another example of linguistic interchange appears in the Hebrew Arthurian Romance, a manuscript dated 1279 and held today by the Vatican Library. In the Hebrew translation, Christological concepts such as "saints" become "kedoshim" (literally, the holy ones) and Christianity's notion of "penance" is judaized into the easily recognizable Hebrew concept of "teshuvah" (repentance). Finally, the

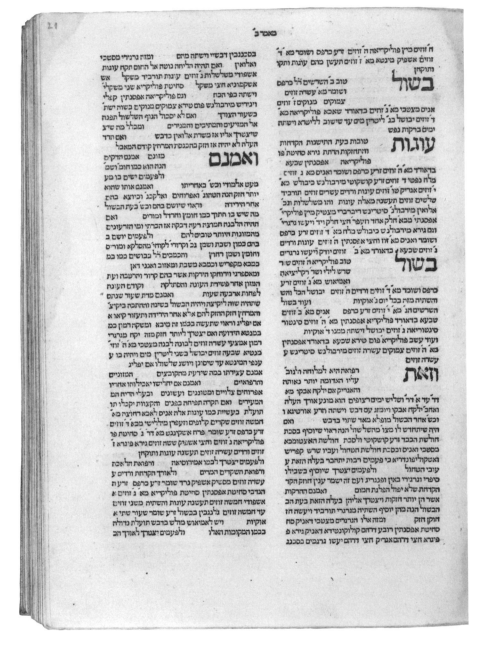

Instructions for various medicinal preparations in the Kanon *of Avicenna (Ibn Sina), printed in Naples by Azriel ben Joseph of Guenzenhausen in 1491. NYPL, Jewish Division [Ex. no. 97]*

Holy Grail, the cup or platter used by Jesus at the Last Supper and the subject of Malory's *Morte d'Arthur,* is transformed in the Hebrew text into *tamḥuy,* in Jewish tradition the plate or dish upon which food was placed for distribution to the poor.[17]

With the expulsion of both the Jews and the Moors from Spain in 1492, the already greatly weakened cultural symbiosis characteristic of the Golden Age collapsed into forced conversions, Inquisitorial fanaticism, and exile. Beginning in the sixteenth century, translating activity from the Hebrew was increasingly carried out by Christian Hebraists and humanists. Some had scholarly objectives, such as the philologists and grammarians Conrad Pellican, the Buxtorfs, or Paul Fagius, while others pursued a keener penetration of Christian theological truths by means of the Hebrew Bible, Jewish antiquities, and the great body of rabbinical literature spanning the Talmud and the medieval Jewish commentators, principally Rashi and David Kimhi. With conversion of the Jews an age-old article of faith for believing Christians, Hebraists and clerics also probed and translated from the Talmud and medieval anti-Christian Jewish texts in search of arguments to harass or intimidate the nation of Israel.

A few noteworthy examples of translations from the Hebrew undertaken for malevolent ends are the publication of Johann Andreas Eisenmenger's *Entdecktes Judenthum* (*Judaism Unmasked;* Koenigsberg, 1711; Frankfurt, 1700, i.e., 1741), Johann Christoph Wagenseil's *Tela ignea Satanae* (*Flaming Arrows of Satan;* Altdorf, 1681), and the tractates of the Mishnah edited with Latin translations by Constantin L'Empereur, the incumbent of a special chair for polemics against Judaism at the University of Leiden. It is not without interest that a great many Christian Hebraists dabbled in the occult sciences, e.g., Kabbalah, gematria, and magic (Pico della Mirandola comes readily to mind), justifying the need for translations of the Zohar and kabbalistic texts, among them the Latin and Hebrew text of the Zohar (*Kabbala denudata*) edited by Christian Knorr von Rosenroth (Sulzbach, 1677–84). Polemics and Kabbalah are effectively joined in the Latin and Hebrew edition of Thomas Aquinas' refutation of paganism, *Summa contra gentiles* (Rome, 1657), translated by Joseph Ciantes but prefaced by a diatribe by Juan Caramuel against the Kabbalah and Judaism as pernicious forms of paganism.

When Jews realized they needed a working knowledge of the New Testament to combat missionary activity, Jacob ben Reuben in the thirteenth century translated parts of the Gospel according to Matthew in his polemical work against Christianity, *Milḥamot ha-Shem,* while in the following century Shem Tob ibn Shaprut included a complete translation of Matthew in his *Even Boḥan.*[18] The proverbial coin, however, has two sides, for Sebastian Münster prepared an edition of Matthew in a Hebrew and Latin translation (*Torat ha-Mashiaḥ;* Basel, 1537), in order to approach the Jews in their own language.

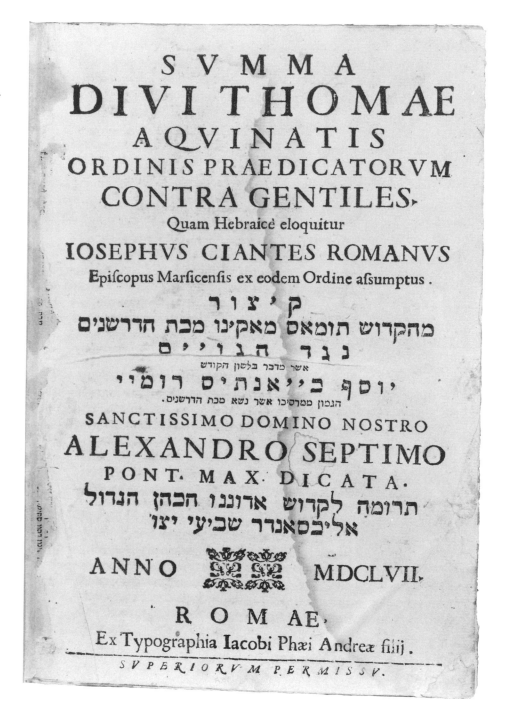

Title page of the Latin and Hebrew edition of Thomas Aquinas' Summa contra gentiles *(Rome, 1657).*
NYPL, Jewish Division [Ex. no. 95]

Italy during the sixteenth century became the center of a considerable amount of translating activity coinciding with the Renaissance. Whereas few Jews in past centuries had achieved any distinction translating Latin texts (Berachiah ha-Nakdan and Hillel ben Samuel are notable exceptions in their fluency in the "language of the Church"), several Italian Jews now excelled. Jacob Mantino translated from Hebrew to Latin medical and philosophical works ranging from Averroës' *De partibus et generatione animalium* (Rome, 1521), an abridgement of Aristotle's *Metaphysics* (Rome, 1521), a paraphrase of Plato's *Republic* (Rome, 1539), and Maimonides' popular *Eight Chapters* (Bologna, 1520). Elijah del Medigo similarly produced Latin translations of the Greek philosophers from texts already translated from the Arabic into Hebrew. Del Medigo's translation of Averroës' compendium of Aristotle's *Meteora* (1488) is "among the first productions of a living Jewish writer to be printed."[19] During the sixteenth century, Jews were also reclaiming their long-ignored apocryphal books from the Church Fathers, as in the translation by Azariah de Rossi (1514–1578), from readily available Latin texts, of the *Letter of Aristeas* into Hebrew (*ha-Ḥibur*), contained in his *Me'or 'Enayim* (Mantua, 1573–75). Although he did not work from the Greek original, it has been claimed that this account of the Septuagint's origins is the first piece of ancient Greek literature rendered into Hebrew.[20]

Christian interest in the so-called Lost Tribes of Israel may partially account for the Oxford, 1691, Latin edition of Abraham Farissol's geography, *Igeret Oreḥot 'Olam,* prepared by Thomas Hyde, a leading English orientalist, under the title *Itinera mundi.* Benjamin of Tudela's twelfth-century narrative of his travels to exotic Jewish communities in Asia enjoyed an early Latin translation in Antwerp, 1575, by the Spanish Hebraist Benito Arias Montano. This travelogue is still highly readable and popular in the frequently reissued English version.

With increased secularization, it was not unknown for learned Jews such as Benedictus de Spinoza to compose scholarly treatises in Latin, or in vernacular languages. A famous example of a vernacular composition is the *Dialoghi d'amore* (Rome, 1535) of Leo Hebraeus (his name also appears in the literature as Judah Abravanel or Leone Ebreo), written in Italian but made available to Hebrew readers only some three hundred years later as *Vikuaḥ 'al ha-ahavah* in David Gordon's Mekitse Nirdamim edition published in Lyck, 1871. Manasseh ben Israel's *The Hope of Israel,* a plea for the readmission of the Jews into England, first appeared in Latin in Amsterdam, 1650, and not originally in Spanish or English as might be assumed. The Hebrew translation (*Mikveh Yisra'el*) was issued in the same city only in 1698. Because of its indirect transmission, *Yeshu'at Yisra'el* (Vienna, 1813), prepared by Samson Bloch from Moses Mendelssohn's German version of *The Hope of Israel,* is an interesting bibliographic example of the circuitous routes that texts may take.

With the rise of the Haskalah (Enlightenment) in Europe at the close of the eighteenth century, we enter the modern period in the development of Hebrew translations as Jews increasingly sought intellectual, educational, and cultural integration into Western society. The secularization of Hebrew was a key element in the Haskalah program, so much so that the "revival of Hebrew" and "revival of the people" are intertwined to the point of being inseparable.[21] To David Franco Mendes, a representative of the Dutch branch of the Enlightenment, Hebrew was not only as useful as other languages, "it rose above the others in its perfection." An accomplished Hebrew poet, Franco Mendes translated Pietro Metastasio's *Betulia Liberata,* an oratorio drawn from the apocryphal book of Judith (*Teshu'at Yisra'el beyede Yehudit;* Rödelheim, 1804), to recapture from the non-Jewish realm this noncanonical telling of the Hanukkah story. Similarly, Naphtali Herz Wessely translated into Hebrew the apocryphal Wisdom of Solomon (*Sapientia Salomonis,* 1780) to reclaim the book's Jewishness, while an Italian Jew, Jacob Saraval, attempted a free-verse translation from English into Hebrew of the libretto of Handel's oratorio *Esther.*[22]

Racine's drama *Esther* enjoyed a paraphrased Hebrew translation by Shlomo Judah Leib Rapoport, *She'erit Yehudah* (*The Remnant of Judah*), published in 1827 in the Hebrew journal *Bikure ha-'itim.*[23] Racine's text was greatly modified by Rapoport in order to stress God's covenant with the Jewish people, doubly interesting because the "translation" indicates

Beginning of the text of the Gospel according to Matthew in Hebrew and in Latin in Sebastian Münster's Basel edition of 1537. NYPL, Rare Books and Manuscripts Division [Ex. no. 168]

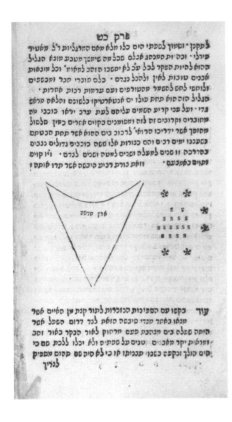

that most Haskalah translators regarded their work as a form of independent creativity. For example, Goethe's *Faust* can hardly be said to be recognizable in Meir Letteris' Hebrew paraphrase, *Ben-Avuyah* (Vienna, 1865), a "betrayal" noteworthy for its hebraization through the deletion of all Christological references and its all-Jewish theme centering around Elisha ben Abuyah, a second-century sage who renounced Judaism. As an example of a seldom-encountered faithfulness to the original among the early nineteenth-century Hebrew translations, one can point to Zvi Ben-David's translation (*Mot Adam;* Prague, 1817) of Friedrich Gottlieb Klopstock's tragedy *Death of Adam,* both a bibliographic rarity and significant for its cultural symbiosis through the introduction of foreign (Christian) elements into a Jewish ambiance.[24]

The rapprochement with the Western classics by Jewish translators, adaptors, and imitators took many shapes and forms. Perhaps the most fascinating example is *Ḥeshbon ha-nefesh* (*The Soul's Reckoning*), by Mendel Levin (Lefin), an ethical treatise first published in Lwow, Galicia, in 1808. Acknowledged as the first Hebrew contact with American literature, Levin's little work contained paraphrased sections of Benjamin Franklin's "Sayings of Poor Richard" and the list of thirteen virtues from Franklin's autobiographical *Art of Virtue.*[25]

Few European Hebraists in the nineteenth century had a command of English, which explains the circumstances surrounding the first complete translation of Shakespeare's

Page of Abraham ben Mordecai Farissol's geography Igeret Oreḥot ʻOlam *in Hebrew (Venice, 1586) with a diagrammatic map of "The New Land" (South America), also showing stars used for navigation and islands which are mentioned in the text.*
NYPL, Jewish Division [Ex. no. 124]

Gemul ʻAtaliah, the Hebrew version of Racine's Athalie *by David Franco Mendes (Amsterdam, 1770).*
NYPL, Jewish Division [Ex. no. 175]

Macbeth into Hebrew (Drohobycz, 1883) from Schiller's German and not from the English original. A few decades later, the Hebrew poet laureate Ḥayyim Naḥman Bialik, not knowing Spanish, translated Cervantes' *Don Quixote* into Hebrew (Odessa, 1912) from readily available Russian and German editions.[26]

In Peretz Smolenskin's preface to Isaac Edward Salkinson's Hebrew translation of *Othello*, entitled *Itiel* (Vienna, 1874), the notion of translation as an act of revenge introduces the first complete Shakespeare play to appear in Hebrew:

Come let us inflict our vengeance this day upon the sons of Albion! They have taken unto themselves our holy writings and done with them as their own, transcribing them into their own tongue, dispersing them into the four corners of the earth. Now we too shall pay them in their own coin, taking unto our own bosom what they deem holy, the theatricals of Shakespeare, transcribing them into the idiom of our holy tongue. Is not this the most sweet manner of revenge? This is a day of triumph to our beloved holy tongue. . . .[27]

Salkinson's later translation of *Romeo and Juliet* (Vienna, 1878) was, to some extent, judaized for a Jewish audience in that the name of Romeo becomes the Hebrew Ram, while Juliet is now Yael. One of the few Hebraists with a mastery of English, Salkinson had previously translated Milton's *Paradise Lost* into Hebrew blank verse (*Va-yegaresh et ha-Adam;* Vienna, 1871). A curious fact is that Salkinson, a very accomplished Hebraist, had long before converted

to Christianity and, not surprisingly, turned his attention to a Hebrew translation of the *New Testament* (Vienna, 1886).[28]

Missionary endeavors to approach the Jews also produced one of the greatest oddities of the translator's craft, a lithographed Hebrew translation of the Church of England's *Book of Common Prayer* (Dublin, 1829), intended for missionary use among the "Christian Israelites" in Smyrna, Turkey. The copyist, Marianne Nevill, explains on the verso of the title page that lest she give offence to the devoted Jewish users of the prayerbook, "I abstained from eating anything forbidden by the Law of Moses, nor did I use any pens but new ones, that had not been used in

Ben-Avuyah, *the reworking of Goethe's* Faust *by Meir (Max) Letteris (Vienna, 1865).*
NYPL, *Jewish Division [Ex. no. 145]*

any other writing" while translating and copying the text.[29]

The nineteenth century saw the first modern Hebrew novel, Abraham Mapu's *Ahavat Tsiyon* (1853). Although an immediate success, with 1,200 copies sold by 1857, this bestseller was outdistanced not by another Hebrew novel but by Kalman Schulmann's Hebrew translation of Eugène Sue's *Mystères de Paris;* 2,000 copies of its first part were sold in 1858 alone. Jewish traditionalists scorned both novels as unwelcome sources of moral corruption.[30] It is entirely likely that the first modern Hebrew novel to appear in English translation was Mapu's *Ahavat Tsiyon,* translated by Frank Jaffe and published in London in 1887 under the title *Amnon: Prince and Peasant, A Romantic Idyll of Judaea.* Although aided by Israel Zangwill, the pioneering Jaffe (and seemingly all contemporary translators, who characteristically confess to enormous feelings of inadequacy when reshaping Hebrew into English) encountered uncommon obstacles, described at some length in his preface (pp. ix–x):

I have had great difficulty in modification and the shaping of sentences, and in many cases was reluctantly compelled to content myself with reproducing the substance of the passage alone. . . . Translations from one language into another generally lose the vigour of the original, but in none more so than in those from the Hebrew. Its highly synthetical qualities make the rendering of it extremely difficult; the parallelism and repetition of Hebrew Poetry and Poetical Prose, would, if literally rendered and slavishly adhered to, sound very uncouth to the general reader.

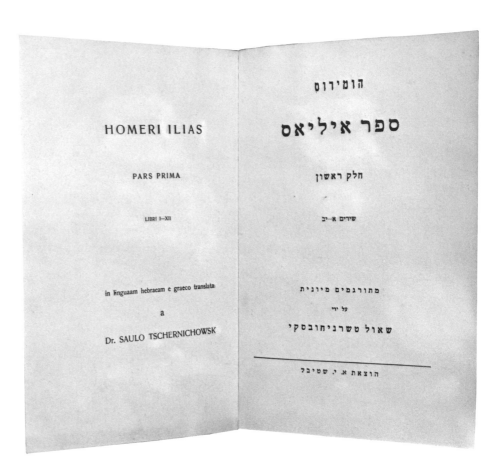

Latin and Hebrew title pages of Saul Tchernichovski's translation of the Iliad, *published in Berlin by Stybel in 1930.*
NYPL, Jewish Division [Ex. no. 134]

Compare this with the apologetic translator's note by Robert Alter, a deservedly famous contemporary critic and essayist, as he attempted an English version of Chapter 1 of Samuel Joseph Agnon's novel *Wayfarer Stopped for a Night* (1940):

Agnon has created a remarkable personal style: he writes in a basically medieval Hebrew that achieves a fine balance between the literally archaic and the simplicity of the language of folklore. This unique style not only endows the most matter-of-fact statements in Agnon with a special charm, but it also means that a body of rich and complex associations and echoes lies behind what is explicitly stated. Such associations must be lost at the outset of any translation, and to avoid the patent absurdities of translating into an archaic English, I have had to abandon most of the poetic effects in the original. The result is inescapably a much flatter, paler Agnon than the real writer.[31]

With the rapid growth of the Zionist movement and the Jewish colonization and repopulation of the Land of Israel both before and after Israeli statehood in 1948, it is not surprising to observe that Hebrew literature is now the repository of an immense body of the world's literature in translation. As is well known, the beginnings of the Jewish national revival were marked by enormous difficulties on all fronts. Ninety years ago, spoken Hebrew was such a novelty that Jewish teachers in Turkish-ruled Palestine were without any suitable plays for children to stage in Hebrew. This very real cultural and linguistic problem was solved by translations, however stilted, from such diverse sources as Schiller's *Wilhelm Tell,* Racine's *Esther,* and Chekov's *The Bear.*[32]

The enterprise of translating American and European literature into Hebrew was for the most part a haphazard one with little or no coordination. Although Mark Twain's *Prince and the Pauper,* a relatively minor work, was translated and published in Warsaw in 1898, translations into Hebrew of *The Adventures of Huckleberry Finn* and *Tom Sawyer* were not published until 1926 and 1911, respectively.

A major endeavor to achieve much-needed coordination of effort was the ambitious and well-financed program of the Stybel publishing house (Warsaw, Berlin, Tel Aviv). Founded in Moscow in the inauspicious year 1917 by Abraham Stybel, a wealthy patron of Hebrew letters, the house published low-priced standard editions of enduring literature by such representative writers as Dostoevsky, Turgenev, and Tolstoy in Hebrew translation. In addition to providing work for translators and aspiring authors in the years between the two world wars, Stybel nourished in an embryonic Hebrew reading public literary standards for character, plot, and realism without which original Hebrew creativity as we now know it would not have flourished.[33]

A great many translators into Hebrew are themselves authors or poets of great distinction. Saul Tchernichovski's translations of the *Iliad* and the *Odyssey,* made directly from the original Greek, are undeniably classics in their own right. Others— among them Joseph Haim Brenner,

Abraham Shlonsky, David Frischmann, A. A. Kabak, Gershon
Schoffmann, Reuven Avinoam, Isaac
Lamdan, Leah Goldberg, Simon
Halkin, and Meir Wieseltier—figure
prominently in any catalog of Hebrew translators who are at the same
time respected as important creative
forces in modern Hebrew literature.
Nahum Sokolov and Zeev Jab-
otinsky, both of whom were Zionists
and accomplished journalists and
men of letters, were active translators. It is not generally known that
Sokolov's translation of Theodor
Herzl's *Altneuland* (*Old-New Land*)
was entitled *Tel-Aviv,* from Ezekiel
3:15, and directly inspired the naming of the new metropolis on the
sand dunes next to Jaffa. Yiddish literature, for example, the works of I.
B. Singer and Sholem Aleichem, also
requires translation into Hebrew as
the European-born settlers in Israel
advance in years and are replaced
by a younger generation, including
settlers from Sephardic and Middle
Eastern backgrounds, born and
nourished in a Hebrew-speaking
environment.

Israeli literature, to be sure, continues to be widely translated for
Western readers, though few ever remember the translator's name (unless
his name is Hillel Halkin, the acknowledged master in the field) and
even fewer Israelis pause to express
their gratitude to the translator of
our exports in the form of Allen

Theodor Herzl's Altneuland (Old-New
Land)*, called* Tel-Aviv *(after Ezekiel 3:15)
in the Hebrew translation of Nahum Sokolow
(Warsaw, 1902).*
NYPL, Jewish Division [Ex. no. 133]

Drury's *Advise and Consent,* Erica
Jong's *Fear of Flying,* the Travis
McGee novels of John D. Mac-
Donald, or such recent blockbusters
as *The Hunt for Red October* by Tom
Clancy.

Jewish consciousness in Western
readers is defined and molded, in
part, by their awareness of and identification with Israeli society and Hebrew culture. The relationship must
also be defined as a reciprocal one in
that the Israelis, highly literate, sophisticated, and surrounded by enemies, have overcome their
geographic and cultural claustropho-
bia in the Arab world by seeking intellectual nourishment through
extensive translations of foreign literature and current affairs. The effects
on the Hebrew literary scene of
world literature in translation are important; for instance, translations of
Soviet authors in the 1920s and 1930s
can be credited with having infused
social realism into the Hebrew novel,
whereas thousands of neologisms in
the rapidly expanding Hebrew linguistic universe can be traced to the
unrelenting creativity of translators
in coining terms and phrases where
none hitherto existed.[34] The great
body of translations to and from Hebrew over the centuries forms a remarkable testament to Jewish
resiliency and adaptiveness in interaction with other cultures and bodes
well for the ability of the Jewish people to continually inform the world
at large of their attainments and distinctive traditions in the family of
nations.

Notes

1 Zvi Woislawski, "The Task of Translation," in *An Anthology of Hebrew Essays,* ed. Israel Cohen and B. Y. Michali, 2 vols. (Tel Aviv, 1966), I:192.

2 Moritz Steinschneider, "An Introduction to the Arabic Literature of the Jews," *Jewish Quarterly Review* 13 (1901): 456.

3 George Sarton, *Introduction to the History of Science,* 3 vols. in 6 (Baltimore, 1927–48; reprinted New York, 1975), II, pt. 1:118. A treasure of valuable data is to be found in the remarkably concise essay by David C. Lindberg, "The Transmission of Greek and Arabic Learning to the West," in *Science in the Middle Ages,* ed. David C. Lindberg (Chicago, 1978), pp. 52–90.

4 Norman Roth, "Jewish Translators at the Court of Alfonso X," *Thought* 60 (1985): 439–455; Norman Daniel, *The Arabs and Mediaeval Europe* (London, 1975), p. 288; Moritz Steinschneider, *Die hebräischen Übersetzungen des Mittelalters und die Juden als Dolmetscher* (Berlin, 1893; reprinted Graz, 1956), pp. 578–580. It should not be overlooked that the Jewish tradition of astrology was widely received among the Christians. See, for example, Lynn Thorndike, "The Latin Translations of the Astrological Tracts of Abraham Avenezra," *Isis* 35 (1944): 293–302.

5 Martin Levey, "The Encyclopedia of Abraham Savasorda: A Departure in Mathematical Methodology," *Isis* 43 (1952): 257.

6 Lynn Thorndike, *Michael Scot* (London, 1965), p. 28; Charles Homer Haskins, *Studies in the History of Mediaeval Science* (New York, 1960), esp. chapters "Science at the Court of the Emperor Frederick II" and "Michael Scot"; Wolfgang Kluxen, "Maimonides and Latin Scholasticism," *Maimonides and Philosophy; Papers Presented at the Sixth Jerusalem Philosophical Encounter, May, 1985,* ed. Shlomo Pines and Yirmiyahu Yovel (Dordrecht, 1986), pp. 224–232; Louis Israel Newman, *Jewish Influence on Christian Reform Movements* (New York, 1925), p. 297.

7 Sarton, *History of Science,* II, pt. 2:709.

8 Averroës, *Commentarium medium in Porphyrii Isagogen et Aristotelis Categorias,* ed. Herbert A. Davidson (Cambridge, Mass., 1969), pp. x–xiii.

9 Steven Harvey, "The Hebrew Translation of Averroës' Proemium to His Long Commentary on Aristotle's Physics," *American Academy for Jewish Research Proceedings* 52 (1985): 59.

10 Muhsin Mahdi, ed. and trans., *Alfarabi's Philosophy of Plato and Aristotle* (New York, 1962), pp. 151–152; Israel Efros, "Palquera's *Reshit ḥokhmah* and Alfarabi's *Iḥṣa al'ulum,*" *Jewish Quarterly Review,* n.s. 25 (1934/35): 227–235; Gad B. Sarfatti, "The Hebrew Translations of Alfarabi's 'Classification of Sciences'" (in Hebrew), *Sefer ha-shanah Bar-Ilan* 9 (1972): 413–422.

11 Regarding "Tibbonian" Hebrew, see William Chomsky, "The Growth of Hebrew during the Middle Ages," in *The Seventy-Fifth Anniversary Volume of the Jewish Quarterly Review,* ed. Abraham A. Neuman and Solomon Zeitlin (Philadelphia, 1967), pp. 121–136, and Gad B. Sarfatti, *Munḥe ha-matematikah be-sifrut ha-mada'it ha-'ivrit shel yeme ha-benayim* (Jerusalem, 1968), pp. 166–214 (English title, *Mathematical Terminology in Hebrew Scientific Literature of the Middle Ages*). In addition to Georges Vajda, "An Analysis of the *Ma'amar yiqqawu ha-Mayim* by Samuel b. Judah Ibn Tibbon," *Journal of Jewish Studies* 10 (1959): 137, three studies are directly relevant to the Ibn Tibbons: Lawrence V. Berman, "Greek into Hebrew: Samuel ben Judah of Marseilles, Fourteenth-Century Philosopher and Translator," in *Jewish Medieval and Renaissance Studies,* ed. Alexander Altmann (Cambridge, Mass., 1967), pp. 289–320; I. Twersky, "Aspects of the Social and Cultural History of Provencal Jewry," in *Jewish Society Through the Ages,* ed. H. H. Ben-Sasson and S. Ettinger (New York, 1971), pp. 184–207; and David Romano, "La Transmission des sciences arabes par les Juifs en Languedoc," in *Juifs et judaïsme de Languedoc* (Toulouse, 1977), pp. 363–386. An overview of translating activity in the Middle Ages and, by extension, attempts at reconciliation with Greek wisdom are provided by Meyer Waxman, *A History of Jewish Literature,* 5 vols. in 6 (New York, 1960), II:201–207 for "Philosophy, Theology and Ethics," and ibid., II:311–314 for "Science." Materia medica is treated by Harry Friedenwald, "Use of the Hebrew Language in Medical Literature," in *The Jews and Medicine,* 2 vols. (Baltimore, 1944; reprinted New York, 1967), I:146–180, esp. pp. 177–180.

12 Charles Singer and Dorothea Singer, "The Jewish Factor in Medieval Thought," in *The Legacy of Israel,* ed. Edwyn R. Bevan and Charles Singer (Oxford, 1927), pp. 233–234.

13 David Wilk, "One Thousandth Anniversary of the Birth of Ibn Sina," *Korot* (Israel Institute of the History of Medicine) 8, nos. 1–2 (June 1981): 91–95 (English section). Avicenna's medical knowledge was dependent in large part on the Greek Galen whose works can be found in over one hundred extant Hebrew manuscripts translated from the Arabic. See Elinor Lieber, "Galen in Hebrew: The Transmission of Galen's Works in the Mediaeval Islamic World," in *Galen: Problems and Prospects,* ed. Vivian Nutton (London, 1981), pp. 167–186.

14 Heinrich Graetz, *History of the Jews,* 6 vols. (Philadelphia, 1891–98), IV:193.

15 "Preface of Alharizi" to *Maimonides' Introduction to the Talmud,* trans. and annotated by Zvi L. Lampel (New York, 1975), p. [21]. In addition, see the widely quoted letter of Maimonides (1199) to Samuel ibn Tibbon with rules for translating from Arabic to Hebrew, in *Masterpieces of Hebrew Literature,* ed. Curt Leviant (New York, 1969), pp. 331–335.

16 Moshe Gottstein, "Translations and Translators in the Middle Ages" (in Hebrew), *Tarbits* 23 (1952): 210–216.

17 Curt Leviant, ed. and trans., *King Artus, A Hebrew Arthurian Romance of 1279* (New York, 1969), pp. 70–72.

18 Judah M. Rosenthal, "Early Hebrew Translations of the Gospels" (in Hebrew), *Tarbits* 32 (1963): 48–66.

19 Cecil Roth, *The Jews in the Renaissance,* Chapter 4, "The Latin Renaissance and the Jewish Translators" (Philadelphia, 1959), p. 74.

20 Shlomo Dykman, "Athens and Jerusalem: Literary Relations between the Jews and the Greeks," *Ariel,* no. 12 (1965): 13; Joanna Weinberg, "Azaria de'Rossi and Septuagint Traditions," *Italia* 5 (1985): 7–35.

21 Moshe Pelli, *The Age of Haskalah: Studies in Hebrew Literature of the Enlightenment in Germany* (Leiden, 1979), pp. 73–90.

22 Jacob Raphael Saraval, "A Hebrew Translation of Handel's Oratorio 'Esther'" (in Hebrew), ed. Moshe Gorali, *Tatslil*, no. 2 (1962): 73–84.

23 Bettina L. Knapp, "Jean Racine's Esther and Two Hebrew Translations of the Drama," in *Salo Wittmayer Baron Jubilee Volume on the Occasion of His Eightieth Birthday,* ed. Saul Lieberman and Arthur Hyman, 3 vols. (New York, 1974), II:591–621.

24 Yehuda Friedlander and Chaim Shoham, "F. G. Klopstock's 'Death of Adam' in a Forgotten Hebrew Translation" (in Hebrew), *Bikoret u-farshanut,* no. 7/8 (1975): 33–40.

25 David Shahar, "The Influence of Benjamin Franklin on the System of Self-Improvement in Menahem Mendel Lapin's 'Ḥeshbon ha-Nefesh'" (in Hebrew), *Tsiyon* 49 (1984): 185–192.

26 H. Chonon Berkowitz, "A Hebrew Version of *Don Quijote,*" *Jewish Forum* 9 (1926): 430–433, 494–498; Ephraim Shmueli, "Why and How Bialik Translated *Don Quixote*" (in Hebrew), *Bitsaron* 27 (October 1952): 45–56.

27 Harai Golomb, " 'Classical' versus 'Contemporary' in Hebrew Translations of Shakespeare's Tragedies," *Poetics Today* 2 (1981): 201.

28 Israel Abrahams, *By-Paths in Hebraic Bookland* (Philadelphia, 1920), pp. 303–310.

29 Joshua Bloch, "An Early Hebrew Translation of the Book of Common Prayer," in *Festschrift für Aron Freimann zum 60. Geburtstage,* ed. Alexander Marx and Hermann Meyer (Berlin, 1935), pp. 145–148.

30 Dan Miron, *A Traveler Disguised: A Study in the Rise of Modern Yiddish Fiction in the Nineteenth Century* (New York, 1973), p. 3.

31 Robert Alter, Translator's Note to *Wayfarer Stopped for a Night,* Chapter 1, by S. J. Agnon, *Mosaic* (Cambridge, Mass.) 2, no. 1 (Winter 1961): 37.

32 Hadassah Shy, "The Hebrew Theater in Palestine before World War 1," in *The Great Transition: The Recovery of the Lost Centers of Modern Hebrew Literature,* ed. Glenda Abramson and Tudor Parfitt (Totowa, N.J., 1985), pp. 150–159 passim.

33 Max Raisin, *Great Jews I Have Known: A Gallery of Portraits* (New York, 1952), pp. 179–189.

34 According to Shlomo Marenof, "Rust'haveli in Hebrew," *Hebrew Abstracts* 13 (1972): 52–54, Boris Gaponov, the translator into Hebrew of Shota Rustaveli's twelfth-century Georgian epic, "A Man Wrapped in a Panther's Skin" (Merḥavyah, 1969), contributed close to a thousand roots and forms, many of them lexicographically accepted, to the Hebrew language. For an appraisal of translations as prerequisites for original Hebrew literature as well as for a viable printing and publishing industry in Palestine, see Zohar Shavit and Yaakov Shavit, "Translated and Original Literature in the Creation of the Literary Center in Erez Israel" (in Hebrew), *ha-Sifrut,* no. 25 (1977): 45–68.

The beginning of the Book of Jonah showing Jonah inside the mouth of a great fish. The marginal note, added in a semi-cursive hand, is a reminder that this is read on the afternoon of Yom Kippur (the Day of Atonement). From the Xanten Bible, Germany, 1294. NYPL, Spencer Collection, Heb. Ms. 1, fol. 189v [Ex. no. 5]

Maimonides' code of law Mishneh Torah (*Germany, 1295–96*), open to the beginning of Book I, the Book of Knowledge, or Fundamentals of the Law. The illustrations are not related to the text, although some are biblical. The one at the bottom of this page shows two knights in combat.
Library of the Hungarian Academy of Sciences, Budapest, Ms. Kaufmann A77/I, fol. 16v [Ex. no. 67]

The Bird's Head Haggadah (southern Germany, ca. 1300), so called because most of the human figures are depicted with bird-like features. Note, too, the Jews' hats. On the left Moses is shown on Mount Sinai with the two tables of the Law. He is then shown passing five tables, for the five books of the Torah, to the children of Israel. On the right the Israelites are shown gathering manna and quail as they fall from heaven (Exodus 16:13–17). Israel Museum, Jerusalem, Ms. 180/57, fols. 23v–24r [Ex. no. 33]

Tripartite Maḥzor *(southern Germany, ca. 1320), Volume III, showing a hymn for the Day of Atonement (Yom Kippur) with an alphabetic acrostic in the right margin. Note the elephant-like creature in the initial word panel.* By permission of the Curators of the Bodleian Library, Oxford, Ms. Michael 619, fol. 130r [Ex. no. 54]

בְּיוֹם כִּפּוּר סְלִיחָה הוֹרֵיתָה
א וּרְמִיחִילָה לְעַם זוּ קָנִיתָ

סְלָחַךְ לַעֲוֹת וּלְחַטָּאֵי עֵרָה
ב עֲשׁוֹר סְמוּכִים מִבֵּית הַוְּעָרָה

מֵרֵי חֲטָאָם בְּאֲנֵי יְשִׁינָה
ג שָׁיֹם אַחַר כִּימֵי שֶׁנָה

וּבְבֵי פִתְחוֹנֵן לִמְחֹל וּסְלֹחַ
ד תַּפְקֵי בִתְשׁוּבָה לִיּוֹצֵר אוֹר וּסְלֹח

חָטָאנוּ יוֹצְרֵנוּ סְלַח לָנוּ יוֹצְרֵנוּ

"Gates of Mercy" from the liturgy for the
Day of Atonement (Yom Kippur) in a four-
teenth-century Maḥzor from Germany.
*NYPL, Jewish Division, **P, fol. 353v [Ex. no.*
59]

King and seer in Meshal ha-Kadmoni *(The Ancient Proverb, based on 1 Samuel 24:14), a collection of fables in rhyme by the thirteenth-century Spanish physician and Hebrew writer Isaac ben Solomon ibn Abi Sahulah. This is one of the earliest manuscripts of the work, copied in southern Germany in 1450. By permission of the Curators of the Bodleian Library, Oxford, Ms. Opp. 154, fols. 44v–45r [Ex. no. 80]*

The First Cincinnati Haggadah *(southern
Germany, ca. 1480–90). The Haggadah
speaks of four sons, one wise, one wicked, one
simple, and one who doesn't know how to
ask, and prescribes the way to tell the story of
Passover to each. For the son who doesn't
know how to ask, the Hebrew states:* At pe-
taḥ lo, *"You open up for him," meaning that
the leader of the seder should start the story
himself. In this illustration, the son wears the
clothes of a medieval jester and the father is
seen actually opening the son's mouth. The father says: "Behold, I throw good words into
the silence."*

Hebrew Union College–Jewish Institute of Religion
Library, Cincinnati, Ohio, Ms. 444, fol. 11v [Ex.
no. 40]

Opening of Ha laḥma ʿanya *(This is the bread of affliction), a paragraph in Aramaic recited at the beginning of the Passover seder. In a Haggadah written by Joel ben Simeon, called Feibush Ashkenazi, probably in Italy, in 1454.*
Courtesy of the Library of the Jewish Theological Seminary of America, New York, Mic. No. 8279, fol.15v [Ex. no. 37]

הא לחמא עניא די אכלו אבהתנא
בארעא דמצרים כל דכפין ייתי

The Washington Haggadah *(probably Northern Italy, 1478). This is the work of Joel ben Simeon, of which a number of examples are known. The Prophet Elijah is viewed as a forerunner of the Messiah and is considered a guest at every Passover seder. A cup of wine is poured for him and is not drunk. At a point in the service the door is opened. Here Elijah is shown arriving on a donkey with the master and mistress of the house and their children seated behind him.*

Library of Congress, Washington, D.C., Hebraic Section, fol. 19v [Ex. no. 39]

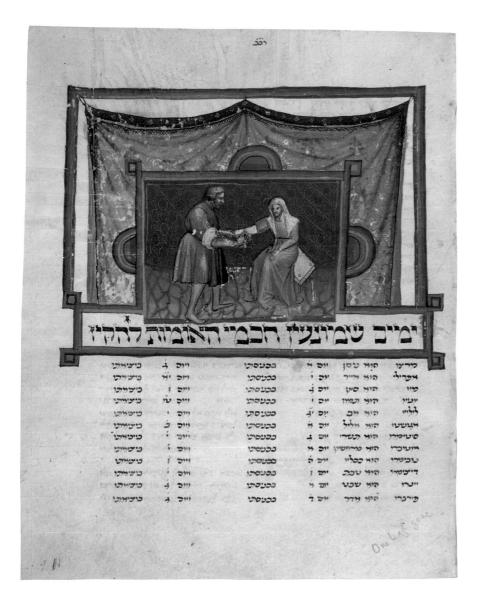

The title of this medical treatise (Italy, fifteenth century) speaks of the days when the gentile sages forbid bloodletting. The illustration shows a physician drawing blood from a woman.

By permission of the Syndics of the Cambridge University Library, Dd. 10.68, fol. 211r [Ex. no. 72]

The Sefer ha-'Ikarim *(Book of Principles)*
of the fifteenth-century Spanish Jewish philoso-
pher Joseph Albo, executed in central Italy, ca.
1460–70. Borders of white vine scrolls were
used in Italy at this time to decorate humanis-
tic books.

Accademia dei Concordi, Rovigo, Ms. Silvestriana
220, fol. 1 [Ex. no. 1]

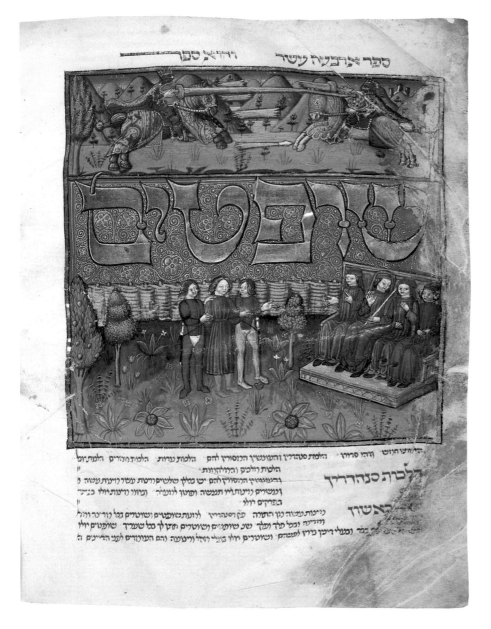

The fourteenth book, called the Book of Judges, of Maimonides' legal code, Mishneh Torah, in a Northern Italian manuscript of the fifteenth century. Gutmann and Metzger have noted that this manuscript complements the Vatican Mishneh Torah (Ms. Ross. 498) and that both are parts of what must originally have been one manuscript. At the top of the page is a jousting scene. Below the initial word Shoftim ("Judges") three men stand before a panel of four judges. Private collection, fol. 298v [Ex. no. 69]

מֶלֶךְ מַלְכֵי הַמְּלָכִים הַקָּבָּה וּגְאָלָם שֶׁנֶּ וַיֹּאפוּ אֶת הַבָּצֵק אֲשֶׁר
הוֹצִיאוּ מִמִּצְרַיִם עֻגוֹת מַצּוֹת כִּי לֹא חָמֵץ כִּי גֹרְשׁוּ מִמִּצְרַיִם וְלֹא
יָכְלוּ לְהִתְמַהְמֵהַּ וְגַם צֵידָה לֹא עָשׂוּ לָהֶם ״

מַצָּה זֶה שֶׁאָנוּ אוֹכְלִים עַל שׁוּם
מָה עַל שׁוּם שֶׁמַּרְרוּ הַמִּצְרִים
אֶת חַיֵּי אֲבוֹתֵינוּ בְּמִצְרַיִם שֶׁנֶּאֱמַר
וַיְמָרְרוּ אֶת חַיֵּיהֶם בַּעֲבוֹדָה קָשָׁה
בְּחוֹמֶר וּבִלְבֵנִים וּבְכָל עֲבוֹדָה בַּשָּׂדֶה אֵת
כָּל עֲבוֹדָתָם אֲשֶׁר עָבְדוּ בָהֶם בְּפָרֶךְ ״

בְּכָל דּוֹר וָדוֹר חַיָּב אָדָם לִרְאוֹת אֶת עַצְמוֹ כְּאִלּוּ הוּא
יָצָא מִמִּצְרַיִם שֶׁנֶּ וְהִגַּדְתָּ לְבִנְךָ בַּיּוֹם הַהוּא לֵאמֹר
בַּעֲבוּר זֶה עָשָׂה יְיָ לִי בְּצֵאתִי מִמִּצְרַיִם וְלֹא אֶת אֲבוֹתֵינוּ גָּאַל
הַקָּבָּה בִּלְבָד אֶלָּא אַף אוֹתָנוּ גָּאַל עִמָּהֶם שֶׁנֶּאֱמַר וְאוֹתָנוּ הוֹצִיא
מִשָּׁם לְמַעַן הָבִיא אוֹתָנוּ לָתֶת לָנוּ אֶת הָאָרֶץ אֲשֶׁר נִשְׁבַּע לַאֲבוֹתֵינוּ ״

לְפִיכָךְ אֲנַחְנוּ חַיָּבִים לְהוֹדוֹת לְהַלֵּל לְשַׁבֵּחַ
לְפָאֵר לְרוֹמֵם לְהַדֵּר לְבָרֵךְ לְעַלֵּה
וּלְקַלֵּס לְמִי שֶׁעָשָׂה נִסִּים לַאֲבוֹתֵינוּ וּ
וְלָנוּ אֶת כָּל הָאוֹתוֹת וְהַמּוֹפְתִים הָאֵלּוּ הוֹצִיאָנוּ מִמִּצְרַיִם מֵעַבְדוּת לְחֵירוּת וּמִיָּגוֹן לְשִׂמְחָה וּמֵאֵבֶל לְיוֹם טוֹב
וּמֵאֲפֵלָה לְאוֹר גָּדוֹל
וְנֹאמַר לְפָנָיו
הַלְלוּ יָהּ

The beginning of Ecclesiastes in the Roths-child Maḥzor (Florence, 1492), with the arms of the Norsa family at top and bottom. The crowned figure at right represents King Solomon, traditionally considered the author of Ecclesiastes. Ecclesiastes is the fourth of the Five Scrolls, and according to most rites it is read in the synagogue on the Sabbath which occurs during the festival of Sukkot (Tabernacles). According to the instructions in this Maḥzor, which follows the Roman Rite, it is to be read on the afternoon of Simḥat Torah (Rejoicing in the Torah), which comes at the end of Sukkot.

Courtesy of the Library of the Jewish Theological Seminary of America, New York, Mic. No. 8892 [Ex. no. 61]

הרואה חכמי ישראל אומר ·

בָּרוּךְ אַתָּה יְיָ אֱמֶּהֿ שֶׁנָתַן מֵחָכְמָתוֹ
לִירֵאָיו :

הרואה מלכי אומות העולם אומר ·

בָּרוּךְ אַתָּה יְיָ אֱמֶּהֿ שֶׁחָלַק מִכְּבוֹדוֹ
לְבָשָׂר וָדָם :

הרואה מקום סנעשו בו נסים לאבותינו אומר ·

בָּרוּךְ אַתָּה יְיָ אֱלֹהֵינוּ מֶּהֿ · שֶׁעָשָׂה
נִסִים לַאֲבוֹתֵינוּ ' בַּמָּקוֹם הַזֶּה ✤

הרואה הקשת אומר :

בָּאֵ אֱמֶּהֿ זוֹכֵר הַבְּרִיתֿ נֶאֱמָן בִּבְרִיתוֹ
וְקַיָם בְּמַאֲמָרוֹ ✤

This illuminated manuscript of blessings to be recited on various occasions, done at Vienna in 1737, is typical of the revival of Hebrew manuscript illumination in the eighteenth century. The illustrations refer to the blessing upon seeing a rainbow and the blessing upon seeing a "King of the gentiles."

Valmadonna Trust Library, London, fols. 12v–13r
[Ex. no. 31]

The first half of Psalm 114 in the Moss Haggadah, A Song of David *(1987). The six hundred figures decorating the Psalm represent the 600,000 Jews believed to have left Egypt in the Exodus. Each head is also a note on a musical staff. The whole, when read from right to left, is a rendition of two Ḥasidic melodies to which the Psalm is sung. The rods in the hands of some of the figures mark the ends of musical bars.*

Collection of Beatrice and Richard D. Levy, fol. 31r (Ex. no. 44)

12 CHAIM POTOK

Text and Texture:
Early Adventures in the Fourth Dimension

I AM SITTING on the bare dark-wood floor in the hallway of our New York apartment: a pale, skinny boy of nine, who, for excitement, races trolley cars along the cobbled streets of his neighborhood and jumps from rooftop to rooftop across the narrow chasms that separate the five-story houses on the block. Propped up on my knees is a Hebrew book, a story about a boy named Chaim Pumpernickel (whose contents I now no longer recall).

It is evening. There are others in the apartment: parents and siblings emitting familiar domestic noises. As the minutes go by, something strange occurs: the book begins gradually to take on the unsubstantiality of air. The words become faint, the paper thins to transparency, the text winks out, the book disappears.

Then I am out of myself and gone from the cold air of the apartment and the bleak winter streets of the neighborhood and the gray despair of the Depression that hangs over our lives like a chilling miasma, and I

דְּקְדּוּק

לְשׁוֹן עֶבְרִית

DICKDOOK LESHON GNEBREET.

A

GRAMMAR

OF THE

Hebrew Tongue,

BEING

An ESSAY

To bring the Hebrew Grammar into English,

to Facilitate the

INSTRUCTION

Of all those who are desirous of acquiring a clear Idea of this

Primitive Tongue

by their own Studies ;

In order to their more distinct Acquaintance with the SACRED ORACLES of the Old Testament, according to the Original. And Published more especially for the Use of the STUDENTS of *HARVARD-COLLEGE* at *Cambridge*, in NEW-ENGLAND.

נֶחְבַּר וְהוּגַּהּ בְּעִיּוּן נִמְרָץ עַל יְדֵי
יְהוּדָה מוֹנִישׁ

Composed and accurately Corrected,

By JUDAH MONIS, M. A.

BOSTON, N.E.

Printed by JONAS GREEN, and are to be Sold by the AUTHOR at his House in *Cambridge.* MDCCXXXV.

The first Hebrew grammar published in America, written by Judah Monis for use at Harvard College (Boston, 1735).
NYPL, Rare Books and Manuscripts Division
[Ex. no. 161]

am inside the world conjured by words that are no longer seen by the naked eye but by the eye of the mind and imagination. I am reading without an awareness of reading. Someone shaped a world out of words and is offering it to me as a gift through the medium of a book that has now vanished. I am enthralled, exhilarated.

I've read books before. (I can't remember a time when I wasn't reading.) But until now there has always been a *weighted presence* of word and book throughout the act of reading. This encounter with a Hebrew book, during which I am in effortless contact with the very heart of the story itself, is my first *pure reading experience*.

When I am done, I close the book and feel the grief of the bereaved: the world of Chaim Pumpernickel is suddenly gone. I am returned to the hallway, dumped back into my drab real world.

In the days that follow, I wonder about what I have experienced. Is this what reading stories is about—this vaulting leap into new worlds? What a spun-gold web of magic and mystery it seems to be! I begin to read in earnest, in Hebrew and English, indiscriminately. For a long time thereafter, my judgment of a writer is contingent upon how swiftly he or she can make the words disappear and catapult me into the time and place of the story.

It is raining. The pelting downpour strikes the tall windows of the classroom, warping and blurring the street. I turn my attention back to the book on my desk.

I am twelve years old. I see the war in the newsreels at our local movie house. Hugely magnified bombs and bodies in grainy, flickering black and white. On occasion I have nightmares about the war. Remote, it nevertheless touches me from time to time and terrifyingly opens to my inner being its hellish maw.

The book we are studying is Genesis, the narrative of the sacrifice of Isaac. A father is commanded by God to slay his son—his beloved only child—as a test of his obedience to God.

I have read this story many times before today—with my father, with teachers in classes—and have followed it twice every year during the Torah readings at Rosh Hashanah and Sabbath services. Until now the words would always easily disappear into a weave of images: the call by God, the journey, the climb up the mountain, the altar, the raised knife, the angel, the ram. But, for some reason (looming adolescence? the frightful war?), this time the words begin to take on resonance and texture. Rather than fading to invisibility, the words have become mountainous, and chasms have opened between them, mysterious spaces that are dark with fearful questions.

I find myself wandering about in the interstices between the words. "God put Abraham to the test. . . ." (What is the story really all about? A test of faith? An argument against

human sacrifice?) "So early next morning. . . ." (Where is Sarah? Does she know? Why no mention of her?) Isaac asks, "Where is the sheep for the burnt offering?" (Does Isaac know? What do father and son talk about on that three-day journey? What did the servants who accompanied them talk about?) I note that the commentator Rashi tells us that Isaac knew where he was being taken, and I ask myself: How did Isaac feel? And I ask myself, further: Why is the narrative so gripping even though none of these questions is answered?

I realize then that there are certain kinds of stories in which the words are not meant to disappear. On the contrary, they lie on the page dense and weighty, at times suddenly luminous as if lit by a flash of lightning—and they yield unforgettable images and shifting kaleidoscopes of meaning and chilling questions to which they offer no hint of a response. I tell myself: Perhaps it's precisely because there is no simple way to understand this narrative that we return to it again and again; perhaps the very mystery of this Hebrew text is much of the reason for its lengthy history.

I now have two kinds of stories to watch out for: the Chaim Pumpernickel kind and the sacrifice of Isaac kind. That's the way I read stories, in Hebrew and English, until my encounter with yet another Hebrew book.

The sacrifice of Isaac in the decoration of an illuminated initial word panel. From a fourteenth-century south German manuscript Maḥzor.

By permission of the Curators of the Bodleian Library, Oxford, Ms. Reggio 1 [Ex. no. 58]

סדר זכרון הנפשות

יזכור ייַ לטובה את נפש רבי פלוני שהלך לחַיֵּי העולם הבא . עם נפש אברהם
יצחק ויעקב אבותינו מן דרהרבי פלוני פיר לו נפש סואו כך לצדקה ואם
היא נקבה יאמר נפש מרת פלונית שהלכה לחַיֵּי העולם הבא עם נפש שרה רב רחל
ולאה אא סורדייה דובדרית בנוחה טובה בגן עדן אי ארבי פלוני אילפמילייה סואה שכר טוב
וחַיִּים טובים אמן :

ובמנחת יום טוב אחרון אומר מה שאו תהלה לדוד ובא לצין וכולי סדראו וקריש עד לעילא וכהפלין הפלה
בלח כסרוד של שחרית ובקריש לילי ימים אחרונים אין אומר שחחינו וגוהגים לקרות מגלת שיר
השירים שחברה שלמה עליו השלום על עיקר גאולה מצרים ושאר הגאולות וכל
השירים קרש ושיר השירים קרש קרשים

השירים אשר לשלמה : יָשָּׁקֵני מנשיקות
פיהו כי טובים דדיך מיין : לריח שמניך
טובים שמן תורק שמך על כן עלמות אהבוך
י מָשכני אחריך נרוצה הביאני המלך חדריו
נגילה ונשמחה בך נזכירה דדיך מיין מישרים
אהבוך : שחורה אני ונאוה בנות ירושלם
כאהלי קדר כיריעות שלמה : אל תראוני
שאני שחרחרת ששזפתני השמש בני אמי
נחרו בי שמני נטרה את הכרמים כרמי שלי
לא נטרתי : הגידה לי שאהבה נפשי איכה
תרעה איכה תרביץ בצהרים שלמה אהיה
כעטיה על עדרי חבריך : אם לא תדעי לך
היפה בנשים צאי לך בעקבי הצאן ורעי את
גדיתיך על משכנות הרעים : לסססתי ברכבי
פרעה דמיתיך רעיתי : נאוו לחייך בתרים

צוארך בחרוזים : תורי זהב נעשה לך עם
נקדות הכסף : עד שהמלך במסבו נרדי
נתן ריחו : צרור המור דודי לי בין שדי ילין :
אשכל הכפר דודי לי בכרמי עין גדי :
הנך יפה רעיתי הנך יפה עיניך יונים : הנך
יפה דודי אף נעים אף ערשנו רעננה :
קרות בתינו ארזים רהיטנו ברותים :
אני חבצלת השרון שושנת העמקים :
כשושנה בין החוחים כן רעיתי בין הבנות :
כתפוח בעצי היער כן דודי בין הבנים בצלו
חמדתי וישבתי ופריו מתוק לחכי : הביאני
אל בית היין ודגלו עלי אהבה : סמכוני
באשישות רפדוני בתפוחים כי חולת אהבה
אני : שמאלו תחת לראשי וימינו תחבקני :
השבעתי אתכם בנות ירושלם בצבאות או

OVER the words of the teacher I hear the rustling of newspapers. I am in my senior year in Yeshiva College. The school authorities have decreed that students of Talmud ought also to be studying Bible. And so each Thursday one hour has been taken from Talmud study and given over to the Bible. For reasons known only to the faculty, the text that has been selected is the Song of Songs.

Most of my classmates are angry at this theft of precious time from Talmud. They manifest their anger by openly reading newspapers in class as the teacher—a mild, mustached Bible scholar in a rumpled gray suit, steel-rimmed spectacles, and a wide-brimmed gray fedora— attempts to cut a path through the text. The noisy pages of the *Post, PM,* the *Times,* the *Herald Tribune* display an open disdain of the harried efforts of the teacher of Song of Songs.

He is teaching the text in the traditional manner: it is a love song between God and His people Israel, written by King Solomon in his lusty youth. How hard he tries to arouse our interest in its bizarre similes! It is all in vain; the air of the classroom is dense with stoney resentment. Clearing his throat, he gazes down at his text. In a suddenly lowered voice, he reads the words, "Your breasts are like two fawns, / Twins of a gazelle, / Browsing among the lilies," and explains them by saying, "This refers to Moses and Aaron." Behind me a newspaper rustles. All around me there is a low buzz of conversation. The classmate to my right yawns audibly and without embarrassment.

Eight months later, I am sitting in a Bible class in the Rabbinical School of the Jewish Theological Seminary of America. We are studying Song of Songs.

The tradition of Solomonic authorship has been briefly explained by our professor, and dismissed. "If Solomon wrote Song of Songs, there is no history of the Hebrew language." He dates the book to the third century B.C.E. (A book of the Bible with a specific date! What a rousing notion that was to me!)

He treats it as a collection of love songs indigenous to the ancient Near East, and reminds us that God is nowhere mentioned in it. He refers to it as a "profane" and "erotic" book, and makes the point that the Hebrew Bible does not look disdainfully upon sexuality in marriage. In close analytic fashion we read the text word for word—as a series of pastoral poems whose syntactic and semantic structures must be clearly understood if the book is to be appreciated as a work of art. "Oh, give me of the kisses of your mouth, / For your love is more delightful than wine. . . . My beloved to me is a bag of myrrh / Lodged between my breasts. . . . Your eyes are like doves / Behind your veil. . . . Your lips are like a crimson thread, / Your mouth is lovely." Week after week, as we study the book, I feel myself enchanted by its allure; it is sensuous, earthy; its similes and metaphors soar with passionate exaggerations, with

heat. There are days in that classroom when I feel myself climbing the spring hills of ancient Israel and thinking that I can actually smell the fragrance of the "vines in the blossom. . . ." I am reading a book of the Bible that pulses with carnal life!

It occurs to me then that orthodoxies will often render a potent text pallid by attenuating it through commentary and allegory. Religion is by and large committed to structure, coherence, community, form, and is therefore understandably fearful of the volcanic forces called to life by the imagination. There is of course imagination in religion: God is everywhere, and Satan will trip you as you enter your home and cause you to tumble into the pit he has dug directly to Hell. But this is a controlled, communal imagination. Indeed, when the religious imagination loses control the result is a special sort of horror: inquisitions, witch burning. But this has not much to do with the passion, the soaring *openness* of the unbridled, mercurial, poetic imagination. I experience a keen sense of the latter precisely because I studied Song of Songs in two such different ways in the course of a single year.

IT IS the early fifties. I have completed my first year at the Jewish Theological Seminary. Sitting alone on a lakeside in a summer camp, I am reading a Hebrew story and feeling the exquisite blaze of my first encounter with a Hebrew writer I have never read before.

The story is *Bilvav Yamim* (*In the Heart of Seas*) by S. J. Agnon. A group of Jews, ten men and their wives, leave their Eastern European town of Buczacz and set out on a phantasmagoric journey to the Land of Israel. The story brings me into a fantasy world that swiftly becomes more real than the grass on which I am sitting and the lake that laps at the shore.

I follow the people on their journey. Inflamed by their passion for the Holy Land, they travel from Galicia in Poland to the Dniester, and then along the Prut and the Danube to the Black Sea and Istanbul. In Istanbul they embark for Jaffa, and from there they proceed on the last leg of their journey and arrive in Jerusalem. Their adventures along the way; the Jews and gentiles they encounter; the man named Chananya, a strange, miraculous figure who lends the story a whimsical and at times a slightly eery quality—the adventures experienced by this group of Jews seem to me a kind of collective quest for meaning and perfection. I am reminded of Huck Finn's journey along the Mississippi, his search for his own inner self, his own vision of the truth.

How intrigued I am by Agnon's style! The pervasive tone of light humor that caresses the story with strokes as gentle as a butterfly's wings and makes the words sing; the folk tales that are woven into the story like iridescent threads. And it is all a carefully wrought artifice. A master hand has manipulated religious motifs, crafting them into a tale possessed of formal and stylistic coherence that adheres to the most

rigorous demands of modern secular literature—and creating thereby a fantasy of astonishing worth and delight.

Secular craft can be brought to bear upon recondite religious material without weakening the craft and demeaning the material! That is one of the most important lessons I learn as I am growing up and teaching myself to write—and I learn it from a Hebrew book.

It was a crucial odyssey for me during my early years—adventurous, fearful, passionate, exhilarating—that odyssey from Chaim Pumpernickel to the sacrifice of Isaac to Song of Songs to the unforgettable image of Chananya in *Bilvav Yamim* traveling over the seas on his handkerchief on his way to Eretz Yisrael.

SHARON LIBERMAN MINTZ

A Selected Bibliography
of the Hebrew Book

Overviews

Assaf, Simcha. *'Am ha-Sefer ve-ha-Sefer.* Safed: Museum of Printing Art, 1964.
An essay on the relationship between Jews and books in the Middle Ages. Examines the sale, purchase, and lending of books, as well as medieval libraries and the theft of books. Summary of text in English.

Bloch, Joshua. "The People and the Book: On the Love, Care, and Use of Books among the Jews." In *Bookmen's Holiday: Notes and Studies Written and Gathered Together in Tribute to Harry Miller Lydenberg.* New York: The New York Public Library, 1943.

Brisman, Shimeon. *A History and Guide to Judaic Bibliography.* Cincinnati: Hebrew Union College Press, 1977.
A guide to the important works of Jewish bibliography, from the work of Johannes Buxtorf (1603) up to 1975.

Cowan, Paul. *A Torah Is Written.* Philadelphia: Jewish Publication Society, 1986.
For youth. Describes the tools and techniques used by Jewish scribes to create a Torah scroll.

Diringer, David. *The Book before Printing: Ancient, Medieval and Oriental.* New York: Dover Publications, 1982. Reprint of a 1953 work published under the title *The Hand Produced Book.*
Focuses on the different ways in which books were made before the beginning of printing. Includes a short chapter on the Dead Sea Scrolls and on Hebrew manuscripts written on parchment.

———. *The Illuminated Book: Its History and Production.* 2d rev. ed. London: Faber and Faber, 1967.
Comprehensive survey of book illustration from ancient times to the sixteenth century. Short chapter on Hebrew book illustration.

Eisenberg, Azriel. *The Book of Books.* New York: The Soncino Press, 1976.
Popular presentation of the Bible. Explanations on the writing of a Torah scroll, the Masorah, and the printed Bible.

Habermann, Abraham Meir. *Ha-Sefer ha-'Ivri be-Hitpathuto.* Jerusalem: Rubin Mass, 1968.
Informative overview which touches briefly on every aspect of the Hebrew book, from ancient scripts to modern typography. Printing is examined century by century.

Mehlman, Israel. "What Makes Antique Hebrew Books So Rare?" *Jewish Book Annual* 39 (1981–82): 7–18.

Posner, Raphael, and Israel Ta-Shema, eds. *The Hebrew Book: An Historical Survey.* Jerusalem: Keter Publishing House, 1975.
General overview of the history of the Hebrew book.

Shunami, Shlomo. *Bibliography of Jewish Bibliographies.* 2d enl. ed. with corrections. Jerusalem: Magnes Press, 1969. Supplement, 1975.
A comprehensive list of Jewish bibliographies, including more than 6,800 entries. The book is arranged topically and contains an index of authors and subjects.

Thompson, James Westfall. *The Medieval Library.* Chicago: University of Chicago Press, 1939.
A chronological study of libraries from the early church period through the Renaissance, concentrating on libraries found in Western Europe. Short chapter on Jewish libraries written by S. K. Padover.

Dead Sea Scrolls

Burrows, Millar. *The Dead Sea Scrolls.* New York: Viking Press, 1955.

———. *More Light on the Dead Sea Scrolls.* New York: Viking Press, 1958.

Cross, F. M. *The Ancient Library of Qumrân.* Rev. ed. Garden City, N.Y.: Doubleday, 1961. Reprint with addendum. Grand Rapids, Mich.: Baker Book House, 1980.

———, and S. Talmon, eds. *Qumrân and the History of the Biblical Text.* Cambridge, Mass.: Harvard University Press, 1975.

Driver, Godfrey Rolles. *The Judean Scrolls: The Problem and a Solution.* New York: Schocken Books, 1965.

Dupont-Sommer, André. *The Essene Writings from Qumrân.* Translated by Géza Vermes. Oxford: Basil Blackwell, 1961.

Fitzmyer, Joseph A. *The Dead Sea Scrolls: Major Publications and Tools for Study.* Missoula, Mont.: Scholars Press for The Society of Biblical Literature, 1975. Reprint with addendum, 1977.

Gaster, Theodor H. *The Dead Sea Scriptures in English Translation.* 3d ed. rev. and enl. Garden City, N.Y.: Anchor Press, 1976.

Habermann, Abraham Meir. *Megilot Midbar Yehudah.* Tel Aviv: Mahbarot le-Sifrut, 1959.

The text of the Judaean desert scrolls is edited with vocalization, introduction, notes, and a concordance. An English translation of the introduction is included.

Jongeling, Bastiaan. *A Classified Bibliography of the Finds in the Desert of Judah 1958–1969.* Leiden: E. J. Brill, 1971.

Koester, C. "A Qumrân Bibliography: 1974–1984." *Biblical Theology Bulletin* 15 (1985): 110–120.

Kutscher, Eduard Yechezkel. *The Language and Linguistic Background of the Isaiah Scroll.* Leiden: E. J. Brill, 1974.

Vaux, Roland de. *Archaeology and the Dead Sea Scrolls.* London: For The British Academy by the Oxford University Press, 1961.

Vermes, Géza. *The Dead Sea Scrolls in English.* 2d ed. New York: Penguin Books, 1975.

———. *The Dead Sea Scrolls: Qumrân in Perspective.* Rev. ed. Philadelphia: Fortress Press, 1981.

———. *Discovery in the Judean Desert.* New York: Desclee Co., 1956.

Yadin, Yigal. *The Temple Scroll: The Hidden Law of the Dead Sea Sect.* New York: Random House, 1985.

Manuscripts and Manuscript Illumination

Avrin, Leila Rachel. "The Illuminations in the Moshe ben-Asher Codex of 895 C.E." Ph.D. dissertation. University of Michigan, 1974.

———. "Micrography as Art." In *Etudes de paléographie hébraïque.* Paris and Jerusalem: Centre National de la Recherche Scientifique and The Israel Museum, 1981.

Beit-Arié, Malachi. *The Only Dated Medieval Hebrew Manuscript Written in England (1189 CE) and the Problem of Pre-Expulsion Anglo-Hebrew Manuscripts.* London: Valmadonna Trust Library, 1985.

———, and Colette Sirat. *Manuscrits médiévaux en caractères hebraïques: portant des indications de date jusqu'à 1540.* 3 vols. in 7. Jerusalem and Paris: National Academy of Sciences, Israel; Centre National de la Recherche Scientifique, Paris, 1972–86.

Detailed descriptions of dated Hebrew medieval manuscripts, arranged chronologically. Text in French and Hebrew.

Bloch, Joshua. *The People and the Book.* New York: The New York Public Library, 1954.

Exhibition catalog of Hebrew illuminated manuscripts and early printed Hebrew books.

Blondheim, D. S. "An Old Portuguese Work on Manuscript Illumination." *Jewish Quarterly Review* 19 (1928): 97–135.
A medieval Portuguese work, written in Hebrew characters, on the art of manuscript illumination.

Cohen, Evelyn M. "The Artist of the Kaufmann Mishneh Torah." In *Proceedings of the Ninth World Congress of Jewish Studies*. Jerusalem: World Union of Jewish Studies, 1986.

Freimann, Aaron. "Jewish Scribes in Medieval Italy." In *Alexander Marx Jubilee Volume*. English section. New York: The Jewish Theological Seminary of America, 1950.

Golb, Norman. *Spertus College of Judaica Yemenite Manuscripts: An Illustrated Catalogue*. Chicago: Spertus College of Judaica Press, 1972.

Goldstein, David. *Hebrew Manuscript Painting*. London and Dover, N.H.: The British Library, 1985.
A presentation of Hebrew illuminated manuscripts found in the British Library. Chiefly illustrations.

Gutmann, Joseph. *Hebrew Manuscript Painting*. New York: George Braziller, 1978.
A study of the art found in medieval Hebrew manuscripts. Contains forty sample pages of illuminated manuscripts.

———. "Thirteen Manuscripts in Search of an Author: Joel Ben Simeon, 15th Century Scribe-Artist." *Studies in Bibliography and Booklore* 9 (1970): 76–95.

———. "When the Kingdom Comes: Messianic Themes in Medieval Jewish Art." *Art Journal* 27, no. 2 (1967–68): 168–174.

———, ed. *No Graven Images: Studies in Art and the Hebrew Bible*. New York: Ktav Publishing House, 1971.
A collection of classic essays on Jewish art, many of which focus on Hebrew illuminated manuscripts.

Haran, Menahem. "Book-Scrolls at the Beginning of the Second Temple Period; the Transition from Papyrus to Skins." *Hebrew Union College Annual* 54 (1983): 111–122.

Hiat, Philip, ed. *A Visual Testimony: Judaica from the Vatican Library*. New York: Union of American Hebrew Congregations, 1987.

Hilgarth, J. N., and Bezalel Narkiss. "A List of Hebrew Books (1330) and a Contract to Illuminate Manuscripts (1335) from Majorca." *Revue des Etudes Juives* 120 (1961): 297–320.

Klagsbald, Victor. *Catalogue des manuscrits marocains de la collection Klagsbald*. Paris: Editions du Centre National de la Recherche Scientifique, 1980.

Landsberger, F. "The Cincinnati Haggadah and Its Decorator." *Hebrew Union College Annual* 15 (1940): 529–558.

———. "The Washington Haggadah and Its Illuminator." *Hebrew Union College Annual* 21 (1948): 73–103.

Leveen, Jacob. *The Hebrew Bible in Art*. Rev. ed. New York: Hermon Press, 1974.

Lieberman, Saul. "Jewish and Christian Codices." Appendix 3 in *Hellenism in Jewish Palestine*. New York: Jewish Theological Seminary of America, 1950.

Mayer, L. A. *Bibliography of Jewish Art*. Edited by Otto Kurtz. Jerusalem: Magnes Press, 1967.
An all-encompassing work listing over 3,000 articles pertaining to every aspect of Jewish art. Arranged alphabetically by author, with a general index.

Metzger, Mendel. *La Haggada enluminée*. Leiden: E. J. Brill, 1973.
Comprehensive study of the art found in illuminated Haggadot.

Metzger, Thérèse. *Les Manuscrits hébreux copiés et décorés à Lisbonne dans les dernières décennies du XVe siècle*. Fundação Calouste Gulbenkian. Paris: Centro Cultural Portugues, 1977.

———, and Mendel Metzger. *Jewish Life in the Middle Ages*. New York: Alpine Fine Arts Collection, 1982.
Contains only a short text concerning medieval Hebrew book production, but includes over 400 illustrations of illuminated manuscripts as well as an appendix with a detailed list of 259 important illuminated manuscripts.

Moreen, Vera Basch. *Miniature Painting in Judaeo-Persian Manuscripts*. Cincinnati: Hebrew Union College Press, 1985.
Exhibition catalog with an introduction to each of the manuscripts and a detailed description of the artwork found in the manuscripts. A microfiche that accompanies the catalog allows the reader to see many of the illuminated pages.

Mortara Ottolenghi, Luisa. "Description of Decorated and Illuminated Hebrew Manuscripts in the Ambrosian Library." In *Hebraica Ambrosiana*. Milan: Il Polifilo, 1972.

Nadav, Mordechai; Rafael Weiser; and Yitzhak Yudlov. *Selected Manuscripts and Prints: An Exhibition from the Treasures of the Jewish National and University Library*. Jerusalem: Jewish National and University Library, 1985.
Exhibition catalog with many illustrations. Text in Hebrew and English.

Narkiss, Bezalel. *Hebrew Illuminated Manuscripts*. 3d ed. Jerusalem: Keter Publishing House, 1978. Rev. Hebrew ed., 1984.
An introduction to Hebrew manuscript art. Contains sample pages from some of the most outstanding Hebrew illuminated manuscripts of all time.

————. *Hebrew Illuminated Manuscripts in the British Isles: A Catalogue Raisonné.* Vol. 1 (in 2 parts): *The Spanish and Portuguese Manuscripts.* Jerusalem and London: Oxford University Press for Israel Academy of Sciences and Humanities and the British Academy, 1982.

————. "Illuminated Hebrew Children's Books from Mediaeval Egypt." *Scripta Hierosolymitana* 24 (1972): 58–71.

————. "On the Zoocephalic Phenomenon in Mediaeval Ashkenazi Manuscripts." In *Norms and Variations in Art: Essays in Honor of Moshe Barasch.* Jerusalem: Magnes Press, 1983.
Examines the many theories that attempt to explain the phenomenon of animal-headed figures in numerous medieval Hebrew manuscripts.

————. "The Relation between the Author, Scribe, Massorator, and Illuminator in Medieval Manuscripts." In *La Paléographie hébraïque médiévale: Colloques Internationaux du Centre National de la Recherche Scientifique.* Paris: Editions du Centre National de la Recherche Scientifique, 1974.

————, and Gabrielle Sed-Rajna. *Index of Jewish Art: Iconographical Index of Hebrew Illuminated Manuscripts.* Jerusalem and Paris: The Israel Academy of Sciences and Humanities and Institut de Recherche et d'Histoire des Textes, vol. 1, 1976; vol. 2, 1981; vol. 3, 1983.
The aim of the *Index of Jewish Art* is to publish a comprehensive subject index of Jewish art; the first three volumes deal with illuminated manuscripts. Each volume consists of a box of cards and an introductory booklet.

Panofsky, Erwin. "Giotto and Maimonides in Avignon: The Story of an Illustrated Hebrew Manuscript." *The Journal of the Walters Art Gallery* 4 (1941): 27–44.

————. "Giotto and Maimonides in Avignon: A Postscript." *The Journal of the Walters Art Gallery* 5 (1942): 124–127.

Roberts, C. H., and T. C. Skeat. *The Birth of the Codex.* London: Oxford University Press, 1983.

Roth, Cecil, ed. *Jewish Art: An Illustrated History.* Rev. 2d ed. by Bezalel Narkiss. Greenwich, Conn.: New York Graphic Society, 1971.
Essays include "Illumination of Hebrew Manuscripts in the Middle Ages and Renaissance" by Franz Landsberger; "The Illumination of Hebrew Manuscripts after the Invention of Printing" by Ernest Namenyi; "The Jewish Art of the Printed Book" by A. M. Habermann.

Sassoon, David Solomon. *Ohel David: Descriptive Catalogue of the Hebrew and Samaritan Manuscripts in the Sassoon Library.* 2 vols. London: Oxford University Press, 1932.

Schubert, Kurt, and Ursula Schubert. *Jüdische Buchkunst*. Graz, Austria: Akademische Druck und Verlagsanstalt, 1983.
Examines the art of Hebrew illuminated manuscripts. It is the first of a planned two-volume set; the authors intend to study the art of the printed Hebrew book in the forthcoming second volume.

Sed-Rajna, Gabrielle. *The Hebrew Bible in Medieval Illuminated Manuscripts*. New York: Rizzoli, 1987.

———. *Le Maḥzor enluminé; les voies de formation d'une programme iconographique*. Leiden: E. J. Brill, 1983.
A comparative analysis of the iconographic program of eight medieval German illuminated prayerbooks.

———. *Manuscrits hébreux de Lisbonne*. Paris: Editions du Centre National de la Recherche Scientifique, 1970.

———. "The Renaissance of Narrative Art: Illuminated Manuscripts." In *Ancient Jewish Art: East and West*. Neuchâtel: Imprimerie Paul Attinger, 1985.

Sirat, Colette. *Les Papyrus en caractères hébraïques trouvés en Egypte*. Paris: Centre National de la Recherche Scientifique, 1985.

Sokolof, M., and J. Yahalom. "Christian Palimpsests from the Cairo Geniza." *Revue d'Histoire des Textes* 8 (1978): 109–132.

Steinschneider, Moritz. *Vorlesungen über die Kunde Hebräischer Handschriften deren Sammlungen und Verzeichnisse*. Leipzig, 1897. Reprint. *Hartsa'ot 'al Kitve-Yad 'Ivriyim*. Translated by Israel Eldad. Edited by Abraham Meir Habermann. Jerusalem: Mossad Harav Kook, 1965.
A collection of Steinschneider's lectures on Hebrew manuscripts.

Turner, Eric. *The Typology of the Early Codex*. Philadelphia: University of Pennsylvania Press, 1977.

Weinstein, Rochelle. "The 1686 Esther Scroll Written and Illustrated by Raphael Montalto; Spencer Collection Heb. Ms. 2." (In preparation.)
Study of a manuscript in the Spencer Collection of The New York Public Library.

Illuminated Manuscripts Reproduced in Facsimile

The Ashkenazi Haggadah. Introduction by David Goldstein. New York: Harry N. Abrams, 1985. British Library, Add. Ms. 14762.

Bilder-Pentateuch von Moses da Castellazzo. Introduction by Kurt Schubert and Ursula Schubert. 2 vols. Vienna: Bernthaler and Windischgraetz, 1983–86. Jewish Historic Institute, Warsaw, Cod. 1164.

The Bird's Head Haggada. Introduction by E. D. Goldschmidt, H. L. C. Jaffé, B. Narkiss, M. Shapiro, and M. Spitzer. 2 vols. Jerusalem: Tarshish Books, 1965–67. Israel Museum, Jerusalem, 180/57.

Canon of Avicenna (partial). Milan: Lepetit, 1953. Biblioteca Universitaria di Bologna, Ms. 2197.

The Copenhagen Haggadah: Altona-Hamburg, 1739. Introduction by Chaya Benjamin. Tel Aviv: Nahar Publishing, 1986.

Die Darmstädter Pessach-Haggadah. Introduction by Bruno Italiener, Aron Friemann, August L. Mayer, and Adolph Schmidt. 2 vols. Leipzig: K. W. Hiersmann, 1927. Hessische Landes- und Hochschulbibliothek, Darmstadt, cod. or 8.

Die Darmstädter Pessach-Haggadah. Introduction by Joseph Gutmann, H. Knaus, P. Pieper, and E. Zimmermann. 2 vols. Berlin: Propyläen Verlag, 1971. Text in English and German. Hessische Landes- und Hochschulbibliothek, Darmstadt, cod. or 8.

Esther Rolle (The *Kaniel Megilla*). Introduction by Bezalel Narkiss and Michael Kaniel. Graz: Akademische Drucke und Verlagsanstalt, 1984. Collection of Michael Kaniel, Jerusalem.

The Golden Haggadah. Introduction by Bezalel Narkiss. 2 vols. London: Eugrammia Press, 1970. British Library, Add. Ms. 27210.

Grace after Meals and Other Benedictions. Introduction by Rafael Edelmann. Copenhagen: Forlaget Old Manuscripts, 1969. Reprinted in 1983 with a new introduction by Iris Fishof. Royal Library, Copenhagen, Cod. Hebr. 32.

Haggadah (German *Sassoon Haggadah*). Zürich: Lichtdruck AG, 1985. Floersheim Collection, Zürich.

Die Haggadah von Sarajevo. Introduction by David Heinrich Müller, Julius von Schlosser, and David Kaufmann. 2 vols. Vienna: Alfred Hölder, 1898. National Museum, Sarajevo.

The Kaufmann Haggadah. Introduction by Alexander Scheiber. Budapest: Hungarian Academy of Sciences, 1957. Hungarian Academy of Sciences, Budapest, Ms. A422.

The Kennicott Bible. Introduction by Bezalel Narkiss and Aliza Cohen-Mushlin. 2 vols. London: Facsimile Editions, 1985. Bodleian Library, Oxford, Ms. Kenn. 1.

Machsor Lipsiae. Introduction by Elias Katz and Bezalel Narkiss. 2 vols. Vaduz: Société pour le Commerce Intercontinental Trust, 1964. Text in English and German. Universitätsbibliothek, Leipzig, Ms. 5 1102/1–2.

A Májmúni Kódex (The *Kaufmann Mishneh Torah*). Introduction by Alexander Scheiber and Gabrielle Sed-Rajna. Budapest: Corvina, 1980. English Edition: *Codex Maimuni; Moses Maimonides' Code of Law*. Budapest: Corvina, 1984. Hungarian Academy of Sciences, Budapest, Ms. A77.

Pessah Haggadah: Ashkenaz 1729. Introduction by Chaya Benjamin. Tel Aviv: Nahar Publishing, 1985. Private collection, Israel.

The Rosenthaliana Leipnik Haggadah. Introduction by Emile G. C. Schrijver. Tel Aviv: W. Turnowsky, 1987. Bibliotheca Rosenthaliana, Amsterdam, Ms. HS, RO5, 382.
Short introductory pamphlet in English and Hebrew.

The Rothschild Mahzor. Introduction by Evelyn M. Cohen and Menahem Schmelzer. New York: The Jewish Theological Seminary of America, 1983. The Jewish Theological Seminary of America, New York, Mic. 8892.

The Rothschild Miscellany. London: Facsimile Editions, 1988 (in press). Israel Museum, Jerusalem, 180/51.

The Sarajevo Haggadah. Introduction by Cecil Roth. London: W. H. Allen, 1963. National Museum, Sarajevo.

The Sarajevo Haggadah. Introduction by Eugene Weber. Beograd: Prosveta, 1984. National Museum, Sarajevo.

A Song of David. Designed and illustrated by David Moss. Rochester, N.Y.: Bet Alpha Editions, 1987.
The original manuscript was commissioned in 1980 by Richard and Beatrice Levy of Florida.

The Worms Mahzor. Introduction by Malachi Beit-Arié, Bezalel Narkiss, and Aliza Cohen-Mushlin. 2 vols. London: Cyelar Publishing, 1985. Jewish National and University Library, Jerusalem, Ms. Heb. 4 781/1.

For more information on the history of illuminated manuscripts in facsimile, see Leila Avrin's article "Art for the Masses: Hebrew Facsimile Publishing" in *AB Bookman's Weekly* 77, no. 16: 1807–1812.

Palaeography

Avrin, Leila. "Modern Hebrew Calligraphy and Calligraphers." *Calligraphy Idea Exchange* 4 (1986): 43–54.

Beit-Arié, Malachi. *Hebrew Codicology: Tentative Typology of Technical Practices Employed in Hebrew Dated Medieval Manuscripts*. 2d ed., rev. Jerusalem: The Israel Academy of Sciences and Humanities, 1981.

Bernheimer, Carlo. *Paleografia ebraica*. Florence: Leo S. Olschki, 1924.
Development of the Hebrew alphabet. Ashkenazic, Sephardic, and rabbinic scripts are examined.

Birnbaum, Solomon Asher. *The Hebrew Scripts.* Vol. 1: Leiden: E. J. Brill,
1971; Vol. 2: London: Paleographia, 1954–57.
Volume 1, the text volume (published almost twenty years after volume 2), contains
a comprehensive study of the Hebrew scripts including Phoenician, Aramaic, and Karaitic. Volume 2 presents over 300 script facsimiles and 188 alphabet charts.

Cross, F. M. "The Development of the Jewish Scripts." In *The Bible and the
Ancient Near East: Essays in Honor of W. F. Albright.* Garden City, N.Y.: Doubleday and Co., 1961.

Diringer, David. *The Story of the Aleph Beth.* New York: Philosophical Library,
1958.

Glenisson, J., and Colette Sirat, eds. *La Paléographie hébraïque médiévale: Colloques Internationaux du Centre National de la Recherche Scientifique.* Paris: Editions
du Centre National de la Recherche Scientifique, 1974.

Hebräische Schrift von der Steinschrift zum Poster. Zurich: Kunstgewerbemuseum,
1976.
Exhibition catalog.

Leaf, Reuben. *Hebrew Alphabets: 400 B.C.E. to Our Days.* New York: Bloch
Publishing Company, 1976.
Presents examples of the Hebrew alphabet over a period of 2,000 years. Explanatory
and introductory notes in English and Hebrew. Chiefly illustrations.

Ory, S. "Un Nouveau Type de muṣḥaf." *Revue des Etudes Islamiques* 33 (1965):
87–149.

Sirat, Colette. *Ecriture et civilisations.* Neuilly-sur-Seine: Institut de Recherche et
d'Histoire des Textes, 1976.
Studies in Hebrew palaeography.

———. "La Lettre hébraïque et sa signification." In *Etudes de paléographie
hébraïque.* Paris and Jerusalem: Centre National de la Recherche Scientifique
and The Israel Museum, 1981.

Spitzer, Moshe, ed. *Ot Hi le-'Olam.* Jerusalem: Ministry of Education and The
Society for Jewish Art, 1981.
A collection of essays on the Hebrew letter and on the Hebrew script.

Haggadot

Fischer, Yona, ed. *Illustrated Haggadot of the Eighteenth Century.* Translated by
Jeffrey Green. Jerusalem: Ben-Zvi Printing Enterprises, 1983.
Catalog essays in both English and Hebrew.

Habermann, Abraham Meir. *Ha-Haggadah ha-Metsuyeret.* Safed: Museum of
Printing Art, 1963.
An exhibition catalog of illustrated Haggadot, including manuscripts and printed
works.

Rivkind, Isaac. *Haggadot Pesaḥ be-Aspaklariah shel ha-Dorot.* New York: Futuro Press, 1961.
A review of and supplement to Ya'ari (see below).

Wengrov, Charles. *Haggadah and Woodcut: An Introduction to the Passover Haggadah Completed by Gershom Cohen in Prague Sunday 26th of Teveth 5267.* New York: Shulsinger Bros., 1967.

Ya'ari, Abraham. *Bibliyografiyah shel Haggadot Pesaḥ.* Jerusalem: Bamberger and Wahrmann, 1960.
The standard bibliography of the Passover Haggadah, containing 2,713 entries arranged chronologically. Ya'ari's work includes that of Samuel Weiner, an earlier writer who had published a list of Haggadot up to the year 1900. Several people have published supplements to Ya'ari's book; for the most recent supplement, see Tzivia Atik, "Addenda to Bibliographies of the Passover Haggadah" in *Studies in Bibliography and Booklore* 12 (1979): 29–36.

Yerushalmi, Yosef Hayim. *Haggadah and History: A Panorama in Facsimile of Five Centuries of the Printed Haggadah from the Collections of Harvard University and the Jewish Theological Seminary of America.* Philadelphia: Jewish Publication Society of America, 1974.
Reproduces 200 sample plates from a variety of Haggadot throughout the ages.

Printing

Adler, Elkan Nathan. "The Romance of Hebrew Printing." In *About Hebrew Manuscripts.* London: H. Frowde, 1905. Reprint. New York: Hermon Press, 1970.

Amram, David Werner. *The Makers of Hebrew Books in Italy.* Philadelphia: J. H. Greenstone, 1909. Reprint. London: The Holland Press Ltd., 1963.

Anselmo, Artur. *Les Origines de l'imprimerie au Portugal.* Paris: J. Touzot, 1983.
An overview of the origins of printing in Portugal with short discussions of Hebrew typography 1487–95, and of three Jewish printers.

Benayahu, Meir. *Ha-Defus ha-'Ivri be-Krimonah.* Jerusalem: Machon Ben-Zvi and Mossad Harav Kook, 1971.
A history of Hebrew printing in Cremona.

———. *Haskamah u-Reshut be-Defuse Venetsiah.* Jerusalem: Machon Ben-Zvi and Mossad Harav Kook, 1971.
An examination of the function of haskamah or "approbation and authorization" in Hebrew books printed in Venice from the sixteenth through the eighteenth centuries.

Benjacob, Isaac. *Otsar ha-Sefarim.* Vilna, 1880. Reprint. New York: Hotsa'at Yerushalayim, 1944.
A listing of all Hebrew books published up to 1863, arranged alphabetically by title.

Ben-Menahem, Naphtali. "Ha-Defusim ha-Rishonim shel ha-Shulḥan Arukh." In *Rabi Yosef Karo*. Jerusalem: Mossad Harav Kook, 1969.
An account of the first printings of the Shulḥan Arukh.

Berger, Abraham; Lawrence Marwick; and Isidore S. Meyer, eds. *The Joshua Bloch Memorial Volume: Studies in Booklore and History*. New York: The New York Public Library, 1960.
Includes: "The New Ornament of Jewish Books" by Joseph Reider; "Medieval Hebrew Manuscripts as Bindings in the Libraries of Hungary" by Alexander Scheiber; and "Elias Hutter's Hebrew Bible" by Herbert C. Zafren.

Berlin, Charles, ed. *Hebrew Printing and Bibliography: Studies by Joshua Bloch and Others*. New York: The New York Public Library and Ktav Publishing House, 1976.
Includes: "Venetian Printers of Hebrew Books," "Early Hebrew Printing in Spain and Portugal," and "Hebrew Printing in Naples" by Joshua Bloch as well as "A Gazetteer of Hebrew Printing" by Aron Freimann.

Berthold, H., Messinglinienfabrik Schriftgiesserei, A.-G., Berlin. *Berthold. Shriftgiseray un Mesingliniye Fabrikn.* . . . Berlin, 1924.
A catalog of Hebrew types. Preface in English.

Bühler, Curt Ferdinand. *The Fifteenth Century Book: The Scribes, the Printers, the Decorators*. Philadelphia: University of Pennsylvania Press, 1960.
Interesting general overview; contains no information specifically regarding the Hebrew book.

Cohen, Gershon. *Sifre ha-Defus ha-Rishonim*. New York: Yeshiva University Press, 1984.
A study of the Hebrew incunabula of the Mendel Gottesman Library of Hebraica and Judaica, Yeshiva University.

Dr. Moshe Spitzer: Books, Typography, Design. Jerusalem: Israel Bibliophiles, 1981.
Exhibition catalog of the books printed by Tarshish Press as well as a list of other books designed by Dr. Spitzer.

Eisenstein, Elizabeth. *The Printing Press as an Agent of Change*. Cambridge: Cambridge University Press, 1979.

Feigensohn, Samuel Shraga. "Le-Toledot Defus Romm." In *Yahadut Lita*. Vol. 1. Tel Aviv: Am ha-Sefer, 1959.

Frank, Rafael. *Über hebräische Typen und Schriftarten*. Berlin: Berthold, 1926.
An essay on Hebrew typefaces and fonts.

Freimann, Aron. *Thesaurus Typographiae Hebraicae Saeculi XV; Hebrew Printing during the Fifteenth Century*. Berlin: Marx and Co., 1924–31. Reprint. Jerusalem: Universitas Booksellers, 1967–69.
Facsimiles of pages from Hebrew incunabula.

Friedberg, Bernhard. *Bet 'Eked Sefarim*. Antwerp, 1928–31. Rev. ed. 4 vols. Tel Aviv: M. A. Bar Juda, 1951–56.
A comprehensive Hebrew bibliography from the beginning of Hebrew printing until 1950. The book is arranged alphabetically by title and contains a separate listing of incunabula.

———. *Toledot ha-Defus ha-'Ivri be-Eropah*. Antwerp, 1937.
The history of Hebrew printing in Western Europe, including biographies of the first printers and their successors.

———. *Toledot ha-Defus ha-'Ivri be-Eropah ha-Tikhonah*. Antwerp, 1935.
The history of Hebrew printing in Central Europe, including biographies of the first printers and their successors.

———. *Toledot ha-Defus ha-'Ivri be-Medinot Italyah, Aspamyah-Portugalyah, Togarmah ve-Artsot ha-Kedem*. 2d ed. rev. Tel Aviv: M. A. Bar-Juda, 1956.
The history of printing in Italy, Spain, Portugal, Turkey, and the Orient.

———. *Toledot ha-Defus ha-'Ivri be-Polanyah*. 2d ed. rev. Tel Aviv: Baruch Friedberg, 1950.
The history of Hebrew printing in Poland.

Friedlaender, Henri. *The Making of Hadassah Hebrew*. Jerusalem: Central Press Ltd., 1975.

———. *Melekhet ha-Sefer*. Jerusalem: Hadassah Apprentice School of Printing, 1962.

———. "Modern Hebrew Lettering." *Ariel* 4 (1962): 6–15.

Fuks, L. "The Hebrew Production of Plantin-Raphelengius Presses in Leyden 1585–1615." *Studia Rosenthaliana* 1 (1970): 1–24.

———, and R. G. Fuks-Mansfeld. *Hebrew Typography in Northern Netherlands 1585–1815*. Leiden: E. J. Brill, 1984.
Focuses on the development of printing in the cities of Leiden, Franeker, and Amsterdam as well as the close relationship between the Hebrew printers and the universities.

Goff, Frederick R. *Incunabula in American Libraries*. Corrected and rev. ed. Millwood, N.Y.: Kraus Reprint Co., 1973.
Hebrew incunabula are listed in a separate section.

Goldschmidt, Lazarus. *Hebrew Incunables: A Bibliographical Essay*. Translated from German by Immanuel Goldschmidt. Oxford: B. H. Blackwell, 1948.
Entertaining account of the author's study of incunabula.

Goldstein, David. *Hebrew Incunables in the British Isles: A Preliminary Census*. London: British Library, 1985.

Habermann, Abraham Meir. *Ha-Madpis Dani'el Bombirgi u-Reshimat Sifre Bet Defuso*. Safed: Museum of Printing Art, 1978.
    An essay on the printer Daniel Bomberg. Short English foreword.

————. *Ha-Madpisim Bene Sontsino*. Vienna: David Frankel, 1933.
    The history of the Soncino family of printers.

————. *Ha-Madpis Kornilyo Adil Kind u-Veno Dani'el u-Reshimat Sefarim she-Nidpesu al Yedeyhem*. Jerusalem: Rubin Mass, 1980.
    The history of the printer Cornelio Adel Kind.

————. *Ha-Madpis Zoan Di Garah u-Reshimat Sifre Bet Defuso (1564–1610)*. Completed and edited by Yizchak Yudlov. Jerusalem: Habermann Institute for Literary Research, 1982.
    A study of the printer Giovanni di Gara and a list of books printed at his press.

————. *Nashim 'Ivriyot be-Tor Madpisot, Mesadrot, Motsiot la-Or ve-Tomhot ba-Mehabrim*. Berlin: Rubin Mass, 1933.
    A study of women who were involved in book production.

————. *Perakim be-Toledot ha-Madpisim ha-'Ivriyim ve-'Inyane Sefarim*. Jerusalem: Rubin Mass, 1978.
    Studies in the history of Hebrew printers and Hebrew books.

————. *Toledot ha-Defus be-Tsefat*. Safed: Museum of Printing Art, 1962.
    Exhibition catalog of the beginnings of printing in Safed. Summary of text in English.

Haiman, György. *Nicholas Kis: Hungarian Punch-Cutter and Printer, 1650–1702*. San Francisco: Greenwood Press in association with John Howell Books, 1983.

Halevy, Shoshana. *Sifre Yerushalayim ha-Rishonim*. 2d rev. ed. Jerusalem: Machon Ben-Zvi Hebrew University, 1975.
    The first Hebrew books printed in Jerusalem, 1841–91.

Henri Friedlaender: Typography and Lettering. Jerusalem: Israel Museum, 1973.
    A short exhibition catalog of the work of Henri Friedlaender. Text in English and Hebrew.

Hill, Brad Sabin. *Incunabula, Hebraica and Judaica*. Ottawa: National Library of Canada, 1981.
    An exhibition catalog of the Jacob M. Lowy Collection. Books are arranged thematically with ample notes and many illustrations. Text in English and French.

Hirsch, Rudolf. *Printing, Selling and Reading 1450–1550*. Wiesbaden: Otto Harrassowitz, 1967.
    A general introduction to the early history of printing. No specifically Jewish content.

Kagan, Berl. *Sefer ha-Prenumerantn*. New York: The Library of the Jewish Theological Seminary, 1975.
A massive compilation of the lists of presubscribers to printed rabbinic books. Introduction in English and Yiddish.

Levy, Jane, and Florence B. Helzel. *The Jewish Illustrated Book*. Berkeley: Judah L. Magnes Museum, 1986.
An exhibition catalog of the modern illustrated Jewish book.

Le Livre hébraïque. Paris: Services Culturels, Ambassade d'Israel, 1962.
An exhibition catalog of various Israeli publications as well as an annotated list by Israel Adler of the Hebrew incunabula of the Bibliothèque Nationale.

Marx, Alexander. *Bibliographical Studies and Notes on Rare Books and Manuscripts in the Library of The Jewish Theological Seminary of America*. Edited by Menachem H. Schmelzer. New York: Ktav Publishing House, 1977.
Register reports of the purchases, acquisitions, and donations to the library, 1917–73.

————. "The Choice of Books by the Printers of Hebrew Incunabula." In *To Dr. R*. Philadelphia, 1946.

Marx, Moses. *Gershom Soncino's Wander-Years in Italy 1498–1527*. Cincinnati: Society of Jewish Bibliophiles, 1969. Reprinted from *Hebrew Union College Annual* 11 (1936): 420–571.

————. "On the Date of Appearance of the First Printed Hebrew Books." In *Alexander Marx Jubilee Volume*. English section. New York: The Jewish Theological Seminary of America, 1950.

Mehlman, Israel. *Genuzot Sefarim*. Jerusalem: The Jewish National and University Library Press, 1976.
Essays on Hebrew printing, including "The First Hebrew Printed Books 1475–1500," "Hebrew Printing Houses in Salonika," and "Unique Hebrew Books and Single Pages."

Offenberg, A. K. "Catalogue of Hebrew Incunabula in the Bibliotheca Rosenthaliana." *Studia Rosenthaliana* 5 (1971): 125–143, 246–267; 7 (1973): 128–150.

Olitzky, Joseph. *Omanut ha-Defus*. Safed: Museum of Printing Art, 1973.
Comprehensive study of the history of printing in Israel.

Pollak, Michael. "The Daily Performance of a Printing Press in 1476: Evidence from a Hebrew Incunable." *Gutenberg-Jahrbuch* (1974), pp. 66–76.

Rabinowitz, Raphael Nathan. *Ma'amar al Hadpasat ha-Talmud*. Completed and edited with corrections and supplements by Abraham Meir Habermann. Jerusalem: Mossad Harav Kook, 1965.
A study of the printing of the Talmud.

Rosenthal, Avraham. "Some Remarks on 'The Daily Performance of a Printing Press in 1476.'" *Gutenberg-Jahrbuch* (1979), pp. 39–50.

Roth, Cecil. *Studies in Books and Booklore.* Farnborough, England: Gregg International Publishers, 1972.
    Essays include: "The Origin of Hebrew Typography in England," "The Marrano Typography in England," "Pledging a Book in Medieval England," and "A Jewish Printer in Naples, 1477."

Schonfield, Hugh Joseph. *The New Hebrew Typography.* London: Denis Archer, 1932.
    Interesting attempt to introduce a modern romanized Hebrew type.

Slatkine, Menachem Mendel. *Otsar ha-Sefarim: Ḥelek Sheni.* Jerusalem: Kiryat Sefer, 1965.
    An updating of Benjacob's *Otsar ha-Sefarim.* Annotates nearly one-third of the titles and includes an index.

———. *Shemot ha-Sefarim ha-'Ivriyim.* 2 vols. Neuchâtel and Tel Aviv, 1950–54.
    Essays on unusual titles of books, arranged topically with a general index.

Soifer, Israel. "The Pioneer Work of Dr. Maurice Spitzer." *Penrose Annual* 63 (1970): 127–142.

Spitzer, Moshe. "The Development of Hebrew Lettering." *Ariel* 37 (1974): 4–28. Translated by Shirley Shpira.

Steinschneider, Moritz. *Catalogus Librorum Hebraeorum in Bibliotheca Bodleiana.* Berolini, 1852–60. Reprint. Hildesheim: G. Olms, 1964.
    A catalog of the Hebrew books in the Bodleian Library.

———, and David Cassel. *Jüdische Typographie und jüdische Buchhandel.* 2d ed. Jerusalem: Bamberger and Wahrmann, 1938.
    Originally appeared in *Ersch and Gruber Allgemeine Encyclopädie der Wissenschaften und Künste.* Vol. 28. Leipzig: F. A. Brockhaus, 1850. Moritz Steinschneider was the father of modern Jewish bibliography, and this is his authoritative treatise on Jewish typography and the Jewish book trade.

Studies in Jewish Bibliography and Related Subjects in Memory of Abraham Solomon Freidus. New York: The Alexander Kohut Memorial Foundation, 1929.
    Essays include: Carlo Bernheimer, "The Library of the Talmud Torah at Leghorn"; H. G. Enelow, "Isaac Belinfante—An Eighteenth Century Bibliophile"; Joseph Reider, "Non-Jewish Motives in the Ornament of Early Hebrew Books"; Cecil Roth, "A Seventeenth Century Library and Trousseau"; and Wilberforce Eames, "On the Use of Hebrew Types in English America before 1735."

Tamani, G. "Nel secondo centenario dell'inizio dell'attività accademica di Giovanni Bernardo De Rossi." *Aurea Parma* 53 (1969): 165–180.

Tamari, Ittai. *New Hebrew Letter Types.* Jerusalem: Keter Publishing House, 1985.
An examination of the development of the Hebrew printed letter. Eight modern types are reviewed. Text in Hebrew and English.

Thomas, Alan. *Great Books and Book Collectors.* New York: Putnam, 1975.
Short chapter on early printed Hebrew books.

Tishby, P. "Hebrew Incunabula." In *Kiryat Sefer* 58 (1983): 808–857; *Kiryat Sefer* 60 (1985): 865–962; *Ohev Sefer* 1 (1987): 23–50 (Hebrew), 29–30 (English).

Ya'ari, Abraham. *Ha-Defus ha-'Ivri be-Artsot ha-Mizraḥ.* 2 vols. Jerusalem: University Press, 1936–40.
Volume 1 contains the history of Hebrew printing in Safed, Damascus, Aleppo, Cairo, Alexandria, and Aden. Volume 2 includes India and Bagdad.

———. *Ha-Defus ha-'Ivri be-Kushta.* Jerusalem: Magnes Press, 1967.
Surveys the history of Hebrew printing in Constantinople and includes a list of books printed there.

———. *Meḥkere Sefer.* Jerusalem: Mossad Harav Kook, 1958.
Contains articles on unusual aspects of Hebrew booklore as well as an essay on the printers Foa.

Zafren, Herbert C. "Early Yiddish Typography." *Jewish Book Annual* 44 (1986/87): 106–119.

———. "Variety in the Typography of Yiddish: 1535–1635." *Hebrew Union College Annual* 53 (1982): 137–163.

Technology of the Book
Bookbindings

Goldschmidt, Ernest Philip. *Gothic and Renaissance Bookbindings.* 2 vols. London, 1928. Reprint. Amsterdam: N. Israel, 1967.
Contains a short section on Mair Jaffe, a medieval Jewish bookbinder.

Katzenstein, Ursula E. "Mair Jaffe and Bookbinding Research." *Studies in Bibliography and Booklore* 14 (1982): 17–28.

Bookplates

Goodmann, Philip. *American Jewish Bookplates.* New York: American Jewish Historical Society, 1956.

———. *Illustrated Essays on Jewish Bookplates.* New York: Ktav Publishing House, 1971.
Collection of the author's earlier articles; includes extensive bibliography.

Habermann, Abraham Meir. *Tave Sefer Yehudiyim*. Ramat Gan: Massada Publishing, 1972.
    History of the Jewish bookplate; chiefly illustrations. Text in Hebrew and English.

Horodisch, Abraham. *Die Exlibris des Uriel Birnbaum: gefolgt von einer Selbstbiographie des Künstlers*. Amsterdam: Erasmus Antiquariat, 1957.
    Contains a collection of the bookplate art of Uriel Birnbaum. The artist explains the symbolism of each bookplate.

Weiss, Avrom. *Tave Sefer Yehudiyim*. Safed: Museum of Printing Art, 1961.
    Exhibition catalog of Jewish bookplates. Text in Hebrew and English.

Printers' Marks

Ya'ari, Abraham. *Digle ha-Madpisim ha-'Ivriyim*. Jerusalem: Hebrew University Press, 1943. Reprint with additional material. Farnborough, England: Gregg International Publishers, 1971.
    A collection of Hebrew printers' marks from the beginning of Hebrew printing until the end of the nineteenth century.

Title Pages

Ben-Yehudah, Meir. *Sha'are Sefarim ve-Kotarot*. Tel Aviv: Ha-Merkaz le-Tarbut ule-Ḥinukh, 1967.
    An examination of the many types of title pages and headings found in Hebrew books.

Habermann, Abraham Meir. *Sha'are Sefarim 'Ivrim*. Safed: Museum of Printing Art, 1969.
    Title pages of Hebrew books. English introduction, chiefly illustrations.

Collectors and Collecting

Adler, Elkan Nathan. "An Ancient Booksellers Catalogue." In *About Hebrew Manuscripts*. London: H. Frowde, 1905. Reprint. New York: Hermon Press, 1970.

Faber, Salamon. "Selected Private Jewish Library Collections." *Jewish Book Annual* 29 (1971–72): 39–46.

Freehof, Solomon B. "On the Collecting of Jewish Books." *Jewish Book Annual* 38 (1980–81): 6–17.

Habermann, Abraham Meir. *Anshe Sefer ve-Anshe Ma'aseh*. Jerusalem: Rubin Mass, 1974.
    Forty short essays on great Jewish bibliographers, bookdealers, and printers.

Homeyer, Fritz. *Deutsche Juden als Bibliophilen und Antiquare*. Tübingen: J. C. B. Mohr, 1963.

Marx, Alexander. *Studies in Jewish History and Booklore.* New York: The Jewish Theological Seminary of America, 1944.

Includes: "Some Jewish Book Collectors," "The History of David Oppenheimer's Library," "The Literature of Hebrew Incunabula," and "Notes on the Use of Hebrew Type in Non-Hebrew Books 1475–1520."

Mehlman, Israel. "From a Bibliophile's Memoirs." *Jewish Book Annual* 44 (1986–87): 184–198.

Munby, A. N. *Connoisseurs and Medieval Miniatures, 1750–1850.* Oxford: Clarendon Press, 1972.

Rabinowicz, Harry. *The Jewish Literary Treasures of England and America.* New York: Thomas Yoseloff, 1962.

Describes some of the most important collections of Hebraica and Judaica in the libraries of England and America.

Roth, Cecil. "Jewish Book Collections and Collectors." *Jewish Book Annual* 25 (1967–68): 75–80.

Wachstein, Bernhard. *Hebräische Autographen von Gelehrten und Schriftstellern in Faksimile.* Vienna: Waldheim-Eberle, 1927. Reprint. Jerusalem: ha-Makhon le-Bibliyografiyah, 1981.

Hebrew autographs of scholars and writers.

Censorship

Berliner, Abraham. *Censur und Confiscation: hebräischer Bücher im Kirchenstaate.* Berlin: H. Itzkowski, 1891.

A study of censorship in the papal territories.

Carmilly-Weinberger, Moshe. *Censorship and Freedom of Expression in Jewish History.* New York: Sepher Hermon Press, 1977.

Discusses Jewish internal self-censorship of Hebrew books through the ages.

Popper, William. *The Censorship of Hebrew Books.* New York, 1899. Reprint, with an introduction by Moshe Carmilly-Weinberger. New York: Ktav Publishing House, 1969.

Sonne, Isaiah. "Expurgation of Hebrew Books." In *Hebrew Printing and Bibliography: Studies by Joshua Bloch and Others.* New York: The New York Public Library and Ktav Publishing House, 1976.

Stow, K. "The Burning of the Talmud in 1553, in Light of the Sixteenth Century Catholic Attitudes toward the Talmud." *Bibliothèque d'Humanisme et Renaissance* 34 (1972): 435–459.

Ya'ari, Abraham. *Serefat ha-Talmud be-Italyah.* Tel Aviv: A. Tsiyoni, 1953.

Journals

Alei Sefer. Ramat Gan: Bar-Ilan University Press, 1975– .

Areshet. Jerusalem: Mossad Harav Kook, 1958– .

Hed Hadefus. Israel: National Union of Printing Workers, 1948–57.
   Articles on the history of Hebrew printing and on modern printing in Israel. Vols.
9–12 contain brief English summaries of the articles.

Israel Bibliophiles Newsletter. Israel, 1980– .

Jewish Book Annual. New York: Jewish Book Council, 1942– .

Journal of Jewish Art. Jerusalem: Center for Jewish Art of The Hebrew University, 1974– .

Journal of Jewish Bibliography. New York: J. Bloch, 1939–43.

Judaica Book News. New York: Book News, 1969– .

Judaica Librarianship. New York: Association of Jewish Libraries, 1983– .

Kiryat Sefer. Jerusalem: Magnes Press, 1924– .
   This bibliographic quarterly essentially constitutes Israel's national bibliography.
Works of Jewish interest published in other countries are also listed.

Ohev Sefer. Jerusalem: High Tech Graphics and Publishing, 1987– .

Soncino-Blätter. Berlin, 1925–30.

Studies in Bibliography and Booklore. Cincinnati: Library of Hebrew Union College–Jewish Institute of Religion, 1953– .

For more information on the background and history of journals of Jewish bibliography, see the article "Jewish Bibliographic Journals" by Charles Berlin in the *Jewish Book Annual* 29 (1971–72): 23–38.

Reference Works
General

Carter, John. *ABC for Book Collectors.* 5th ed., rev. New York: Knopf, 1981.

Glaister, Geoffrey Ashall. *Glossary of the Book: Terms Used in Paper Making, Printing, Bookbinding and Publishing.* London: G. Allen and Unwin, 1960.

Roberts, Matt T., and Don Etherington. *Bookbinding and the Conservation of Books: A Dictionary of Descriptive Terminology.* Washington, D.C.: Library of Congress, 1982.

Judaica

Alcalay, Reuben. *The Complete English-Hebrew Dictionary.* 2 vols. Ramat-Gan and Jerusalem: Massadah Publishing Co., 1986.

———. *The Complete Hebrew-English Dictionary.* Ramat-Gan and Jerusalem: Massadah Publishing Co., 1986.

Ashkenazi, Shmuel, and Dov Jarden. *Otsar Rashe Tevot: Thesaurus of Hebrew Abbreviations.* Jerusalem: Rubin Mass, 1978.

Chajes, Saul. *Otsar Beduye ha-Shem.* Vienna, 1933. Reprint. Hildesheim: Georg Olms, 1967.
Hebrew and Yiddish pseudonyms.

Cutter, Charles, and Micha Falk Oppenheim. *Jewish Reference Sources: A Selective Annotated Bibliographic Guide.* New York: Garland Publishing, 1982.

Encyclopaedia Judaica. 16 vols. Jerusalem: Keter Publishing House, 1971.

Even-Shoshan, Abraham. *Ha-Milon he-Hadash.* 2d rev. ed. 4 vols. Jerusalem: Kiryat Sefer, 1985.

Frank, Ruth, and William Wollheim, eds. *The Book of Jewish Books: A Reader's Guide to Judaism.* San Francisco: Harper and Row, 1986.

Ha-Entsiklopediyah ha-'Ivrit. 32 vols. plus 2 Supplement vols. Israel: Encyclopaedia Publishing Co., 1949–83.

Hoogewoud, F. J.; Ulf Haxen; A. K. Offenberg; and G. Weill, comps. *A Guide to Libraries of Judaica and Hebraica in Europe.* Copenhagen: Det Kongelige Bibliotek, 1985.

The Jewish Encyclopedia. 12 vols. New York and London: Funk and Wagnalls Company, 1906.

Lubetski, Edith, and Meir Lubetski. *Building a Judaica Library Collection: A Resource Guide.* Littleton, Colo.: Libraries Unlimited, 1983.

Checklist of the Exhibition

This checklist includes manuscripts and printed books exhibited in "A Sign and a Witness: 2,000 Years of Hebrew Books and Illuminated Manuscripts," presented in the D. Samuel and Jeane H. Gottesman Exhibition Hall, The New York Public Library, Fifth Avenue and 42nd Street, October 15, 1988–January 14, 1989. The symbol * indicates items illustrated in black and white; the symbol § indicates items illustrated in color. An index of illustrations begins on p. 219. The abbreviation "NYPL" refers to The New York Public Library.

Manuscripts

I
§ Joseph Albo, fifteenth century
ספר העקרים
Sefer ha-'Ikarim
Central Italy, ca. 1460–70
Accademia dei Concordi, Rovigo, Ms. Silvestriana 220

2
§ Bible
Aleppo Codex
Tenth century
Page containing text of 2 Chronicles 35:25 through 36:19
Ben-Zvi Institute for the Study of Jewish Communities in the East, Jerusalem

3
Bible
Ambrosian Bible
Germany, 1236–38
Biblioteca Ambrosiana, Milan, Ms. B. 32, Inf.

4
§ Bible
Burgos Bible
Spain, 1260
The Jewish National and University Library, Jerusalem, Ms. Heb. 4° 790

5
§ Bible
Xanten Bible
Germany, 1294
NYPL, Spencer Collection, Heb. Ms. 1

6
§ Bible
Cervera Bible
Spain, 1300
Biblioteca Nacional, Lisbon, Ms. 72

7
Bible
Schocken Bible
Southern Germany, ca. 1300
Schocken Collection, Jerusalem, Ms. 14840

8
* Bible
Northern Spain or Provence, 1301
Royal Library, Copenhagen, Cod. Hebr. II

9
§ Bible
Harley Catalan Bible
Northern Spain, 1350–75
The British Library, London, Harley Ms. 1528

10
Bible
Written by Simeon ben Samuel
Provence, December 1422
The Pierpont Morgan Library, New York, The William S. Glazier Collection, deposited in 1963, given in 1984

11
* Bible
Spain, 1460–80
Royal Library, Copenhagen, Cod. Hebr. V

12
§ Bible
Lisbon Bible
Lisbon, 1482
The British Library, London, Ms. Or. 2627

13
Bible
Ibn Musa Bible
Lisbon, 1475
With box binding
Hebrew Union College–Jewish Institute of Religion Library, Cincinnati, Ohio, Ms. 2

14
* Bible
Aberdeen Bible
Naples, 1493/94
Aberdeen University Library, Scotland, Ms. 23

15
Bible
Probably Spain, fifteenth century
Staatsbibliothek Preussischer Kulturbesitz, Orientabteilung, Berlin (West), Ms. Hamilton 81

16
* Bible. Esther
מגילת אסתר
Megillat Ester
Copied and illustrated by Raphael Montalto
Netherlands, 1685/86
NYPL, Spencer Collection, Heb. Ms. 2

Beginning of an Esther Scroll copied and illustrated by Raphael Montalto, Netherlands, 1685/86. Raphael Montalto's father, Elijah Montalto, was personal physician to Marie de Médicis of France.

NYPL, Spencer Collection, Heb. Ms. 2 (Ex. no. 16)

17
* Bible. Five Scrolls
Written in micrography by Aaron Wolf
Herlingen of Gewitsch
Vienna, 1752
Collection of Richard D. Levy

18
§ Bible. Numbers
שלח-לך
Shelaḥ-Lekha
Egypt, 1106/07
Weekly Torah reading containing text of
Numbers 13–15
The Jewish National and University Library,
Jerusalem, Ms. Heb 8° 2238

19
* Bible. Pentateuch
Samaritan Torah
Land of Israel, thirteenth century
NYPL, Rare Books and Manuscripts Division

20
* Bible. Pentateuch
Written by Moses of Ebermannstadt
Southern Germany, 1290
Royal Library, Copenhagen, Cod. Hebr. XI

21
* Bible. Pentateuch
Germany, 1294/95
Bibliothèque Nationale, Paris, Ms. Hebr. 5

22
* Bible. Pentateuch
Sussex German Pentateuch
With Masorah, Targum Onkelos, Five
Megillot, and Haftarot
Copied and illuminated by Ḥayyim
Southern Germany, ca. 1300
The British Library, London, Add. Ms. 15282

23
* Bible. Pentateuch
Coburg Pentateuch
With Megillot and Haftarot
Copied by Simḥah ben Samuel ha-Levi
Coburg, 1395
The British Library, London, Add. Ms. 19776

24
* Bible. Pentateuch
Spain, ca. 1460
Royal Library, Copenhagen, Cod. Hebr. VII

25
§ Bible. Pentateuch
San'a Pentateuch
With Masorah and Maḥberet ha-Tijan
Written and illuminated by Benayah ben
Se'adyah
Yemen, 1469
The British Library, London, Ms. Or. 2348

Fragment of the Naḥum Commentary
(Péšer Naḥum).
*The Shrine of the Book, D. Samuel and Jeane H.
Gottesman Center for Biblical Manuscripts, Israel
Museum, Jerusalem (Ex. no. 28)*

26
* Bible. Pentateuch
Written by Benayah ben Se'adyah ben
Zacharia
Yemen, 1470
Valmadonna Trust Library, London

27
* Bible. Psalms
Italy, fifteenth century
Staatsbibliothek Preussischer Kulturbesitz,
Orientabteilung, Berlin (West), Ms. Hamilton
547

28
§* Dead Sea Scrolls
Naḥum Commentary
After 63 B.C.E.
The Shrine of the Book, D. Samuel and Jeane
H. Gottesman Center for Biblical Manu-
scripts, Israel Museum, Jerusalem

29
§ Geniza
Children's Primer
Tenth or eleventh century
Cambridge University Library, T-S. K5.13

30
Liturgy for Saying Grace
Pressburg, 1731
Hebrew Union College–Jewish Institute of Re-
ligion Library, Cincinnati, Ohio, Ms. 814

31
§ *Grace after Meals*
Vienna, 1737
Valmadonna Trust Library, London

32
* Haggadah
Fragment from Geniza
Oriental, ca. 1000
Annenberg Research Institute for Judaic and
Near Eastern Studies, Merion, Penn., Halper
211

33
§* Haggadah
Bird's Head Haggadah
Southern Germany, ca. 1300
Israel Museum, Jerusalem, Ms. 180/57

34
§ Haggadah
Rylands Spanish Haggadah
Spain, mid-fourteenth century
The John Rylands University Library of Manchester, Ms. 6

35
§ Haggadah
Golden Haggadah
Spain, fourteenth century
The British Library, London, Add. Ms. 27210

36
* Haggadah
Kaufmann Haggadah
Spain, fourteenth century
Library of the Hungarian Academy of Sciences, Budapest, Ms. Kaufmann A422

37
§ Haggadah
Written by Joel ben Simeon, called
Feibush Ashkenazi
Italy?, 1454
Library of the Jewish Theological Seminary of America, New York, Mic. No. 8279

38
Haggadah
Second Nuremberg Haggadah
Southern Germany, mid-fifteenth century
Schocken Collection, Jerusalem, Ms. 24087

39
§ Haggadah
Washington Haggadah
Written by Joel ben Simeon
Probably Northern Italy, 1478
Library of Congress, Washington, D.C.,
Hebraic Section

40
§ Haggadah
First Cincinnati Haggadah
Southern Germany, ca. 1480–90
Hebrew Union College–Jewish Institute of Religion Library, Cincinnati, Ohio, Ms. 444

41
Haggadah
Written by Joel ben Simeon
Germany, fifteenth century
Library of the Jewish Theological Seminary of America, New York, Mic. No. 4481

42
Haggadah
Farissol Haggadah
Ferrara, 1515
Library of the Jewish Theological Seminary of America, New York, Mic. No. 4817

43
Haggadah
Second Cincinnati Haggadah
Amsterdam, 1717
Hebrew Union College–Jewish Institute of Religion Library, Cincinnati, Ohio, Ms. 444.1

44
§ Haggadah
הגדת שיר המעלות לדוד
A Song of David
Calligraphy and illumination by David Moss
Completed in Israel, 1987
Collection of Beatrice and Richard D. Levy

45
הנהגות מכל השנה
Hanhagot mi-Kol ha-Shanah
Northern Italy, late fifteenth century
Princeton University Library, Princeton, N.J.,
Robert Garrett Collection of Medieval and Renaissance Manuscripts, Ms. Garrett 26

46
Iehudah Machabeu
Sample Book
Amsterdam, 1660
Collection of Richard D. Levy

47
Isaac ben Joseph, of Corbeil, thirteenth century
ספר מצות קטן
Sefer Mitsvot Katan
Paris, ca. 1288
Bibliothèque Nationale, Paris, Ms. Hebr. 643

48
* Isaac Israeli, fourteenth century
יסוד עולם
Yesod 'Olam
Sicily, 1491
Bibliothèque Nationale, Paris, Ms. Hebr. 1069

49
* עברונות
'Ivronot
Bingen am Rhein, 1651
A work on the calendar
Staatsbibliothek Preussischer Kulturbesitz,
Orientabteilung, Berlin (West), Ms. or. oct. 3150

50
* Kabbalah
Collection of Mystical Texts
Greece, 1468
NYPL, Jewish Division, **P; formerly Sassoon, 56

51
Kabbalistic Omer Book
1743
Hebrew Union College–Jewish Institute of Religion Library, Cincinnati, Ohio, Ms. 803

52
* Maḥzor
Tripartite Maḥzor
Vol. I
Southern Germany, ca. 1320
Library of the Hungarian Academy of Sciences, Budapest, Ms. Kaufmann A384

53
* Maḥzor
Tripartite Maḥzor
Vol. II
Southern Germany, ca. 1320
The British Library, London, Add. Ms. 22413

54
§ Maḥzor
Tripartite Maḥzor
Vol. III
Southern Germany, ca. 1320
Bodleian Library, Oxford, Ms. Michael 619

55
§ Maḥzor
Hamilton Maḥzor
Spain, thirteenth or early fourteenth century
Staatsbibliothek Preussischer Kulturbesitz,
Orientabteilung, Berlin (West), Ms. Hamilton 288

56
* Maḥzor
Germany, thirteenth or fourteenth
century
Württembergische Landesbibliothek, Stuttgart,
Cod. Or. Fol. 42

57
§ Maḥzor
Catalan Maḥzor
Catalonia, fourteenth century
The Jewish National and University Library,
Jerusalem, Ms. 8° 6527

58
* Maḥzor
Southern Germany, fourteenth century
Bodleian Library, Oxford, Ms. Reggio 1

59
§ Maḥzor
Germany, fourteenth century
NYPL, Jewish Division, **P

60
* Maḥzor
Germany, fourteenth century
Staatsbibliothek Preussischer Kulturbesitz,
Orientabteilung, Berlin (West), Ms. or. fol.
388

61
§ Maḥzor
Rothschild Maḥzor
Florence, 1492
Library of the Jewish Theological Seminary of
America, New York, Mic. No. 8892

62
§ Maḥzor
Italy, fifteenth century
NYPL, Jewish Division, **P

63
* Maḥzor
Northern Italy, fifteenth century
Staatsbibliothek Preussischer Kulturbesitz,
Orientabteilung, Berlin (West), Ms. or. quart.
361

64
Maḥzor
Written by Iehudah Machabeu
Amsterdam, 1659
Collection of Richard D. Levy

65
Maḥzor
Liturgy for New Year
China, ca. seventeenth century
In form of Chinese fan book
Hebrew Union College–Jewish Institute of Re-
ligion Library, Cincinnati, Ohio, Ms. 925

66
Moses Maimonides, 1135–1204
משנה תורה
Mishneh Torah
Twelfth century
Two leaves with corrections in Mai-
monides' hand
Library of the Jewish Theological Seminary of
America, New York, ENA 2632

67
§ Moses Maimonides, 1135–1204
משנה תורה
Mishneh Torah
The *Kaufmann Mishneh Torah*
Germany, 1295–96
Library of the Hungarian Academy of Sci-
ences, Budapest, Ms. Kaufmann A 77/I

68
§ Moses Maimonides, 1135–1204
משנה תורה
Mishneh Torah
Copied and illuminated by Solomon Ibn
Alzuk
Lisbon, 1471/72
The British Library, London, Harley Ms. 5699

69
§ Moses Maimonides, 1135–1204
משנה תורה
Mishneh Torah
Northern Italy, fifteenth century
Private collection; formerly Frankfurt am
Main, Stadtbibliothek, MS. Ausst. 6

70
§ Moses Maimonides, 1135–1204
מורה נבוכים
Moreh Nevukhim
Barcelona, 1348
Royal Library, Copenhagen, Cod. Hebr.
XXXVII

71
§ Medical Miscellany
Italy, fourteenth century
Bibliothèque Nationale, Paris, Ms. Hebr. 1181

72
§ Medical Treatises
Italy, fifteenth century
Cambridge University Library, Dd. 10. 68

73
* Medical Work
Northern Spain or Provence, first half fif-
teenth century
Bibliothèque Nationale, Paris, Ms. Hebr. 1135

74
Memorial Service
Prague, 1731
Hebrew Union College–Jewish Institute of Re-
ligion Library, Cincinnati, Ohio, Ms. 453

75
Mohel Book
Copied by Uri Pheibush ben Isaak Eisik,
Sofer (Scribe) of Altona, Hamburg, and
Wandsbek, also known as Philip Isak
Levy
N.p., 1741
Hebrew Union College–Jewish Institute of Re-
ligion Library, Cincinnati, Ohio, Ms. 599

76
Mohel Book
Hildesheim, 1775
Hebrew Union College–Jewish Institute of Re-
ligion Library, Cincinnati, Ohio, Ms. 600

77
* Mohel Book
Copied by Aaron ben Judah Levy
London, 1826
Collection of Richard D. Levy

78
Moses ben Jacob, of Coucy, fl. thirteenth
century
ספר מצות גדול
Sefer Mitsvot Gadol
Italy, ca. 1400
Private collection; formerly Frankfurt am
Main, Stadtbibliothek, MS. Ausst. 7

79
פרק שירה
Perek Shirah
End eighteenth/beginning nineteenth
century
Hebrew Union College–Jewish Institute of Religion Library, Cincinnati, Ohio, Ms. 815

80

§ Isaac ben Solomon ibn Abi Sahulah, thirteenth century

משל הקדמוני

Meshal ha-Kadmoni
Southern Germany, 1450
Bodleian Library, Oxford, Ms. Opp. 154

81

* סדר ברכת המזון

Seder Birkat ha-Mazon
Nikolsburg, 1728
Royal Library, Copenhagen, Cod. Hebr.
XXXII

82

* Shahin

ארדשיר נאמה

Ardashir Nama
Persia, seventeenth century
Staatsbibliothek Preussischer Kulturbesitz,
Orientabteilung, Berlin (West), Ms. or. quart.
1680

83

Shahin

ארדשיר נאמה

Ardashir Nama
Persia, seventeenth/eighteenth century
Library of the Jewish Theological Seminary of
America, New York, Mic. No. 8270

84

* Shahin

Moses Book
Persia, late seventeenth century
Staatsbibliothek Preussischer Kulturbesitz,
Orientabteilung, Berlin (West), Ms. or. oct.
2885

85

* Siddur
Aragon or Catalonia, second half fif-
teenth century
Bibliothèque Nationale, Paris, Ms. Hebr. 593

86

Theodosius Tripolitanus (first century
B.C.E.)
Sphaerica
Translated from the Arabic into Hebrew
by Moses ibn Tibbon, 1271
and:

Menelaus of Alexandria (first century
C.E.)
Sphaerica
Translated from the Arabic into Hebrew
by Jacob ben Makhir, 1271
Aix-en-Provence, 1332
Library of the Jewish Theological Seminary of
America, New York, Mic. No. 8182

87

Treatises on Calendar, etc.
Germany, seventeenth/eighteenth century
Hebrew Union College–Jewish Institute of Re-
ligion Library, Cincinnati, Ohio, Ms. 906

*The hanging of Haman's ten sons, from a sev-
enteenth-century Judeo-Persian manuscript of
Ardashir Nama by Shahin, a Jewish poet
from Shiraz who lived in the fourteenth
century.*

*Staatsbibliothek Preussischer Kulturbesitz, Orient-
abteilung, Berlin (West), Ms. or. quart. 1680, fol.
93r (Ex. no. 82)*

Printed Books

88
* Abraham bar Ḥiyya, fl. 1136
צורת הארץ
Tsurat ha-Arets
Sphaera Mundi
Basel: H. Petrus, 1546
Astronomy
NYPL, Jewish Division

89
Isaac Abravanel, 1437–1508
ראש אמנה
Rosh Amanah
Constantinople: David and Samuel Ibn Naḥmias, 1505
Discussion of Maimonides' thirteen articles of belief
Bound with the author's *Naḥalat Avot* and *Zevaḥ Pesaḥ*. All three are thought to have been issued together.
NYPL, Jewish Division

90
David ben Joseph ben David Abudarham, fourteenth century
פירוש סידור התפלות
Perush Sidur ha-Tefilot
(*Commentary on the Prayerbook*)
Lisbon: Eliezer Toledano, 1489
NYPL, Jewish Division

91
* Samuel Joseph Agnon, 1888–1970
מעשה רבי גדיאל התינוק
Ma'aseh Rabi Gadi'el ha-Tinok
(*Tale of the Baby Rabbi Gadiel*)
Berlin, 1925
Gift for members of Soncino-Gesellschaft der Freunde des jüdischen Buches
NYPL, Jewish Division

92
* Samuel Joseph Agnon, 1888–1970
כלב חוצות
Kelev Ḥutsot
(*A Stray Dog*)
Illustrated by Avigdor Arikha
Jerusalem: Tarshish, 1960
Fiction
NYPL, Jewish Division

93
Joseph Albo, fifteenth century
ספר העקרים
Sefer ha-'Ikarim
(*Book of Principles*)
Soncino: Joshua Solomon Soncino, 1485
NYPL, Jewish Division

94
Moses ben Baruch Almosnino, 1510–1580
הנהגת החיים
Hanhagat ha-Ḥayim
Salonica: Joseph ben Isaac Jabez, 1564
Ethics
NYPL, Jewish Division

95
* Thomas Aquinas, 1225?–1274
קיצור
Kitsur
(*Summa contra gentiles*)
Rome: Ex typographia Iacobi Phaei Andreae filij, 1657
Philosophy
NYPL, Jewish Division

96
* Averroës, 1126–1198
כל מלאכת הגיון
Kol Melekhet Higayon
Riva di Trento: Jacob ben David Marcaria, 1559
Paraphrase of Aristotle's *Organon*
NYPL, Jewish Division

97
* Avicenna (Husain Ibn 'Abd Allāh Ibn Sina), 980?–1037
קאנון
Kanon
Naples: Azriel ben Joseph of Guenzenhausen, 1491. 5 parts in 3 volumes
Medicine
NYPL, Jewish Division

98
Baḥya ben Asher ben Ḥalawa, d. 1340
ביאור על התורה
Be'ur 'Al ha-Torah
(*Commentary on the Pentateuch*)
Naples: Joseph ben Jacob of Guenzenhausen, 1492
NYPL, Jewish Division

99
Baḥya ben Joseph, eleventh century
חובות הלבבות
Hovot ha-Levavot
(*Duties of the Heart*)
Naples: Joseph ben Jacob of Guenzenhausen, 1489
Ethics
NYPL, Jewish Division

100
Barlaam and Josaphat
בן המלך והנזיר
Ben ha-Melekh veha-Nazir
(*The Prince and the Hermit*)
Mantua: Venturin Ruffinello, 1557
NYPL, Jewish Division

101
* Shabbethai ben Joseph Bass, 1641–1718
שפתי ישינים
Sifte Yeshenim
Amsterdam, 1679/80
Bibliography of Hebrew literature
NYPL, Jewish Division

102
בראשית *
be-Reshit
(*In the Beginning*)
Vol. 1
Moscow and Leningrad (printed in Berlin), 1926
Literary collection
NYPL, Jewish Division

103
Eliezer Ben-Yehudah, 1858–1922
מלון הלשון העברית
Milon ha-Lashon ha-'Ivrit
(*Complete Dictionary and Thesaurus of the Hebrew Language*)
Berlin, Jerusalem, 1908–59. 16 volumes
NYPL, Jewish Division

104
* Ḥayyim Naḥman Bialik, 1873–1934
שירים
Shirim
Cracow: Hovevei ha-Shira ha-'Ivrit, 1907/08
Poetry
NYPL, Jewish Division

105
* Bible
Vol. 4
Venice: Daniel Bomberg, 1525
NYPL, Jewish Division

106
Bible
Vol. 1
Antwerp: Christopher Plantin, 1566
With Robert Browning's signature
Library of the Jewish Theological Seminary of
America, New York, Acc. No. 174561

107
Bible
דרך הקדש
Derekh ha-Kodesh
(*Via Sancta*)
Hamburg: Typis Elianis, per Iohannem
Saxonem, 1587
Known as "Hutter's Hebrew Bible"
NYPL, Jewish Division

108
* Bible
Biblia Hebraica
Prepared by Manasseh ben Israel
Amsterdam: Sumptibus Henrici Lauren-
tii, 1635
NYPL, Jewish Division

109
* Bible
תורה נביאים וכתובים
Torah Nevi'im u-Khetuvim
(*Biblia Hebraica*)
Philadelphia: Thomas Dobson, Typis
Gulielmi Fry, 1814. 2 volumes
The first Hebrew Bible printed in
America
NYPL, Jewish Division

110
* Bible. Ecclesiastes
קהלת יעקב
Kehilat Ya'akov
Safed: Abraham Ashkenazi by Eliezer
ben Isaac Ashkenazi, 1577–78
NYPL, Jewish Division

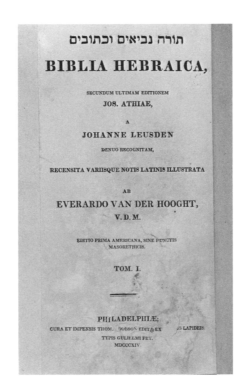

Title page of the first Hebrew Bible published
in America (Philadelphia, 1814).
NYPL, Jewish Division [Ex. no. 109]

111
Bible. Lamentations
איכה
Eykhah
Calligraphy and printing by Jonathan
Kremer
Elkins Park, Pa.: Kesset Press, 1985
NYPL, Jewish Division

112
* Bible. Minor Prophets
תרי עשר
Tre 'Asar
Paris: Robertus Stephanus, 1539–40
NYPL, Jewish Division

113
Bible. Pentateuch
חמשה חומשי תורה
Hamishah Humshe Torah
Bologna: Abraham ben Hayyim for
Joseph ben Abraham Caravida, 1482
On vellum
NYPL, Jewish Division

114
Bible. Pentateuch
תורת האלהים
Torat ha-Elohim
(*The Law of God*)
Edited by Isaac Leeser
Philadelphia: K. Sherman, 1845.
5 volumes
NYPL, Jewish Division

115
* Bible. Pentateuch
חמשה חומשי תורה
Hamishah Humshe Torah
Berlin: Soncino-Gesellschaft, 1929/30–
1932/33. 2 volumes
NYPL, Jewish Division

116
* Bible. Pentateuch
תורה
Torah
Jerusalem: Korén, 1959
NYPL, Jewish Division

117
* Bible. Polyglot
Biblia Polyglotta Ximenii
(*The Complutensian Bible*)
Alcalá de Henares, 1514–17. 6 volumes
NYPL, Jewish Division

118
Bible. Polyglot
Biblia Sacra
Antwerp: Christopher Plantin, 1569–72.
8 volumes
NYPL, Jewish Division

Beginning of Jeremiah in The Complutensian Bible *(Alcalá de Henares, 1514–17).
The biblical text appears in Hebrew with roots
in the margin, in Jerome's Latin translation,*
*and in the Septuagint Greek version with an
interlinear Latin translation.*
NYPL, Jewish Division (Ex. no. 117)

119
Bible. Polyglot
Biblia Sacra Polyglotta
London: Thomas Roycroft, 1655–57.
6 volumes
Known as the London or Walton's
Polyglot
NYPL, Jewish Division

120
Johannes Böschenstein, 1472–1540
Contenta In Hoc Libello . . .
Augsburg: Erhard Oeglin, 1514
An elementary Hebrew textbook for
Christians
NYPL, Jewish Division

121
* John Calvin, 1509–1564
חנוך *hoc est Catechesis*
Leiden: Ex Officina Plantiniana, Apud
Franciscum Raphelengium, 1591
Christian catechism with Hebrew and
Greek translations
NYPL, Jewish Division

122
* Joseph Caro, 1488–1575
שלחן ערוך
Shulḥan 'Arukh
(*The Set Table*)
Venice: A. Bragadin, 1564–65
Code of Jewish Law
NYPL, Jewish Division

123
Elijah ben Moses Gershon, eighteenth
century
מלאכת מחשבת
Melekhet Meḥashevet
Berlin: Isaac Jacob Speier, 1765
Mathematics
NYPL, Jewish Division

124
* Abraham ben Mordecai Farissol, 1451–
1525
אגרת ארחות עולם
Igeret Oreḥot 'Olam
Venice: Giovanni di Gara, 1586
Geography
NYPL, Jewish Division

125
Abraham b. Samuel Firkovich, 1786–
1874
מסה ומריבה
Masah u-Merivah
Eupatoria: Tirishkan, 1838
Karaitic polemic
NYPL, Jewish Division

126
Solomon ibn Gabirol, 1021?–1069?
מבחר הפנינים
Mivḥar ha-Peninim
(*Choice of Pearls*)
Soncino: Joshua Solomon Soncino, 1484
Maxims, proverbs, and moral reflections
NYPL, Jewish Division

127
David ben Solomon ben Seligman Gans,
1541–1613
נחמד ונעים
Neḥmad ve-Naʿim
Jessnitz: Israel ben Abraham, 1783
Astronomy
NYPL, Jewish Division

128
Haggadah
Prague: Gershom Kohen, 1527
Library of the Jewish Theological Seminary of
America, New York, Acc. No. 66245

129
Haggadah
Amsterdam: Asher Anshel ben Eliezer
Ḥazan and Issachar Ber ben Abraham
Eliezer, 1695
NYPL, Jewish Division

130
Haggadah
The Haggadah
Executed by Arthur Szyk
Edited by Cecil Roth
London: Beaconsfield Press, printed in
1939 but not bound and published until
about 1949
NYPL, Spencer Collection

131
*Haggadah
A Passover Haggadah
For the Central Conference of American
Rabbis
Drawings by Leonard Baskin
New York: Grossman Publishers, 1974
NYPL, Jewish Division

132
Haggadah
Illustrated, Written, and Executed by
Yaʿakov Boussidan
London, 1974
NYPL, Jewish Division

133
*Theodor Benjamin Herzl, 1860–1904
תל־אביב
Tel-Aviv
Warsaw: Russian Zionist Organization,
1902
Translation of *Altneuland*
NYPL, Jewish Division

134
*Homer
איליאס
Iliyas
Berlin: Stybel Pub. Co., 1930
The *Iliad*, translated by Saul
Tchernichovski
NYPL, Jewish Division

135
*Joseph ben David Ibn Yaḥya, 1494–1539
תורה אור
Torah Or
Bologna: The Jewish Silkweavers,
1537–38
Theology
NYPL, Jewish Division

136
Immanuel ben Solomon, ca. 1265–1330
המחברות
ha-Maḥbarot
Brescia: Gershom Soncino, 1491
Poems
NYPL, Jewish Division

137
*Jacob ben Asher, ca. 1269–ca. 1340
ארבעה טורים
Arbaʿah Turim
(*The Four Columns*)
Piove di Sacco: Meshullam Kuzi, 1475
Code of Jewish Law
On vellum
NYPL, Jewish Division

138
Jacob Joseph Ha-Kohen of Polonnoye, d.
ca. 1782
תולדות יעקב יוסף
Toledot Yaʿakov Yosef
Korzec: Zebi Hirsch ben Aryeh Loeb and
Samuel ben Issachar Baer Segal, 1780
First Ḥasidic work published
NYPL, Jewish Division

139
*Abraham Jona, 1745?–1815
*The Diary of the Last Rabbi of the Vene-
tian Ghetto, 1783–1814*
Manuscript bound with *Ḥesed le-
Avraham,* a daily prayerbook, and other
special prayers including one for the suc-
cess of Napoleon and his armies
NYPL, Jewish Division

140
Joseph bin Gorion ha-Kohen
יוסיפון
(*Josippon*)
Calcutta, 1841
A popular chronicle of Jewish history,
based mainly on Josephus
NYPL, Jewish Division

141
*Judah ben Jeḥiel, Messer Leon, fifteenth
century
נפת צופים
Nofet Tsufim
(*The Honeycomb*)
Mantua: Abraham Conat [1474–76?]
Rhetoric
NYPL, Jewish Division

142
David Kimḥi, 1160–1235
ספר השרשים
Sefer ha-Shorashim
(*Book of Roots*)
Naples, 1490
Dictionary
NYPL, Jewish Division

143
Naḥman Krochmal, 1785–1840
מורה נבוכי הזמן
Moreh Nevukhe ha-Zeman
(*Guide to the Perplexed of the Time*)
Leopoli, 1851
Philosophical work
NYPL, Jewish Division

144
Jonah ben Elijah Landsofer, 1678–1712
מעיל צדקה
Me'il Tsedakah
Prague: Judah and Lipman Bak, 1756
Rabbinic decisions and responsa, containing notes on Euclid
NYPL, Jewish Division

145
* Meir Letteris, 1800–1871
בן־אבויה
Ben-Avuyah
Vienna: In Commission, J. Schlossberg's Buchhandlung, 1865
A re-working of Goethe's *Faust*
NYPL, Jewish Division

146
Mendel Levin, ca. 1741–1819
חשבון הנפש
Ḥeshbon ha-Nefesh
Vilna: M. Romm & Sons, 1844
Ethics; includes paraphrases from *Poor Richard's Almanac*
NYPL, Jewish Division

147
* Elijah Levita, 1468–1549
פרקי אליהו
Pirke Eliyahu
Basel: J. Froben, 1527
Hebrew grammar
NYPL, Jewish Division

148
Yom-Tov ben Solomon Lipmann-Muelhausen, fifteenth century
ספר נצחון
Sefer Nitsaḥon
Altdorf, 1644
Polemics
NYPL, Jewish Division

149
Isaac Lombroso, d. 1752
זרע יצחק
Zera Yitsḥak
Tunis: Yeshuah ha-Cohen Tanugi, 1768
Talmud commentaries
NYPL, Jewish Division

150
* Moses Ḥayyim Luzzatto, 1707–1747
לישרים תהלה
La-Yesharim Tehilah
Amsterdam: Proops, 1743
Poetry
NYPL, Jewish Division

151
* Maḥzor
Soncino, Casalmaggiore: Joshua Solomon Soncino, 1485–86. 2 volumes
Festival prayers
NYPL, Jewish Division

152
* Maḥzor
Bologna: Jeḥiel ben Solomon of Ravenna et al., 1540. 2 volumes
Festival prayers, Roman Rite
On vellum
NYPL, Jewish Division

153
Moses Maimonides, 1135–1204
מורה נבוכים
Moreh Nevukhim
(*Guide to the Perplexed*)
[Rome, 1473–75?]
NYPL, Jewish Division

154
* Abraham Mapu, 1808–1867
אהבת ציון
Ahavat Tsiyon
2d ed.
Vilna: Romm, 1864
Historical novel
NYPL, Jewish Division

155
* Raymundus Martini
Pugio Fidei
Leipzig: Sumptibus Haeredum F. Lanckisi, 1687
NYPL, Jewish Division

156
* המאסף
ha-Me'asef
(*The Gatherer*)
Koenigsberg, 1784–1811
The earliest successful periodical published in Hebrew
NYPL, Jewish Division

157
Moses Mendelssohn, 1729–1786
אור לנתיבה
Or la-Netivah
Berlin, 1783
Introduction to Mendelssohn's Bible translation
NYPL, Jewish Division

158
* ספר מדות
Sefer Midot
(*Book of Ethics*)
Isny, 1542
NYPL, Jewish Division

159
* Mishnah. Abot
פרקי אבות
Pirke Avot
Sententiae Vere Elegantes
(*The Chapters of the Fathers*)
Isny: Paul Fagius, 1541
NYPL, Jewish Division

160
Mishnah. Abot
אבני יהושע
Avne Yehoshu'a
New York: Printed at "Jewish Messenger" Office, 1860
Commentary on Abot
NYPL, Jewish Division

161
* Judah Monis, 1683–1764
Dickdook Leshon Gnebreet
(*A Grammar of the Hebrew Tongue*)
Boston: J. Green, 1735
NYPL, Jewish Division

162
* Moses ben Jacob of Coucy, thirteenth century
ספר מצות גדול
Sefer Mitsvot Gadol
(*Great Book of Precepts*)
[Rome, 1473–75?]
NYPL, Jewish Division

163
* Sebastian Münster, 1489–1552
הויכוח
ha-Vikuah
(*The Disputation*)
Basel: Froben, 1529
NYPL, Jewish Division

164
Sebastian Münster, 1489–1552
ספר השרשים
Sefer Ha-Shorashim
Basel: Froben, 1564
With Ben Jonson's signature
Library of the Jewish Theological Seminary of America, New York, Acc. No. 128961

165
* Moses Nahmanides, 1195–1270
חדושי התורה
Hidushe ha-Torah
Lisbon: Eliezer Toledano, 1489
Commentary on the Pentateuch
NYPL, Jewish Division

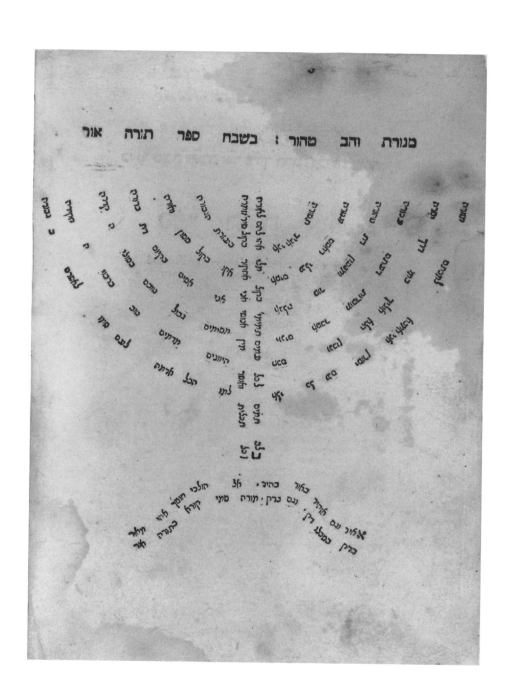

166
* Naphtali Hirsch ben Menahem, sixteenth century
פירוש למדרש חמש מגילות רבה
Perush la-Midrash Hamesh Megilot Rabah
Cracow: Isaac ben Aaron of Prostitz, 1569
Commentary on *Midrash Rabbah* to the Five Scrolls
NYPL, Jewish Division

An introductory poem in the form of a menorah, in Torah Or *(Bologna, 1537–38), an eschatological work by Joseph ben David Ibn Yahya.*
NYPL, Jewish Division (Ex. no. 135)

Page of the diary of Abraham Jona (1745?–1815), last rabbi of the Venetian Ghetto, which is bound with a printed prayer for the success of Napoleon and his armies.
NYPL, Jewish Division (Ex. no. 139)

167
Nathan ben Jeḥiel, ca. 1035–1106
ערוך
'Arukh
[Rome: Obadiah, Manasseh and Benjamin, ca. 1469–72]
Dictionary of the Talmud
NYPL, Jewish Division

168
∗ New Testament. Gospels. Matthew. Hebrew
. . . *Evangelivm Secvndvm Matthaevm In Lingva Hebraica, cum uersione latinae atque succinctis annotationibus Sebastiani Munsteri*
Basileae: Apud Henricvm Petrvm, 1537
NYPL, Rare Books and Manuscripts Division

169
Occasional Prayers
סדר תפלות
Seder Tefilot
Amsterdam: Proops, 1757
According to the custom of the Cochin Jews
NYPL, Jewish Division

170

* Occasional Prayers
סדר הקונטריס
Seder ha-Kunteres
Avignon, 1765
Prayers in the rite of the Jews of Avignon
NYPL, Jewish Division

171

Omar Khayyām
אמר קים
(*The Rubaiyat*)
Manchester, 1907
Translated by Joseph Massel
NYPL, Jewish Division

172

On Confiscation of the Talmud
Venice, October 21, 1553
Printed broadside
Library of the Jewish Theological Seminary of
America, New York, Acc. No. 04501

173

Joseph Perl, 1773–1839
מגלה טמירין
Megaleh Temirin
Wien: A. Strauss, 1819
Anti-Ḥasidic satires
NYPL, Jewish Division

173a

Josiah ben Joseph Pinto, ca. 1565–1648
כסף נבחר
Kesef Nivḥar
Damascus: Abraham ben Mattathiah Bat-
Sheva, printed by Isaac & Jacob, sons of
Abraham Ashkenazi, 1605–06
Sermons on Genesis, Exodus, and Levi-
ticus. The only Hebrew book printed in
Damascus
NYPL, Jewish Division

174

Menaḥem Zion Cohen Porto, d. ca. 1660
עובר לסוחר
'Over la-Soḥer
Venice: Giovanni Caleoni appresso
Pietro, Aluise & Lorenzo Bragadini, 1627
Arithmetic
NYPL, Jewish Division

175

* Jean Baptiste Racine, 1639–1699
גמול עתליה
Gemul 'Ataliah
Amsterdam: J. Jansson in the house of J.
Mondavi, 1770
Athalie, translated by David Franco
Mendes
NYPL, Jewish Division

176

Research Institute for Hebrew Poetry
מבחר השבעים
Mivḥar ha-Shiv'im
Tel-Aviv: Ha-Arets, 1947
Medieval poetry
NYPL, Jewish Division

*Prayerbooks for local usage provide information
about the history of standard prayers and about
local tastes and traditions in religious poetry.
These Occasional Prayers are in the rite of the
Jews of Avignon.*
NYPL, Jewish Division [Ex. no. 170]

The Tractate America of the Yankee Tal-
mud (*Masekhet Amerikah min Talmud
Yanka'i*), *a parody by Gerson Rosenzweig
(New York, 1907).*
NYPL, Jewish Division (Ex. no. 178)

177

* Johann Reuchlin, 1455–1522
De Arte Cabalistica Libri Tres . . .
Hagenau: Apud Thomam Anshelmum,
1517
Kabbalah
NYPL, Rare Books and Manuscripts Division

178

* Gerson Rosenzweig, 1861–1914
תלמוד ינקאי
Talmud Yanka'i
(*Yankee Talmud*)
New York: Druckerman, 1907
Parody
NYPL, Jewish Division

The stag preaching to the animals, from
Meshal ha-Kadmoni *(The Ancient
Proverb, after 1 Samuel 24:14; Venice, ca.
1547), a collection of fables in rhymed Hebrew*
by the thirteenth-century Spanish Hebrew poet
*Isaac ben Solomon Ibn Abi Sahulah.
NYPL, Jewish Division (Ex. no. 181)*

179
Azariah ben Moses dei Rossi, 1513?–
1578
מאור עינים
Me'or 'Eynayim
Mantua, 1573–75
History
NYPL, Jewish Division

180
Giovanni Bernardo de Rossi, 1742–1831
De Hebraicae Typographiae
Parma: Ex Regio Typographeo, 1776
NYPL, Jewish Division

181
∗ Isaac ben Solomon Ibn Abi Sahulah, thir-
teenth century
משל הקדמוני
Meshal ha-Kadmoni
Venice: Meir ben Jacob Parenz, ca. 1547
Fables
NYPL, Jewish Division

182
Abraham Shlonsky, 1900–1973
דוי
Devay
Tel-Aviv: Hedim, 1924
Poetry
NYPL, Jewish Division

183
∗ Talmud
Venice: Daniel Bomberg, 1520–23.
21 volumes
NYPL, Jewish Division

184
Zohar
הזוהר
Cremona: Vicenzo Conti, 1558–60.
3 parts in 2 volumes
NYPL, Jewish Division

185
Zohar
הזהר
Mantua: Meir Sofer ben Ephraim of
Padua and Jacob ben Naphtali ha-Cohen,
1558–60. 5 parts in 3 volumes
NYPL, Jewish Division

Glossary

For the spellings of the words and expressions listed below, which appear in an English context, *Webster's Third New International Dictionary of the English Language, Unabridged* and other standard reference works served as guides. *The Encyclopedia of the Jewish Religion,* edited by R. J. Zwi Werblowsky and Geoffrey Wigoder (Jerusalem and Tel Aviv, 1966) was very useful for definitions. Meanings are from the Hebrew unless another language is given.

AGGADA, noun; AGGADIC, adj. – Literally, "narration." The nonlegal parts of the TALMUD and MIDRASH, including ethical and moral teaching, legends, folklore, anecdotes, and maxims, as distinct from HALAKA, which has to do with law. The word HAGGADAH is very close to AGGADA, but is often used in a more specific way, described below. (Variant spellings: AGGADAH, HAGGADAH.)

ASHKENAZ, noun; ASHKENAZI, ASHKENAZIC, adjs. – A biblical name which, from around the ninth century of the Common Era, was identified with Germany. Jews in medieval England, northern France, Germany, and Central and most of Eastern Europe and their descendants are said to be ASHKENAZIM (singular ASHKENAZI). Most American Jews are ASHKENAZIM.

GABBAI – Treasurer of a synagogue or communal institution and, later, a community official in general. The term is shortened from GABBAI TSEDAKAH, "collector of charity."

GEMARA – Aramaic, "completion." The discussion and commentary which amplifies the MISHNAH and together with it makes up the TALMUD. Sometimes GEMARA is used to refer to the TALMUD as a whole.

GEMATRIA – Calculation of the numerical value of Hebrew words—made possible because every Hebrew letter has a numerical value—and the substitution of other words or phrases of equal value. This was used as a device in explaining Scripture and later became a feature of KABBALISTIC interpretation and the practice of magic. The word GEMATRIA is derived from the Greek *geometria* and is related to the English *geometry.*

GENIZA – Literally, "hiding." A hiding place or storeroom, usually part of a synagogue, where sacred books were put when they were too worn to be used. The term is sometimes used specifically with reference to the Cairo GENIZA, which belonged to the synagogue at Fostat, built in 882 C.E., and was found to contain a wealth of early texts, including some which had been lost. Today, Orthodox Jews collect unusable sacred writings and bury them in the cemetery. (Sometimes written GENIZAH.)

HAFTARAH, plural HAFTAROT – Literally, "concluding." A definite selection from the Prophets which is read in the synagogue following its corresponding TORAH reading, or weekly PARASHAH.

HAGGADAH, plural HAGGADOT – "Narration." Used now to designate the separate book containing the text of the Passover SEDER ritual, including the story of redemption from slavery in Egypt. MAHZORIM often contain the HAGGADAH, as well, as part of the yearly cycle of festival prayers.

HAKHAM – "Wise man, sage." The title is used for a rabbi in SEPHARDI communities and, in particular, for the Chief Rabbi of British SEPHARDIM.

HALAKA, noun; HALAKIC, adj. – "The way to walk," law. The legal part of Jewish traditional literature. (Variant spellings: HALAKHA, HALAKHAH, HALACHA, HALACHAH.)

HASKALAH – "Enlightenment." A movement among Jews in Western and Central Europe, especially Germany, during the late eighteenth century which spread eastward during the nineteenth century. It advocated the acquisition and propagation of secular culture.

KABBALAH, noun; KABBALIST, noun; KABBALISTIC, adj. – "Receiving, that which is received, tradition." Generally refers to a movement in Jewish mysticism which began in the twelfth century. (Variant spellings: CABALA, CABBALA, KABBALA, QABBALA, QABBALAH.)

MAHZOR – "Cycle." A book containing the prayers for the cycle of the year. In common modern usage MAHZOR denotes the festival prayerbook as distinct from the SIDDUR, where Sabbath and weekday prayers are found.

MASORAH, noun; MASORETIC, adj. – Collection of notes the purpose of which is to ensure the correct transmission of the text of the Hebrew Bible. A MASORETE was one of the scholars who in antiquity and the early Middle Ages contributed to formulating the notes and rules which became the MASORAH. A MASORATOR was the person who added the MASORAH to a Bible manuscript. (Variant spellings: MASORA, MASSORA, MASSORAH.)

MEGILLAH – "Scroll." May mean a scroll in general. Five books of the Bible are especially designated the Five Scrolls: Song of Songs, Ruth, Lamentations, Ecclesiastes, and Esther. The term, when used alone, often refers to the Book of Esther.

MIDRASH – A type of rabbinic literature whose name indicates an attempt "to seek out" the meaning of Scripture. It is homiletical in nature, being based on biblical text. MIDRASH HALAKA deals with the law; MIDRASH AGGADA is varied, includes ethical teaching, and makes much use of legend. Early MIDRASH is associated with the period of the MISHNAH (compiled in about 220 C.E.). MIDRASH continued to be written into the Middle Ages.

MISHNAH – A systematic collection of several hundred years of rabbinic discussion, opinion, and rulings compiled in its final form around 220 C.E. This is the basic codification of the Oral Law (as distinct from what is written in the Bible). Its contents are organized into six broad categories or "orders" (SEDER, plural SEDARIM). These are ZERAIM (Seeds), MOED (Appointed Times), NASHIM (Women), NEZIKIN (Damages), KODASHIM (Holy Things), TOHAROT (Purity).

MISHNEH TORAH (also known as HA-YAD HA-HAZAKAH) – Code of Jewish law compiled by Moses ben Maimon, also known as Maimonides and Rambam, who lived in Spain and in Egypt from 1135 to 1204 C.E.

MOHEL – A person who performs circumcision in accordance with Jewish law. Jewish male children in good health are generally circumcised on the eighth day after birth. This is viewed as entering into a covenant with God in the manner of Abraham (Gen. 17:11–12).

PARASHAH, plural PARASHOT or PARASHIYOT; also called a SIDRA (SIDRAH) – One of fifty-four definite portions of the TORAH or PENTATEUCH read in the synagogue on Sabbaths, Mondays, and Thursdays throughout the year. There are additional portions for festivals and special Sabbaths. An alternate three-year cycle also existed in ancient times.

PENTATEUCH – English, from the Greek, the first five books of the Hebrew Bible, in Hebrew called TORAH or ḤUMASH. The other main sections of the Hebrew Bible are the PROPHETS (Hebrew, NEVI'IM) and HAGIOGRAPHA or WRITINGS (Hebrew, KETUVIM).

RESPONSA – English, from Latin, in Hebrew SHE'ELOT U-TESHUVOT, "questions and answers." Replies and rulings of rabbis to questions in Jewish law which have been submitted to them. It has been the practice to collect and publish the RESPONSA of important rabbinic scholars.

SEDER, plural SEDARIM – "Order." The celebration on the first two evenings of Passover which includes recital of the HAGGADAH and partaking of a festive meal. It usually takes place in the home. SEDER may also refer to one of the six main sections of the MISHNAH and TALMUD.

SEFER – "Book." May be used to indicate a book in general, but is sometimes used to connote a religious work specifically.

SEPHARAD; also SEFARAD – A place name in the Bible which from the early Middle Ages came to be identified with the Iberian peninsula. The SEPHARDI (or SEPHARDIC) traditions of liturgy and ritual differ from those of the ASHKENAZIM. After the expulsion of Jews from Spain and Portugal at the end of the fifteenth century, SEPHARDIM settled in North Africa, Italy, the Balkans, and the eastern Mediterranean as well as in France, the Netherlands, the Hamburg region, and, later, England. Today's SEPHARDIM are their descendants. The term is also used generally to denote Jews belonging to communities in North Africa and the Middle East which follow the SEPHARDIC rite.

SHNORRER – Yiddish, "a beggar, a sponger."

SIDDUR – Now commonly refers to the prayerbook which contains weekday and Sabbath prayers, as distinct from the MAḤZOR, where the liturgy for festivals is found.

SIDRA – see PARASHAH

TALMUD – Literally, "study, learning, instruction." There are two TALMUDS, the Babylonian or Bavli, and the TALMUD of the Land of Israel, also inaccurately called the Jerusalem TALMUD or Yerushalmi, of which the Babylonian is both much longer and the one considered more authoritative. When reference is made simply to the TALMUD, it is assumed that the Babylonian is meant. Each consists of the text of the MISHNAH (the same in both) and a GEMARA which is different for each. For a number of tractates of the MISHNAH there is no GEMARA extant in one TALMUD or the other and some-times it is lacking in both. Each TALMUD constitutes a compendium of rabbinic thought, discussion, interpretation, law, and lore spanning some eight hundred years. Compilation of the TALMUD of the Land of Israel was finished in about 400 C.E.; the Babylonian was virtually completed about a hundred years later. Partly because of persecutions, there survives only one complete manuscript of each TALMUD. A standard printed set of the Babylonian TALMUD contains twenty volumes. The English translation consists of thirty-five.

TARGUM – The translation into and, to some extent, paraphrase of the Bible in Aramaic made in the early centuries of the Common Era.

TORAH – "Teaching, doctrine"; later, "the Law." In its narrowest sense the term denotes the first five books of the Bible or PENTATEUCH. Jewish lore speaks of the written TORAH, which is taken to mean Scripture as a whole, and the divinely inspired oral TORAH, consisting of the tradition of rabbinic study and interpretation, part of which was written down in the MISHNAH and TALMUD. In its broadest sense, therefore, TORAH may also be taken to mean the entire teaching of Judaism, understood as the result of divine revelation.

TOSAPHOT – "Additions." Collections of comments on the TALMUD arranged according to the tractates of the TALMUD, written by the pupils of Rashi and their followers, who flourished in France and Germany from the twelfth to the fourteenth centuries.

Contributors

LEILA AVRIN teaches at the School of Library and Archive Studies of the Hebrew University and at the School of Information and Library Studies of the University of Michigan. She has written on the illuminations of the Moshe ben Asher codex of 895 C.E., on Hebrew micrography, and on modern book arts.

MALACHI BEIT-ARIÉ is Director of the Jewish National and University Library, Jerusalem. Earlier, he was Head of the Institute of Micro-filmed Hebrew Manuscripts. He has done much original work in Hebrew pal-aeography and codicology and is also a published poet.

EVELYN M. COHEN is Curator of Graphic Materials at the Library of The Jewish Theological Seminary of America. She has published a study of the *Rothschild Maḥzor.*

FRANK MOORE CROSS is Hancock Professor of Hebrew and Other Oriental Languages at Harvard University. He is a distinguished semi-tist and an authority on the Dead Sea Scrolls.

MORDECHAI GLATZER is lecturer on Talmud and Hebrew pal-aeography and printing at the Hebrew University, Jerusalem. He has written a book on *Sefer ha-'Itur* by Isaac ben Abba Mari and an extensive study of the *Aleppo Codex.*

MICHAEL W. GRUNBERGER is Head of the Hebraic Section at The Library of Congress. Previously, he was Librarian of Gratz College, Philadelphia.

JOSEPH GUTMANN is Professor of Art History at Wayne State University, Detroit, and Adjunct Curator at the Detroit Institute of Arts. He has written extensively on Hebrew illuminated manuscripts and on Jewish art.

SHARON LIBERMAN MINTZ is a doctoral candidate in art history at Columbia University.

CHAIM POTOK, the well-known novelist, is the author of *The Chosen* and *My Name Is Asher Lev,* among other works.

MOSHE N. ROSENFELD, a chemist by profession, lives in London. He is devoted to the history of Hebrew and Yiddish printing and has brought to light new information in this field. He has written a book on Jewish printing in Augsburg.

DAVID B. RUDERMAN is Frederick P. Rose Professor of Jewish History at Yale University. His *World of a Renaissance Jew: The Life and Thought of Abraham ben Mordecai Farissol* received a National Jewish Book Award in 1982.

MENAHEM SCHMELZER is now Professor of Medieval Hebrew Literature and Jewish Bibliography at The Jewish Theological Seminary of America. For many years he was Librarian of the Seminary.

ROBERT SINGERMAN is Head of the Isser and Rae Price Library of Judaica at the University of Florida. He has compiled a number of book-length bibliographies.

INDEX OF ILLUSTRATIONS

Lenders to the Exhibition

Aberdeen University Library, Scotland

Accademia dei Concordi, Rovigo, Italy

Annenberg Research Institute for Judaic
and Near Eastern Studies, Merion,
Pennsylvania

Ben-Zvi Institute for the Study of Jewish
Communities in the East, Jerusalem

Biblioteca Ambrosiana, Milan

Biblioteca Nacional, Lisbon

Bibliothèque Nationale, Paris

Bodleian Library, Oxford

The British Library, London

Cambridge University Library, England

Hebrew Union College–Jewish Institute
of Religion Library, Cincinnati, Ohio

Israel Museum, Jerusalem

The Jewish National and University
Library, Jerusalem

The John Rylands University Library of
Manchester, England

Beatrice and Richard D. Levy

Library of Congress, Washington, D.C.

Library of the Hungarian Academy of
Sciences, Budapest

Library of the Jewish Theological
Seminary of America, New York

The Pierpont Morgan Library, New York

Princeton University Library, Princeton,
N.J.

Royal Library, Copenhagen

Schocken Collection, Jerusalem

The Shrine of the Book, D. Samuel and
Jeane H. Gottesman Center for Biblical
Manuscripts, Israel Museum, Jerusalem

Staatsbibliothek Preussischer Kulturbesitz, Orientabteilung, Berlin (West)

Valmadonna Trust Library, London

Württembergische Landesbibliothek,
Stuttgart

A private collector

PHOTOGRAPH CREDITS

Numbers refer to pages. Unless otherwise indicated, photographs were provided by lenders to the exhibition. All photographs of items from The New York Public Library are by Robert D. Rubic.

José Manuel Costa Alves: 26

Israel Museum/Moshe Caine: 11, 19, 48, 157, 200

Jewish National and University Library: 126, 127, 129

Library of the Jewish Theological Seminary of America/Peter Bittner: 162, 168

Marzola Dino: 165

Robert D. Rubic: 39, 166, 169, 170

Ray M. Wiener Photography: 69, 78

STUDIES IN JEWISH HISTORY

Published by Oxford University Press
Jehuda Reinharz, General Editor

Jacques Adler
The Jews of Paris and the Final Solution:
Communal Response and Internal Conflicts, 1940–1944

Leonard Singer Gold, ed.
A Sign and a Witness:
2,000 Years of Hebrew Books and Illuminated Manuscripts, paperback edition (co-published with The New York Public Library)

Ben Halpern
A Clash of Heroes:
Brandeis, Weizmann, and American Zionism

Hillel Kieval
The Making of Czech Jewry:
National Conflict and Jewish Society in Bohemia, 1870–1918

Michael A. Meyer
Response to Modernity:
A History of the Reform Movement in Judaism

Jehuda Reinharz
Chaim Weizmann:
The Making of a Zionist Leader, paperback edition

David Sorkin
The Transformation of German Jewry, 1780–1840

Michael F. Stanislawski
For Whom Do I Toil?
Judah Leib Gordon and the Crisis of Russian Jewry

Jack Wertheimer
Unwelcome Strangers:
East European Jews in Imperial Germany

Moshe Zimmermann
Wilhelm Marr:
The Patriarch of Antisemitism

Other volumes are in preparation.

THIS BOOK was set by The Sarabande Press, New York City, in a Merganthaler Linotronic 300 version of the typeface Bembo. The display type for the title of the book is Monotype Spectrum, set by Mackenzie & Harris, Inc., San Francisco. The Hebrew type is Narkiss, set by Spectrum Multilanguage Communications, Inc., New York City.

Bembo, first used in 1495, was a copy of a roman type cut by Francesco Griffo for the Venetian printer Aldus Manutius. The italic was based upon a script of the writing-master Giovantonio Tagliente, published in Venice circa 1524. Today's versions of Bembo derive from the revival of classical faces carried out by Stanley Morison for the Monotype Corporation in 1929.

Forty-five hundred copies were printed and bound by the Meriden-Stinehour Press, Meriden, Connecticut. The paper used is Mohawk Superfine, with Warren's Lustro Dull for the color plates and Carolina for the cover.

The book was designed by Marilan Lund at The New York Public Library.

Scribe's colophon inside the initial word of a *piyyut* or liturgical hymn, in a fourteenth-century German Maḥzor. NYPL, Jewish Division, **P, fol. 506r (Ex. no. 59)

Temple Israel

Minneapolis, Minnesota

IN MEMORY OF
MARC A. DORENFELD
FROM
HIS CLOSE NEIGHBORS